READING DERRIDA'S *OF GRAMMATOLOGY*

Also available from *Continuum*:

Alienation After Derrida, Simon Skempton
Badiou and Derrida, Antonio Calcagno
Between Deleuze and Derrida, edited by Paul Patton and John Protevi
Derrida: Writing Events, Simon Morgan Wortham
Derrida and Disinterest, Sean Gaston
Derrida and Theology, Steven Shakespeare
The Derrida Dictionary, Simon Morgan Wortham
Derrida's Writing and Difference: A Reader's Guide, Sarah Wood
Derrida, Literature and War, Sean Gaston
Derrida: A Guide for the Perplexed, Julian Wolfreys
Derrida: Profanations, Patrick O'Connor
The Domestication of Derrida, Lorenzo Fabbri
Encountering Derrida, edited by Alison Weiner and Simon Morgan Wortham
The Impossible Morning of Jacques Derrida, Sean Gaston
Jacques Derrida: A Biography, Jason Powell
Jacques Derrida: Live Theory, James K.A. Smith
Starting with Derrida, Sean Gaston
Understanding Derrida, edited by Jack Reynolds and Jonathan Roffe

READING DERRIDA'S *OF GRAMMATOLOGY*

EDITED BY
SEAN GASTON AND
IAN MACLACHLAN

continuum

Continuum International Publishing Group

The Tower Building	80 Maiden Lane
11 York Road	Suite 704
London SE1 7NX	New York NY 10038

© Sean Gaston, Ian Maclachlan and Contributors, 2011

Derrida, Jacques. Translated by Gayatri Chakravorty Spivak.
Of Grammatology © 1998 The Johns Hopkins University Press. Reprinted
with permission of The Johns Hopkins University Press.

British Library Cataloguing-in-Publication Data
A catalogue record for this book is available from the British Library.

ISBN: HB: 9781441146762
PB: 9781441152756

Library of Congress Cataloging-in-Publication Data
Reading Derrida's Of grammatology / edited by
Sean Gaston and Ian Maclachlan.
p. cm.
Includes bibliographical references (p.) and index.
ISBN 978-1-4411-4676-2 – ISBN 978-1-4411-5275-6
1. Derrida, Jacques. De la grammatologie. 2. Language and languages–
Philosophy. I. Gaston, Sean. II. Maclachlan, Ian, 1960–

P105.D533R43 2011
401–dc22

2010041951

Typeset by Newgen Imaging Systems Pvt Ltd, Chennai, India
Printed and bound in India

READING DERRIDA'S OF GRAMMATOLOGY

Derek Attridge
Geoffrey Bennington
Timothy Clark
Clare Connors
Paul Davies
Sean Gaston
Christopher Johnson
Peggy Kamuf
Ian Maclachlan

J. Hillis Miller
Forbes Morlock
Michael Naas
Jean-Luc Nancy
Nicholas Royle
Ann Smock
Gayatri Chakravorty Spivak
Michael Syrotinski
Julian Wolfreys
Sarah Wood

CONTENTS

Prefatory Note and Acknowledgements   xi

Introduction   xiii
Sean Gaston, Punctuations

Preface   xxix
Gayatri Chakravorty Spivak, Reading *De la grammatologie*

PART 1   WRITING BEFORE THE LETTER

1. The End of the Book and the Beginning of Writing   3
   Christopher Johnson, Epoch, Event, Context   3
   Michael Syrotinski, Origins: 'the most original and
      powerful ethnocentrism'   5
   Sean Gaston, Even Leibniz   10
   Christopher Johnson, The Cybernetic Imaginary   11
   Julian Wolfreys, Of Dark Sentences and Gnomes   14
   Forbes Morlock, Deconstruction – A Little Note   22
   Michael Syrotinski, From Etymology (*etumos logos*)
      to Translation, via Badiou and Paulhan   23
   Michael Naas, Pneumatology, *Pneuma*, *Souffle*, Breath   28
   Sarah Wood, Good Writing   31
   Ian Maclachlan, The Idea of the Book   32
   Peggy Kamuf, A Certain Way of Inhabiting   36

2. Linguistics and Grammatology   38
   J. Hillis Miller, Exergue   38
   J. Hillis Miller, *Brisure*   41
   J. Hillis Miller, *Jeu*   43

CONTENTS

J. Hillis Miller, Trace   47
Nicholas Royle, Bizarre   51
Derek Attridge, The Arbitrary   58
Sean Gaston, Writing and World   68
Ian Maclachlan, Embarrassing Experience   70
Ann Smock, This Concept Destroys its Name   72
Ian Maclachlan, A Hinge   74
Ian Maclachlan, Something Other Than Finitude   76

3. **Of Grammatology as a Positive Science**   79
Christopher Johnson, Grammatology as a 'Positive' Science   79
Paul Davies, Why Leibniz?   81
Christopher Johnson, Writing in Evolution,
    Evolution as 'Writing'   91
Peggy Kamuf, Grammatology as General Science   93
Forbes Morlock, Differance – A Little Note   95
Sarah Wood, The Constitution of Good and Bad Objects   96
Jean-Luc Nancy, L'ouverture blanche   98
Jean-Luc Nancy, Blank Opening   99

PART 2   NATURE, CULTURE, WRITING

1. **The Violence of the Letter: From Lévi-Strauss to Rousseau** 113
Michael Naas, *Leurre*, Lure, Delusion, Illusion   113
Forbes Morlock, The Subject of Reading-1   117

2. **'. . . That Dangerous Supplement . . .'**   119
Michael Naas, *Entamer, Entamé*, To Initiate or Open Up,
    to Breach or Broach   119
Forbes Morlock, The Subject of Reading-2   123
Forbes Morlock, The Subject of Reading-3   124
Peggy Kamuf, *L'habitation des femmes*   126

3. **Genesis and Structure of the 'Essay on the Origin
   of Languages'**   129
   3.1 The Place of the 'Essay'   129
   Sean Gaston, Pity, Virtuality and Power   129
   Clare Connors, Preference and Force   131
   Peggy Kamuf, Being-in-Nature   133
   Clare Connors, *Dynamis* and *Energeia*   134

3.2 Imitation   136
    Ann Smock, *Estampe*   136
    Geoffrey Bennington, Fractal Geography   137
    Ann Smock, Accents   145
    Forbes Morlock, The Copyist   147
    Clare Connors, Articulation, Accent and Rhyme   149

3.3 Articulation   151
    Michael Naas, Butades, the Invention of Drawing
      and the 'immediate sign'   151
    Peggy Kamuf, The Eye at the Centre of Language   154
    Forbes Morlock, The Subject of Reading-4   158
    Forbes Morlock, The Subject of Reading-5   159
    Clare Connors, *Presque*   160
    Timothy Clark, Climate and Catastrophe:
      A Lost Opening?   161
    Sarah Wood, The *Point d'Eau* or the Water-Holes
      that are Imperceptibly Present in Writing   168

4. From/Of the Supplement to the Source:
The Theory of Writing   173
    Sean Gaston, Kafka, Literature and Metaphor   173
    Forbes Morlock, The Subject of Reading-6   175
    Forbes Morlock, The Subject of Reading-7   175
    Peggy Kamuf, On Naïveté   176
    Ann Smock, Theatre Without Theatre   177
    Sean Gaston, Periodicity   179
    Peggy Kamuf, Habitation in General   181
    Peggy Kamuf, 'From somewhere where we are'   182

Biographical Notes – Intervals   184
Contributors   195
Notes   196
Bibliography   206
Index   219

PREFATORY NOTE AND ACKNOWLEDGEMENTS

The following collection of readings is organized as far as possible on the division into parts, chapters and sub-sections of Derrida's *Of Grammatology*. One can read it following the sequence of the original text or, by using the table of contents, follow the intervals, gaps and punctuations of an individual reader.

In all cases, the page numbers of Spivak's 1976 English translation will be designated by *OG* and will be followed, where necessary, by the page numbers of the 1967 French edition, which will be designed by *DG*. When Spivak's translation has been modified in some fashion this will be noted by trans. mod., while still giving the page numbers for the Spivak edition. Where no published translation is referenced, translations are the contributors' own. We have also displayed Jean-Luc Nancy's contribution in a parallel French text and English translation.

The work ends with a short biographical reflection by each participant on their first reception and reading of *Of Grammatology*. This is followed by a list of our contributors' institutional affiliations. We are fortunate to have so many readers who have shaped our ongoing understanding of the work of Jacques Derrida.

We would like to thank Nicholas Royle for his support and encouragement during various stages of this project from its inception in 2006. We are especially grateful to the original group who took the time and trouble to attend the one-day meetings at Brunel University in 2007 and Oxford University in 2009, all of whom also brought other keen readers to the project when we decided on a collection of readings. We would also particularly like to thank Jonathan Culler, J. Hillis Miller and Geoffrey Bennington for their kind and ready assistance in the preparation of this work. We are indebted to Sarah Campbell and David Avital at Continuum for their consistent enthusiasm for this distinctive publication.

Sean Gaston and Ian Maclachlan
July 2010

INTRODUCTION

PUNCTUATIONS

So I would answer you by saying, first, that I am trying, precisely, to put myself at a point so that I do not know any longer where I am going.

Jacques Derrida (1966)[1]

I

This project began in 2006 as an attempt to address the question of how to mark the coming fortieth anniversary of the publication of *De la grammatologie*. In the wake of the recent death of Jacques Derrida in 2004 how could one mark this anniversary without reconstituting an absent and idealized head of the family or falling into a celebratory hagiography? How could we read *Of Grammatology* today, forty years after its first publication and thirty years after its translation into English?[2] At the same time, it is also perhaps difficult now to appreciate how remarkable Derrida's work was when it first appeared in 1967. From its opening attempts to rethink language as an aspect of writing in general, to the assertion of a comprehensive logocentrism, to a contrast between linguistics and the work of Heidegger that culminates in an oscillating reading that at once marks the limitations of Heidegger's thought and pushes it towards an engagement with *différance*, to the conclusion 'that the undertaking of deconstruction is always in a certain way carried away [*emportée*] by its own work', *De la grammatologie* was the startling announcement of a formidable and adventurous philosophical project (*OG* 24; *DG* 39, trans. mod.).

As is well known, Gayatri Chakravorty Spivak's 1976 translation of *Of Grammatology* played a significant role in the reception of Derrida's work in the Anglo-American academy in the 1970s and 1980s. This reception, especially in English, French and Philosophy departments, was often shaped by existing theoretical conflicts and institutional battles. As *Of Grammatology* became part of these battles it gained the status of 'The Book of Derrida', a status that it still enjoys. Throughout the Humanities it has been much mentioned, hardly read and sometimes reduced to a single catchphrase. At times it has seemed as if Derrida's work was undergoing the very processes of idealization that he warned about in *Of Grammatology*.

In October 2007, a number of the contributors to this work met at Brunel University in West London for a one-day workshop. The participants were from English, Philosophy and French departments in British universities and the workshop opened with each person reflecting on how they first encountered Derrida's most well-known work and how this reception was influenced by existing institutional and departmental contexts. A few admitted that they had always found *Of Grammatology* a difficult work. Its combination of a contracted and closely argued opening (chiefly reading Heidegger, Hegel and Saussure), followed by a short section on Claude Lévi-Strauss and an almost two-hundred-page reading of a thirty-five-page essay by Jean-Jacques Rousseau on the origin of language is often hard to grasp as a complete work. One can contrast this seemingly disjointed and disproportionate work to the elegant articles collected in Derrida's *Writing and Difference* (1967) or the sustained analysis of Husserlian phenomenology in *Speech and Phenomena* (1967). This apparent difficulty was exacerbated by the extraordinary reception of Gayatri Chakravorty Spivak's 1976 translation.

The one-day workshop at Brunel eschewed the convention of a series of read papers and created an open space for close readings of short passages in *Of Grammatology*, taking care to respond in each case to the philosophical, literary and linguistic challenges of the text. In January 2009, a second workshop was held at Merton College, Oxford. On this occasion, each participant presented a close reading of one or more passages in *Of Grammatology*. It was after this meeting that we began to think about a collection of short close readings of Derrida's work. Prompted by a notion that Derrida always took account of the *punctuations* of a work – the necessary discriminations and clarifications that also repeatedly divide and interrupt the work – as a series of intervals or moving gaps that cannot be recollected into a unity, we settled on each contributor writing approximately 3,500 words and offering either a single reading or a series of shorter readings of a number of selected phrases, themes, pages, passages, sections or chapters in *Of Grammatology*.[3] Our aim was to revisit and to rediscover this influential work. Through a series of readings from a number of different academic disciplines and readers that reflect the reception of Jacques Derrida's work over the last forty-five years, we hope to convey the sense that we are perhaps only just beginning to read *Of Grammatology*.

II

De la grammatologie was published in late 1967 in Paris in the 'Collection' Critique. Georges Bataille had founded the review journal *Critique* in 1946 and after Bataille's death in 1962, Jean Piel established the 'Collection' Critique to publish monographs in collaboration with Les Éditions de Minuit. After spending much of the 1950s working on Husserl, Derrida had published an introduction to and translation of Husserl's *L'origine de la géométrie* in 1962. This first work was followed by a series of articles and longer works that appeared in three publications in 1967: *L'écriture et la différence*, *La voix et le phénomène* and *De la grammatologie*.

From 1963 to 1966, Derrida published five review articles in *Critique*. While in this period his important essays on Foucault and Levinas appeared in the *Revue de métaphysique et de morale* and his first articles on Artaud and Freud were published in the newly founded *Tel Quel*, *Critique* saw Derrida's first interventions into the existing debates over language, linguistics and literary interpretation. These essays – 'Force et signification' (1963), 'Edmond Jabès et la question du livre' (1964), 'De la grammatologie I' (1965), 'De la grammatologie II' (1966) and 'Le théâtre de la cruauté et la clôture de la représentation' (1966)—capture Derrida's probing and critical response in the mid-1960s to the phenomenological and structuralist methods of reading and interpretation.[4]

Celebrating the move away from authorial consciousness and philological historicism in these essays, Derrida also challenged the underlying assumption in structuralist projects that a science of language could provide an exhaustive summation of a work based on universal and fundamental linguistic structures. At the outset of 'De la grammatologie I' (1965), Derrida attempted to counteract or redirect the contemporary 'inflation of the sign "language"'.[5] In his revisions to this passage for *De la grammatologie* in 1967, he adds that this sublime gesture of inflation has already sent language wandering 'back to its own finitude' ('renvoyé à sa propre finitude') (*OG* 6; *DG* 15). As with much of his work in the 1960s, Derrida both acknowledges the innovations of structuralism and questions its claims to be an absolute break with the past, notably with a logocentric tradition that centres or orders a work through the authority of an unchanging *logos* (word, speech, reason, reasoning).

In 'De la grammatologie I', Derrida quotes Aristotle's own summary of his treatise *De Anima* as framework for a logocentrism which, Derrida argues, is still at work in the thought not only of Rousseau and Hegel, but also Saussure, Lévi-Strauss and Heidegger. Aristotle writes:

> Words are symbols or signs of affections or impressions of the soul; written words [*graphómena*], are the signs of words spoken [*phonē*]. As writing, so also is speech not the same for all races of men. But the mental affections [*pathēmata tês psukhēs, états de l'âme* in Derrida's translation] themselves, of which these words are primarily signs, are the same for the whole of mankind, as are also the objects of which these affections are representations or likenesses, images, copies.[6]

Derrida would remain preoccupied throughout his work with the pervasive role played by the soul (*psukhē*) in relation to a determined ordering of language, inscription, signs, representation and the senses.[7]

Derrida's two review articles from 1965–66, 'De la grammatologie I' and 'De la grammatologie II', devoted to recent publications on structural linguistics, would provide the first sections of Part I of *De la grammatologie* in 1967. The opening section of Part II, 'The Violence of the Letter: From Lévi-Strauss to Rousseau', also first appeared as an article in the short-lived journal *Cahiers pour l'Analyse* in the autumn of 1966.[8] It is worth recalling that by 1965 Derrida had only published his introduction to Husserl and five articles. Still a relatively junior academic, Derrida was fortunate to find support for his work in *Critique*. The editorial board of *Critique* in the early 1960s included some of the most significant writers, philosophers and historians of the post-war period in France, including Raymond

Aron, Maurice Blanchot, Fernand Braudel, René Char, Jean Wahl, Roland Barthes, Michel Deguy and Michel Foucault. Michel Deguy had published one of the first responses to Derrida's work in *Critique* in 1963, a review of *Introduction à L'origine de la géométrie*. Gérard Granel would also write one of the first reviews of Derrida's three works from 1967 in *Critique*.[9] Derrida would go on to publish the article 'La dissémination' in *Critique* in 1969 and the collections *Marges – de la philosophie* and *Positions* would both appear in the 'Collection' Critique series in 1972.[10] In 1974 he joined the editorial board of *Critique* and today, along with Maurice Blanchot, remains part of the honorary and posthumous board of the journal.

In revisiting *Of Grammatology* nearly forty-five years after its first publication, this French context helps us to appreciate that Derrida's best-known and controversial book initially appeared as part of a series of publications in *Critique* and the 'Collection' Critique that range from 1963 to 1972. One could argue that, for quite conscious strategic reasons, Derrida never published a book or an orthodox academic monograph. Certainly, by 1967 he had only published an introduction and a number of articles and, as he suggested, the three works that appeared that year can be understood as a *series* of works that are each *more and less than a book*. *La voix et le phénomène* was an extension of a planned lecture that was never delivered, *L'écriture et le différence* is a collection of articles and papers from 1959–1967 and *Of Grammatology* is a number of shorter works gathered into one publication.

As Derrida himself states in the *avertissement* of *De la grammatologie*, the first part of the book—'Writing Before the Letter' – can be considered 'as the development of an essay published in the review *Critique* (December 1965–January 1966)' (*OG* lxxxix; *DG* 7, trans. mod.). He also begins *De la grammatologie* by describing the work that will follow as an 'essai' (Spivak translates 'cet essai' as 'this book') (*OG* lxxxix; *DG* 7). In other words, he sees this work as an essay, an attempt, a try, a testing out, a preliminary gesture that has no assurance of becoming a 'book'. The challenge not to take this work as a book, as a monograph or treatise, is highlighted by Derrida in the title for the opening chapter: 'The End of the Book and the Beginning of Writing'.[11] Derrida links the notion of a complete and finished work, the presentation of an exhaustive and encyclopaedic totality on a given subject, to Hegel's claims that the history of spirit can culminate in an 'end' of history in which consciousness gains absolute knowledge. The write-up on the back-cover of *De la grammatologie* ends by referring to Derrida's well-known neologism *différance* and one can perhaps say that Derrida did not want his new work to be taken as 'The Book on *Différance*'. As he observed in early 1968, some three months after the publication of *De la grammatologie*:

> [*la différance*] is not announced by any capital letter. Not only is there no kingdom of *différance*, but *différance* instigates the sub-version of every kingdom. Which makes it obviously threatening and infallibly dreaded by everything within us that desires a king-dom, the past or future presence of a kingdom. And it is always in the name of a kingdom that one may reproach *différance* with wishing to reign, believing that one sees it aggrandize itself with a capital letter.[12]

Very broadly understood as a challenge to a tradition that privileged time over space – notably in the work of Bergson and Heidegger in the first half of the twentieth century – *différance* accounts for space always becoming time and time always becoming space. As Derrida would later argue, this interlacing oscillation (or deferring and differ-ing) of *temporisation* and *espacement* resists projects of self-evident presentation, capitalization, totalization, infinite incompletion and anticipatory programming.[13] Derrida's attempt to have the publication, style and content of his works not enact a Hegelian *Aufhebung* of *différance* (an uplifting that negates and conserves in the name of a teleological idealization) is quite clear in his 1967 interview with Henri Ronse. Derrida remarks:

> In what you call my books, what is first of all put in question is the unity of the book and the unity 'book' considered as a perfect totality, with all the implications of such a concept. [. . .] One can take *Of Grammatology* as a long essay [*comme un long essai*] articulated in two parts (whose juncture is not empirical, but theoretical, systematic) *into the middle* of which one could staple *Writing and Difference*. *Grammatology* often calls upon it. In this case the interpretation of Rousseau would also be the twelfth 'table' of the collection. Inversely, one could insert *Of Grammatology into the middle* of *Writing and Difference*, since six of the texts in that work preceded – *de facto* and *de jure* – the publication in

Critique (two years ago) of the articles that announced *Of Grammatology*.[14]

Derrida refers to *De la grammatologie* not as a book, or the book 'considered as a perfect totality', but as 'a long essay articulated in two parts'. As he observes, his works are an attempt to resist 'the unity of the book'. Part of the intention of this collection of scattered close readings is to counteract the profound temptation to treat *De la grammatologie* as a unified book, as yet another programmatic treatise or philosophical system. This temptation has its own institutional traps and ruses, as academics over the last forty years have attempted to either build a recognized school or body of thought in response to this 'book' or to refute and destroy its apparent claims to legitimacy in the academy. In this collection, we have rather attempted to respond to this remarkable work as a series of intervals or moving gaps that gesture towards the interlacing oscillations that are 'recognized here under the name of *différance*'.

III

This collection of readings also reflects on the history of the reading and reception of *De la grammatologie* and, most notably, its translation into English by Gayatri Spivak in 1976. Having worked on the project from 1970–75, some thirty-five years ago Spivak introduced Derrida's work to the larger Anglo-American academy. By 1976, only a handful of Derrida's articles had been translated into English. This history of translation, which alters the dates of the original French publications, creates its own narrative of reception and reading. Derrida's first work in English was an extract of *Speech and Phenomena* published in 1967.[15] Two years later in 1969 his paper 'The Ends of Man' appeared.[16] It was only in 1970 that the over-anthologized conference paper 'Structure, Sign and Play in the Discourse of the Human Sciences' (1966) came out in English.[17] In the following five years, only a handful of articles were translated: '*"Ousia"* and *"Grammē"*' (1970); 'Freud and the Scene of Writing' (1972); 'White Mythology' (1974); 'The Supplement of Copula' (1975); 'Le facteur de la vérité' (1975).[18] The last of these, Derrida's essay on Lacan and Poe, was the first to be translated into the English in the same year that it was published in France. Derrida's only 'book' in English before *Of Grammatology* was David Allison's translation of *Speech and Phenomena* (1973), which included the articles 'Form and Meaning' and 'Différance'.[19] In 1974, the first chapter of *Of Grammatology* was published in the journal *SubStance*.[20]

From this history of translation one is reminded not only that Derrida was initially known in the English-speaking world for his work on Husserl, but also that his first fully translated work, the 1968 paper 'The Ends of Man' opens with an examination of the politics of the institution. It is worth recalling these opening remarks:

> Every philosophical colloquium necessarily has a political significance. And not only due to that which has always linked the essence of the philosophical to the essence of the political. Essential and general, this political import nevertheless burdens the *a priori* link between philosophy and politics, aggravates it in a way, and also determines it when the philosophical colloquium is announced as an international colloquium. Such is the case here.[21]

At the very time that *Of Grammatology* was being published in 1976, Derrida was already involved in a series of direct institutional interventions in France and writing on the politics of the institution and pedagogical practices. It is one of the more striking examples of how the vagaries of translation can shape the reception and interpretation of a 'body of thought' that this work, published as articles and papers in French from 1976 and collected in *Du droit à la philosophie* (1990), did not fully appear in English until after Jacques Derrida's death in 2004.[22] A host of academic careers have been built on the apparent 'apolitical' and 'ahistorical' nature of Derrida's work, often reducing *Of Grammatology* to a single catch phrase: *'il n'y a pas de hors-texte'* (*DG* 227).

Spivak translates this phrase as *'there is nothing outside of the text'* and 'there is no outside-text' (*OG* 158). This has often been taken as the grand assertion of an ahistorical – and apolitical – textuality that simply 'plays' within the games of language. However, as his earlier work on Husserl and Levinas amply demonstrates, Derrida was keenly aware of the traps and ruses of both historicism and ahistoricism.[23] One can only speculate how Derrida's reception may have differed if his advertised work in 1965 on Heidegger, *La Question de l'histoire*, had been written and published.[24]

It is difficult to pinpoint exactly when the phrase 'il n'y a pas de hors-texte' became a shorthand for summarizing and criticizing

Of Grammatology. In an article from 1978 in *Critical Inquiry* Edward Said brought attention to the phrase in contrasting Derrida and Foucault. He writes:

> Finally – and I am depressingly aware that these prefatory comments are far too schematic – I will discuss Derrida's *mise en abîme* and Foucault's *mise en discours* as typifying the contrast between a criticism claiming that *il n'y a pas d'hors texte* [sic] and one discussing textuality as having to do with a plurality of texts, and with history, power, knowledge, and society.

Said goes on to add that both of these apparent stances 'strike me as indispensable to any cogent critical position'.[25] Towards the end of his article, Said implies that he has been influenced by Foucault's 1972 response to Derrida's paper 'Cogito and the History of Madness' (1963), which ends by describing Derrida's work as 'a pedagogy which teaches the student that there is nothing outside of the text'.[26]

If the widespread reduction of *Of Grammatology* to a single catch phrase did indeed begin with Foucault, the continued inflation and detachment of 'il n'y a pas de hors-texte' should be placed within the context of the contested relation between Foucault and Derrida in France in the 1960s and the reading of Foucault in America in the late 1970s. It is perhaps not that surprising that the association of *Of Grammatology* with an assertion that there is nothing outside text – the claim for an absolute text without any context – has itself undergone a decontextualization. Floating somewhere well beyond Foucault's response in 1972 to a paper given by Derrida in 1963 and Said's article from 1978 juxtaposing Foucault and Derrida, 'il n'y a pas de hors-texte' has become a relentless *Aufhebung* of Derrida's work.

To speak of *Of Grammatology* in terms of this single phrase is already to give way to this history of inflation, idealization and decontextualization and yet it has become unavoidable in the reading of Derrida's work. We are always caught by this catch phrase. 'Il n'y a pas de hors-texte' can be understood not as announcement that there is nothing outside of language or outside of language as writing, but as an affirmation that the *text*, or the traces and interlacing oscillations of *différance*, exceed the programmatic and totalizing sciences of language that were still readily embraced in the early 1960s.[27] It is difficult to see why this gesture would preclude or rule out a response to political, historical, social, economic and ethical discourses. As Derrida himself observed in 1988:

> I wanted to recall that the concept of text I propose is limited neither to the graphic, nor to the book, nor even to discourse, and even less to the semantic, representational, symbolic, ideal, or ideological sphere. What I call 'text' implies all the structures called 'real', 'economic', 'historical', socio-institutional, in short: all possible referents. Another way of recalling once again that 'there is nothing outside the text'.[28]

One can also note in this context the small but profound decision on the part of The Johns Hopkins University Press in 1976 to categorize *Of Grammatology* as a work that should be placed under the 'Literature' section of bookshops (it has since been changed to 'Literary Theory'). On such small decisions, a thousand careers in English studies were launched.

IV

This is not the place to attempt a comprehensive account of the reception of Derrida's work in America, but a provisional sketch of the earliest years may be helpful.[29] The first reference to *De la grammatologie* in the *MLN*, a long-established journal devoted to the study of European literature, appears in the French issue from 1969.[30] In 1970, Edward Said noted in passing in the same journal, 'the relevance of Jacques Derrida's important variations on center, decentering and difference'.[31] In the following year in the *MLN*, both Carol Jacobs and John Heckman cite *De la grammatologie* in footnotes to their articles.[32] The first extended article on Derrida's work in the *MLN*, '"Literature"/Literature' by Alan Bass, appeared in 1972 and celebrates the publication of *La dissémination* that year while also offering an account of *De la grammatologie*. Introducing Derrida, Bass asks: 'Is there a text (for science is as textual, as written-down as literature) in which truth can be made present? What is the relationship between truth, presence and textuality? This question is the brunt of the work of Jacques Derrida, a "philosopher" whose texts are "literary" because they have attacked the fundamental notion of "scientific" truth'.[33]

As is often noted, the arrival of Derrida's work in America is also associated with his participation in a conference at Johns Hopkins

University in October 1966, which also included Jean Hyppolite, Georges Poulet, Roland Barthes and Jacques Lacan. It was at Johns Hopkins that Derrida also first encountered Paul de Man and J. Hillis Miller. Reading over the proceedings and the transcriptions of the discussions, it is striking that Derrida only speaks twice, after the papers of Barthes and Jean-Pierre Vernant. Nonetheless, as Hillis Miller recalls, Derrida's own paper, 'Structure, Sign and Play', received a great deal of attention:

> I could not attend Derrida's paper because I had a class to teach, but I met my close friend and colleague Georges Poulet in the quadrangle after it, and he said 'I have just heard the most important paper of the conference. It puts in question all my work [he was writing essays on centers and circumferences at that point], but it is an absolutely major essay'. That has always seemed to me both extraordinarily perceptive, prescient even, and extraordinarily generous.[34]

It is worth noting that Eugenio Donato actually refers to 'De la grammatologie I' and 'De la grammatologie II' in his own paper at the conference – probably the first references to *Of Grammatology* in the American academy.[35]

In an article from 1970 in the recently founded journal *New Literary History*, 'English Literary History at The Johns Hopkins University', Ronald Paulson notes that the prevailing attitude at the English Department has 'been identified variously as philology, history of ideas, "close-reading", and Geneva School phenomenology'.[36] Inspired by Husserl and represented by Georges Poulet and Jean Starobinski at Johns Hopkins, the so-called Geneva School had influenced both Hillis Miller and Paul de Man and provides one of the contexts for the reception of Derrida's critique of both Husserlian phenomenology and structuralist linguistics and literary criticism.[37] Derrida's first published article, 'Force and Signification' (1963), had been a review of a work by Jean Rousset, who was part of the Geneva School.[38]

As Paulson comments, it was at Johns Hopkins that Starobinksi prepared his 'magisterial study of Rousseau', *Jean-Jacques Rousseau: la transparence et l'obstacle* (1957), and it is Derrida's reading of Rousseau which prompted the first full-length critical response in America to *De la grammatologie*: Paul de Man's 1970 essay,

'The Rhetoric of Blindness: Jacques Derrida's Reading of Rousseau'.[39] One can trace Hillis Miller's early response to Derrida in a number of essays in this period. In 'Geneva or Paris? The Recent Work of Georges Poulet' (1970), Miller suggests that 'all the apparent assumptions of Poulet's criticism are interrogated by Derrida and found wanting'.[40] Poulet himself had offered a remarkable reading of Rousseau in the first volume of his *Etudes sur le temps humain* (1949), vividly describing the fullness of 'the present moment' enjoyed by primitive man before his fall into society and 'the kingdom of time'. Poulet charts Rousseau's unceasing attempts to regain a 'pure timelessness' or the 'abolition of duration and the spiritualization of space'.[41] In an article on Wordsworth in the following year, Miller described 'Structure, Sign and Play' as representative of a 'novel turn' in 'the putting in question of metaphysics', which is distinguished by 'new concepts of language, new ideas of structure, and new notions of interpretation'.[42]

In 1972, the recently founded *Diacritics* published a translation of the first part of Derrida's 1971 interview 'Positions'. In the same year, Richard Klein's 'Prolegomenon to Derrida' was addressed to an audience that was already familiar with 'the monstrous difficulties of reading Derrida'.[43] It was also in 1972 that Jeffrey Mehlman published his translation of Derrida's 'Freud and the Scene of Writing' (1966) in a special issue of the *Yale French Studies*, emphasizing the role played by psychoanalysis as well as literature in the early reception of Derrida's work.[44] Alexander Gelley also undertook the task of offering the first English review of *De la grammatologie* in *Diacritics* in 1972, five years after it had been published in Paris.[45] 1972 does seem to be a critical year in the reception of *De la grammatologie*.

Derrida's 1966 paper at Johns Hopkins University 'Structure, Sign and Play' was published, along with the other contributions from the conference, in English in 1970 in a work entitled *The Languages of Criticism and the Sciences of Man: The Structuralist Controversy*. In 1972, a paperback edition was published, reversing the order of the title and subtitle of the 1970 edition. This reversal led in part to the association of Derrida's work with a move to announce the 'end' of structuralism – and all the proliferating postisms that followed – as opposed to the 'criticism' of structuralism that he had proposed in his paper.[46] In an article from 1973, Eugenio Donato argued: 'Structuralism as a critical concept has outlived its usefulness'.[47]

One can balance this focus on the fortunes of structuralism in America with Lacoue-Labarthe's observation that Derrida's work was also distinguished by its unique engagement with Heidegger. Derrida's '*Auseinandersetzung* with Heidegger', Lacoue-Labarthe argued, offered a stark contrast to the largely uncritical or openly hostile readings of Heidegger in France at that time.[48] It is also worth noting that the English translation of *De la grammatologie* was relatively late: the Italian translation appeared in 1969, the German in 1974 and the Japanese the same year as the American edition in 1976.[49]

The years 1971–72 also marked the beginning of the reaction against Derrida's work within the American academy. In 'Abecedarium Culturae: Structuralism, Absence, Writing' (1971) Said offered a critical analysis of *De la grammatologie*. Associating Derrida's work with a 'nihilistic radicality', Said also compared Derrida to Dostoyevsky (which some would take as a compliment). Said observed: 'Derrida's grasp of the bewildering dilemma of modern critical knowledge resembles, in its awareness of the debilitating paradoxes that hobble knowledge, Dostoevski's'.[50] Fredric Jameson also included an account of Derrida in *The Prison-House of Language* (1972), concluding that Derrida's work was limited by 'the isolation and valorization of script as a unique and privileged type of content' and by a notion of the trace that is 'yet another ontological theory of the type it was initially designed to denounce'.[51]

V

Gayatri Chakravorty Spivak was part of a remarkable generation of scholars, including Alan Bass and the late Barbara Johnson, who began the daunting task of translating Derrida into English. While a corrected version of the 1976 translation of *Of Grammatology* was published in 1997, as Spivak has acknowledged, unavoidably some errors and confusions remain. Derrida himself was acutely aware of the philosophical issues, difficulties and opportunities of translation.[52] In revisiting *De la grammatologie/Of Grammatology* we should not avoid the issue of translation. Indeed, one could take this project as the call for a 'new translation' of *De la grammatologie*.

Spivak also undertook an indispensable task in 1976: a comprehensive introduction of Derrida and *Of Grammatology*. She was fortunate to have both de Man and Hillis Miller as her first readers and the near eighty-page introduction has itself become part of the history of the reception of Derrida in America. At the same time, it was perhaps this very need to introduce Derrida's work on 'de-construction' that led Spivak – despite Derrida's warnings – to describe *Of Grammatology* as a *book*. At the outset of her preface, Spivak reflects on the nature of the preface and puts into question the status of the work that is taken as a 'book'. She writes:

> The preface, by daring to repeat the book and reconstitute it in another register, merely enacts what is already the case: the book's repetitions are always other than the book. There is, in fact, no 'book' other than these ever-different repetitions: the 'book' in other words, is always already a 'text', constituted by the play of identity and difference (*OG* xii).

Despite this, later in her preface while remarking on the differences between the 1965–66 review articles in *Critique* and Derrida's 1967 work, Spivak still describes *De la grammatologie* as a book: 'It is fascinating to study the changes and interpolations made in the text of the review articles as they were transformed into *the book*' (*OG* lxxx, my emphasis).

To complement Spivak's remarkable introduction it is helpful to take note of the brief comments on the back cover of *De la grammatologie*, written in 1967. It is striking that this text, which is most likely by Derrida himself, begins by emphasizing his interest not in the primacy of writing but in the bizarre or uncanny relation between speech and writing, in an interlacing oscillation between presence and absence that cannot be harnessed entirely to a commanding science of language:

> 'Languages are made to be spoken, writing is only used to *supplement* speech. . . . Writing is only the *representation* of speech, it is *bizarre* that one gives more care [*soin*] to the determining of the image than of the object'. ROUSSEAU
> This book is therefore devoted to the bizarre. But in giving its full attention [*soin*] to writing, it subjects writing to a radical re-evaluation. And the routes it takes are necessarily extravagant, as it is a matter of exceeding what presents itself as logic itself in order to think what makes it possible: that logic which must determine the relation of speech and writing by taking its reassurance

from the self-evidence of common sense, from the categories of 'representation' or 'image', from the opposition of inside and outside, of the more and the less, of essence and appearance, of the originary and the derivative.

Analysing the investments that our culture has given to the written sign, Jacques Derrida also demonstrates the written sign's topical and sometimes most unnoticed effects. This is only possible through a systematic displacement of concepts: indeed one could not respond to the question '*what is writing?*' by a 'phenomenological' style of appeal to some wild, immediate and spontaneous experience. The Western interpretation of writing governs all fields of experience, of practice and knowledge, and even the ultimate form of the question ('what is?') that one believes oneself able to free from this grip. The history of this interpretation is not that of a particular prejudice, a localized error or an accidental limit. It forms a finite but necessary structure in the movement that finds itself recognized here under the name of *différance*.

Sean Gaston

PREFACE

READING *DE LA GRAMMATOLOGIE*

Some have found it hard to credit that I did not know Jacques Derrida's name when I bought *De la grammatologie* off the Minuit catalogue because it looked interesting.[1] I bring it up for the record because I saw the following in a biography of Derrida published by Continuum:

> De Man sought to show that the signifier is, like the referent, material, and hence, as a set of mere marks and inscriptions, should not be taken to be something which should immediately, without reflection, guide action. That is, the sign 'Aryan' could mislead one into thinking that there really is an 'Aryan' race, when in fact the materiality of persons and their distinctions cannot, except without great violence, be associated with the linguistic division of persons into separate races according to linguistic, mental signs. G. C. Spivak, Derrida's translator, and one of de Man's students at Yale, makes this point with reference to the term 'Aryan' in her work on post-colonialism (McQuillan 2001, 118). The material signifier in literature means nothing, but it invites us to dream and to become aware of the reality of reality. (Powell, *Jacques Derrida: A Biography* 155)

The details are wrong here. I was Paul de Man's student at Cornell. I left to teach at Iowa in 1965. De Man met Derrida in 1966, at the structuralism conference at Johns Hopkins.[2]

The reader should imagine a foreign female student from Asia, in the United States, in a European field, in 1965, before multiculturalism, but also before Internet, email, fax. There was no reason anyone should send her information about the conference and no way I would know of its importance.

As for the 'Aryan' example, implicitly suggesting that Spivak made deconstruction safe for third-world politics, the author misread his source.[3]

It is important for me that reading *De la grammatologie* was among my chances (Derrida, 'My Chances/*Mes chances*'). I do not remember that first untutored reading at all. The reader will understand and, I hope, forgive my investment in making of my chance encounter an example of the play of chance in that essay. The question of the mark and the proper name being the condition of iterability will relate to the argument about the prohibition of the proper name and oral language in *De la grammatologie* which I will discuss later ('My Chances' 360). Derrida's taking a distance from the necessity Freud avoids in order to think psychoanalysis as 'positive science' will relate to yet another passage in *De la grammatologie* about which I will also write below ('My Chances' 369). But the two special passages that I claim here are: 'more probably, it imposed itself upon my choice as if I had fallen upon it leaving me the illusion of free will' (344, trans. mod.). 'Works befall us; they say or unveil what befalls us *by* befalling us. They dominate us inasmuch as they explain themselves with what falls from above' (361, trans. mod.).

I realize that this sort of resemblance by hindsight is what 'Mes Chances' would call a 'symptom' in the Epicurean sense. If these were memoirs, I would be even more symptomatic and, beginning with my Programme Chair's warning that I was compromising my professional future by suddenly beginning to translate, before receiving tenure, a writer obscure in both senses, continue on with the peculiar ups and downs of my peripheral and tangential trajectory in 'deconstruction', ending with the passage: 'The sign of bad luck [*mal chance ou méchance*] would be inverted; it would be the chance for truth to reveal itself' (366, trans. mod.).

Why was I so taken by the book? Why did I want to translate it when I knew so little French? Why did the University of Massachusetts Press give me a contract to do so when I had no recommendation letters? (Hillis Miller later took it over to Johns Hopkins Press without my knowledge but appropriately, of course.) If favourite passages had emerged at that time, I cannot report them. All for me is excitement recollected in relative tranquillity.

There is even more forgetfulness at the origin. Looking again at the 'Translator's Preface', many years later, I notice that I put 'New Delhi – Dacca [*sic*] – Calcutta' in parentheses, inside the text, inside the list of metropolitan places. That visit to Dhaka held a secret origin for my work, which I forgot for many years. I went on thinking that that new direction in my writing started with 'Can the Subaltern Speak?', where I 'chose' (no chance there!) Derrida over Deleuze and Foucault.[4] But, by a chance conversation a year ago, a forgotten secret starting point opened, with pictures of war-raped women in Bangladesh in 1972:

> I don't quite know where to begin Nayanika, but I very much want to say something. Derrida speaks of destinerrance – that a thing always errs away from its destination. Pulling these pictures up from 71/72 is almost an allegory of that for me.[5] These pictures were not any records of anything for me – I should say here I am not a photographer. This was not being undertaken for any academic transcoding. It was an emotional thing – mother and daughter going back to where mother had been happiest, the city of Dhaka. Going back to where no one in the family had been after 1941, the year before my birth. A luminous secret.

These are words spoken to Nayanika Mookerjee, who has included a version of the conversation in her book *The Spectral Wound*.[6] This conversation is interspersed with looking through photo albums, searching for and talking through photographs of women who were raped in the Bangladesh war of 1971 and were in the Dhaka Rehabilitation Centre from 1972, taken by my mother and me in the Rehabilitation Centre in Dhaka in January 1973.

What I had in turn forgotten in my conversation with Nayanika was that during this trip I was also translating Derrida's book, in the shared austere hotel room, in rickshaws, onto notebooks, now lost, with soft cardboard covers. If translation is the most intimate act of reading, I cannot prefer a passage in that first act of reading, framed in forgetting a scene of origin.

Later, in re-reading for teaching, lecturing, writing, some passages emerged. I did not relate to the reading of Rousseau, paradoxically because during my years at Cornell, de Man had been too deeply in his Rousseau period. Rousseau seemed to belong to finer reading minds than mine.

* * *

The first passage is a description of the double bind resident in wanting to deconstruct. You must live in your object, work as your object and go under in a specific way – dare one say, specific to the object? – Captain Ahab and Moby Dick.

> The movements of deconstruction do not shake up [*sollicitent*] structures from the outside. They are neither possible and effective, nor can they set their aim [*ajuster leur coup*], except by inhabiting those structures. Inhabiting them *in a certain way*, because one always inhabits and all the more when one does not suspect it. Operating necessarily from the inside, borrowing all the strategic and economic resources of subversion from the old structure, borrowing them structurally, that is to say without being able to isolate their elements and atoms, the enterprise of deconstruction is always, in a certain way, swept away by [*emportée par*] its own work. (*OG* 24; *DG* 39, trans. mod.)[7]

What strikes the reader again and again is the responsibility of the critic. You cannot shake up the whole thing from the outside, but you cannot separate the tiny bits from the inside either, work at working *as* your object rather – the thing that developed into *être juste avec* – but not quite *as*, for though you live in it the resources are still borrowed, so you are living without authorization, which implies a certain degree of separation or caution, which might imply a self-consciousness, perhaps (Derrida, 'To Do Justice to Freud')?[8] But this self-consciousness must be prepared to be carried off by its own intimate risk-taking. What is this being-carried-away? How to distinguish it either from falling back within or pushing away from without? Is this the distance between the italics of self-consciousness in the first *in a certain way*, and their absence as the being-carried-away of and by self-consciousness in the end? All these are practical questions, about reading and the limits of reading. I have also always liked *ancienne* – translated as 'old'. I know it can mean simply 'pre-existing', or 'prior'. But I like to think that this is an indication of Derrida's engagement with the classics. Live in them in a certain way, be swept away, but don't be unsuspecting.

If the first passage is about the responsibility of reading, the second passage is about the transactional character of writing:

> The constitution of a science or philosophy of writing is a necessary and difficult task. But, having managed to reach [*parvenue*] these limits [of historical closure] and repeating them without closure, a *thought* of the trace, of differance or of reserve must also point beyond the field of the episteme. Outside of the economic and strategic reference to the name that Heidegger justifies himself in giving to an analogous but not identical transgression of all philosophemes, *thought* is here for us a perfectly neutral name, a textual blank [*blanc textuel*], the necessarily indeterminate index of an epoch of differance to come. *In a certain way, 'thought' means nothing.* Like all openings, this index belongs, by the face that is open to view, to a past epoch. This thought weighs nothing [*ne pèse rien*]. It is, in the play of the system, that very thing which always weighs nothing [*jamais ne pèse rien*]. Thinking, it is what we already know as not having yet begun; doing that which, measured by writing's size, cuts in only within the episteme. Grammato*logy*, this thought, would still hold itself walled-in within presence. (*OG* 93; *DG* 142, trans. mod.) [9]

We have to remember that the trace/differance/reserve thought carries the name of writing in the general sense only in this historical episteme, our mind set, by the face open to our view in Derrida's book. But this passage speaks to me also because it is about writing in one specific narrow sense, considering the question: what is it to write, here, now. Does writing carry thought? Only weightlessly, but also taking the weight of nothing by having an enclosed thingly face. For in the system that can be called writing, thought always weighs nothing because it looks to the future when it will differ from itself and be inhabited, knowingly or unknowingly, by another reader/thinker. And so on indefinitely. Am I empiricizing? Am I wrong in thinking the text would let it pass? Writing in the narrow sense is not only making meaning, it is a sign-system, but it is also pointing, like a trace, if we keep up with 'writing' in the general sense. (This is why, by 'Mes Chances', he is uninterested in the sign as such, seeing every word in a text as having the divisible iterability of the mark or proper name. The syncategoremes are coming loose here. This may be a pointing at the 'closed to view', to which I assign no proper name.)

We arrive with industry at the limits of the historical closure and we fall in, pointing at the way out, as the event escapes into some future anterior. In so far as even a nothing must be thought, in writing.

Because Derrida so expressly takes his distance from Heidegger, even as he points at the similarities, I will spend a moment on Heidegger here. The series of lectures entitled 'What Is Called Thinking?' was delivered by Heidegger at the University of Freiburg during the winter and summer semesters of 1951–52, roughly fifteen years before the summer of 1965, when Derrida wrote the two articles for *Critique* that would become *De la grammatologie*. It is well known that the articles used the Heideggerian word 'destruction' for what would become 'deconstruction' in the book. That more affirmative move, made so early, was a rewriting of the responsibility of thinking. The move, as Derrida points out in the passage I have quoted, is 'outside of the economic and strategic reference to the name that Heidegger justifies himself in giving to an analogous but not identical transgression of all philosophemes'. Heidegger transgresses by redirecting and claiming, Derrida by way of trace/reserve/differance. In one way or the other, the important Heidegger essays by Derrida re-cite the move ('The Ends of Man', 'Heidegger's Hand', 'Geschlecht I', 'Of Spirit', 'Heidegger's Ear').

I have argued elsewhere that Derrida rewrote Kant's transcendental dialectic as trace and have tried to show the trace of the trace in fourteen unrevised paragraphs of the *Critique of Pure Reason*.[10] I have repeated, in much of my commentary on Derrida's early work, including in this essay, that in his early period, Derrida saw the 'thought' of the trace – a perilous necessity to be avoided in order to establish grammatology – as his contribution to a philosophizing that would not 'transgress' in the direction of the universal (Derrida, 'Différance' 12).

'What Is Called Thinking?' may be called the site of such a transgression in the direction of the universal. Here Heidegger claims the *logos* as his ally. In 'Freud and the Scene of Writing' (1966) Derrida warns that logocentrism is not a pathology (197). But Heidegger claims for thinking a specifically logocentric destiny (166–7). He suggests that the naming, by man, of the Being of beings as thinking (or 'thanc' – 'thought, thanks, memory [. . .] in the realm of the unspoken', or *enos emmenai* as in Parmenides) is called for by the very nature of the Being of beings (*What is Called Thinking?* 153). (Heidegger himself gives indications of passages declaring this already in *Being and Time*, and the famous paragraph 22 of the 'Letter on Humanism', as a place where this thought of 'the end of man' is already broached.[11]) Kant's synthetic a priori, Hegel's epistemograph of Absolute Knowledge biting its own tail, and, of course, 'the Greeks' are seen as examples (*What is Called Thinking?* 243, 238).[12] The leap across the aporia to a non-empirical superman-hood – signalled as Nietzsche's 'weightiest thought'; (Derrida sees thought as 'weighing nothing') – is now possible, says Heidegger, although it cannot, of course, be done through a series of lectures (*What is Called Thinking?* 108, 171). Here and there, the entire invest-igation claims Christianity.

These are crucial differences. But it is the uncanny resemblances that strike ('analogous but not identical transgression of all philoso-phemes', writes Derrida). Heidegger seems to include versions of the textual blank that I discuss below (*What is Called Thinking?* 186). 'Being underway' seems linked to the 'to come' (*What is Called Thinking?* 30, 35, 169). We cannot let go of the fact that Derrida sees his philosophy as walled in, because it *is* a thought through system. The event, for him, escapes. By contrast, Heidegger justifies his philo-sophy as the opening needed by truth. The event, of unconcealment, remains concealed as a silent guarantee.

Derrida's harshest judgement of these self-justifying methodolo-gical manoeuvres as the animal automata, without 'humanity', cited by Descartes and others in the eighteenth century, is to be found in *Of Spirit* (129–36).[13]

There is a bit of Mallarmé in the Derridean passage, in the engage-ment with the blank, with nothing. Thought is not just a blank, but a textual blank, a blank organized by *this* text, by the size of writing, 'spacing'.[14] The nothing it weighs is nothing and a (thing named) nothing; Derrida uses the skeleton of a specific language – his own historical closure: both *pèse rien* and *ne pèse rien*, allowed only by French. This is why here too it is 'a certain way'. The text is that way, enclosed in French, each word divisible by translation. You, writer, be careful how you weave, for the web organizes the blank, the noth-ing, no thing thing, for a certain opening. The web's design is locked up. Ulysses as Penelope. You call it masculine hysteria if you want to take away its practicality.[15]

Shailja Patel, an activist writer from Kenya, reminded me recently that I had said at WALTIC (Writers and Literary Translators' Inter-national Conference) in Stockholm, 2008: 'I take this idea extremely seriously, so I am obliged to critique it rigorously. We are self-appointed moral entrepreneurs, our mission predicated on the failure of state and revolution. We fetishize literacy, health, employ-ability'. Alas, I know where I got this 'I'm inside and so must talk and this is our historical moment' stuff. I cringe at the vulgarization. But there was no one to say it there. And Derrida is not compulsory reading for European do-gooders.

* * *

These two passages about reading and writing that I so love come at the end of the section in the book that lays down the terms of his positive science, his 'grammato*logy*', the concluding chapter of Part I of the *Grammatology*: 'Writing Before the Letter'. Derrida reso-lutely remains within the enclosure of presence. Three times he repeats: 'Without venturing up to that perilous necessity', almost like a mantra. (Again, 'Mes Chances' strikes a chord for me, for, as I have indicated, Freud is there shown as not venturing up to certain peril-ous necessities in order to wall in psycho-*analysis* as a 'positive sci-ence'. Derrida's work with Freud was a lifelong engagement with the pointing away. . . .) Must have a definition before I start reading, here Derrida seems to suggest – and all definitions are decided in the night of non-knowledge, without venturing up to the perilous necessities of the conditions of possibility of truth-telling. The section closes with the paragraphs I have quoted before, and goes on to read Lévi-Strauss and Rousseau.

The first necessity avoided is the undoing or shaking up of logo-centrism as a whole. We know from our first passage that he knows that he is borrowing the structures of logocentrism intimately and that this knowledge is a *pharmakon*.

The second necessity avoided is a meditation on the trace. This is so that a historical closure, which necessarily implies an origin, can be described in order further to describe, in its terms, the history of the suppression of writing in the general sense. The thought of the trace would have forbidden it. But of course, a *thought* of the trace, in so far as it is a thought, has always *weighed* nothing, transitively and descriptively. Thus it gives an opening, though not in the justifying Heideggerian mode. And we will not know this until the end of 'Writing Before the Letter'. For now only the alerting that all this material that follows is only possible by sleeping with the enemy.

In other words, we must make our words weigh something in order to weigh nothing and in this chapter, which gives us a task of grammatology as positive science by virtue of the famous French partitive genitive, we get it by clues, like a detective story, a genre I have been obsessed by since high school. Perhaps that's how I knew these were not vain circlings. They offered us a do-it-yourself 'imitative form' philosophizing lesson in how to think, read, write responsibly, in circles – of course necessarily linear by the double bind of intended mistake. A teaching text, multi-tasking.

The third necessity not risked is the question of essence. In order to proceed, it must be assumed that there is something called writing. This grounding error is possible only if this additional necessity nested in the thought of the trace is not risked. But if it is a thought . . . And so on. This obligation is not a strategic use of essentialism, but a necessity to presuppose essence and therefore a necessity to ignore the necessity unearthed by the young philosopher and declared as the definitive solution offered by his philosophy (Derrida, 'Différance' 25–6). *Être juste avec* Kant (to be continued when time and context allow).

I have already said that I remember nothing of my first reading of this exciting book by an unknown author, the reading that changed my life. I do know, however, that when, at the end of his life, the dying philosopher tries to venture up to every perilous necessity, necessarily transformed, in *The Animal That Therefore I Am*, the reading that began at the beginning helped me to see, with wonder, how he breaks form, teaching the limits of reading, multi-tasking, always in a certain way, whodunit style, seriatim, leading us into discoveries. He said in print that I am a poor reader, so perhaps I am wrong, but that is also part of the story (Derrida, 'Marx & Sons' 222–3). It is true that I had thanked Catty in quite the wrong direction in my Introduction.[16]

With these provisos, then, I enter the reading: the shorter one of Lévi-Strauss, not the long one of Rousseau, which provoked de Man's 'Rhetoric of Blindness: Derrida Reading Rousseau' (1970), which Derrida criticized long after de Man's death ('"Le Parjure", *Perhaps*', 'Typewriter Ribbon').

In the Lévi-Strauss reading, I always liked this passage particularly, although all of that reading is impressive in the interrogation of
a benevolent anthropologism ferociously active today:

> [A] people that accedes to the genealogical pattern [*dessin* lit.
> drawing] accedes also to writing in the colloquial sense. [. . .] Here
> one passes from arche-writing to writing in the colloquial sense.
> This [. . .] is not a passage from speech to writing, it operates
> within writing in general. The genealogical relation and social
> classification are the stitched seam of arche-writing, condition of
> the (so-called oral) language, and of writing in the usual sense
> [*sens commun*]. (*OG* 125; *DG* 182, trans. mod.)

I will do a mea culpa here. In this passage, Derrida is speaking
neither of genealogical *memories* as such, nor of the early Freudian
notion of mnemic traces, about which he writes an important essay
just about now ('Freud and the Scene of Writing' 198). His point
about the emergence of the *proper* name as standing in for the
absent person, wrenched as mark from its common meaning, is not
necessarily related to the psychic machine. In order, however, to face
the foolish argument that 'privileging writing ignores orature', I have
routinely twisted Derrida's words to accommodate genealogical
memories and writing as mnemic mark. And no one has cared or
known enough to question me. To measure the extent of my error,
I pore over the body–mind discussions in 'My Chances/ *Mes chances*',
looking specifically at such lines as 'one must not confuse what refers
to the biophysical and organic in the drive with what is represented
of it in the physical world [*le monde physique*]' (369), and recall that
other warning that Derrida places as an epigraph to 'Freud and the
Scene of Writing:' 'in what the fraying [of the mnemic material] does
consist remains an open question' (198, trans. mod.).

* * *

Now more and more passages crowd my memory, and demand attention. It is like those forgotten first days, perhaps, when the whole
book had to be given equal time. Any ending will be abrupt, an
unwilling cut. I leave you with this short list, then: reading, writing,
sheltering and the argument from the proper name transgressed.
Nothing, ever, about the Aryans.

Postscript. Although there is an altogether important discussion of auto-eroticism in *De la grammatologie*, there is not much play of sexual difference here. Did I wait for *Spurs*? In the 'Translator's Preface' my philosopher was a 'she'. I was uncharacteristically unmindful of the historical problems of such careless reduction of gendering to choice of grammatical gender. Still working on that one . . .

Gayatri Chakravorty Spivak

PART 1

WRITING BEFORE THE LETTER

THE END OF THE BOOK AND THE BEGINNING OF WRITING

CHRISTOPHER JOHNSON, EPOCH, EVENT, CONTEXT (*OG* 3–5; *DG* 11–14)

Cette inadéquation avait toujours déjà commencé à donner le mouvement. Mais quelque chose aujourd'hui la laisse apparaître comme telle, en permet une sorte de prise en charge, sans qu'on puisse traduire cette nouveauté dans les notions sommaires de mutation, d'explicitation, d'accumulation, de révolution ou de tradition. (*DG* 13; *OG* 4)

Each time that I return to *Of Grammatology*, I am struck and fascinated by the rhetoric of its introduction. The Exergue is an extremely dramatic piece of writing, with a very strong sense of historical conjuncture. It announces the closure of an epoch, or at least our emergent apprehension of such a closure, and anticipates a monstrous future. The epoch is that of *logocentrism*, the metaphysics of phonetic writing which is also an *ethnocentrism*, to the extent that the 'Western' variant of alphabetic writing is accepted as the most evolved and most effective transcription of human speech, a variant which, at the time of writing, the author asserts, is in the process of colonizing the planet. The time of writing, of course, is far from indifferent, and this is what particularly fascinates me about the Exergue and its framing of the *Grammatology* as a whole. As with all seminal texts, the thinking of *Grammatology* both transcends its historical context and is indelibly marked by this context, so much so that by the time of the appearance of its English translation in

1976 the world, it could be argued, had already moved on. I will focus here on two elements of context.

1. The first element of context is clearly geo-political: the italicization of *ethnocentrism* in the first sentence reminds the reader of the immediate proximity, in 1967, of decolonization, a world-event more explicitly referenced in 'Structure, Sign and Play' (1966), where it is presented as a *decentring* of the West convergent with the end of logocentrism (*Writing and Difference* 282). The reference to ethno-centrism also reminds us that *Of Grammatology* was a dramatic intervention into a discursive field which in 1960s France was dominated by structuralism, most notably through the anthropology of Claude Lévi-Strauss. Lévi-Strauss's formulation of a 'structural' anthropology not only set in train a new kind of thinking or *theoriza-tion* characteristic of the so-called human sciences, it also positioned anthropology, within the context of decolonization, as the self-reflexive voice and conscience of Western civilization, the critique of ethno-centrism being one of its central themes. What Derrida's opening reference to ethnocentrism does, therefore, is re-open the question of ethnocentrism from the point of view of speech and writing, a question which will lead him, quite inevitably, to his engagement with Lévi-Strauss in the second part of *Of Grammatology*.

2. The second element of context has to do with science, or rather what science had become in the post-war period. Under this reading, the apprehension of the limits of logocentrism is not simply some-thing that happens within philosophy, within a certain history of metaphysics, but something that happens *between* philosophy and science. On the one hand, '*the concept of science* or the scientificity of science', of science as logic, has always been a philosophical concept. On the other hand, the *practice* of science has always contested the 'imperialism of the logos' in its recourse to non-phonetic writing (*OG* 3). The specific example given here is mathematical symbolism, but if science in practice has always already been out of step with logocentrism, there is something different, something *peculiar*, about the present epoch:

> It could not have been otherwise. Nonetheless, it is a peculiarity of our epoch that, at the moment when the phoneticization of writing – the historical origin and structural possibility of philosophy as of science, the condition of the *epistémè* – begins to lay hold on world culture, science can no longer, in any of

its areas of advancement, be satisfied with it. This inadequation had always already begun to make its presence felt. But today something lets it appear as such, allows us in a way to take charge of it, without our being able to translate this novelty into clear cut notions of mutation, explication, accumulation, revolution, or tradition. (*OG* 3–4; *DG* 12–13, trans. mod.)

The disengagement of decolonization does not mean an end to Western hegemony, rather it is accompanied in the post-war period by the definitive globalization of Western thought and science. At the same time, what has been the necessary, structural blindness of logocentrism to its internal contradictions ('It could not have been otherwise') is giving way, *within science itself*, to the insight of the limits of logocentrism. The dramatic message of the Exergue is that there is 'something' today, a 'peculiarity of our epoch' which enables such a revealing, and which makes a grammatology finally possible. If the traditional discourse of historical change (mutation, accumulation, revolution, etc.) is inadequate to the description of such an epoch, its novelty or monstrosity, nevertheless the reader is drawn, inexorably, to the question of what this conditioning 'something' might be. And if that 'something' is not reducible to a singular event or set of events, then one is left with the question of the different *contexts* of post-war science, the different areas of 'advancement' that might have produced qualitatively new ways of thinking the world.

MICHAEL SYROTINSKI, ORIGINS: 'THE MOST ORIGINAL AND POWERFUL ETHNOCENTRISM' (*OG* 3; *DG* 11)

The opening page of the Exergue. An opening and an origin, the beginning of the story we know all too well about the impossibility of the origin (of language, for example), in a text many would identify as the very 'origin of poststructuralism':

This triple exergue is intended not only to focus attention on the *ethnocentrism* which, everywhere and always, had controlled the concept of writing. Nor merely to focus attention on what I shall call *logocentrism*: the metaphysics of phonetic writing (for example, of the alphabet) which was fundamentally – for enigmatic yet essential reasons that are inaccessible to a simple

historical relativism – nothing but the most original and powerful
ethnocentrism, in the process of imposing itself upon the world.
(*OG* 3)

The triple exergue points to three interrelated realms, which are all
controlled or determined by logocentrism: (1) the concept of writing;
(2) the history of metaphysics; and (3) the concept of science, as
logic. These three realms will be mirrored in Rousseau's three stages
which lead dialectically, as Hegel will also tell us at far greater length,
and with the utmost philosophical rigour, to the equation of civilization with writing.

Writing (*écriture*), or 'arche-writing', is thus announced at the
outset as the concept through which Derrida will deconstruct
Western metaphysics, its fundamental ethnocentrism, and its onto-
theological privileging of *logos* as speech, presence, the proper, and
so on, and it will become for him the first of a long series of quasi-
transcendental and ever-changing place-holding terms that are all,
in essence, saying and doing the same thing (*différance, supplement,
pharmakon, trace, dissemination, cinders, signature, shibboleth, subjectile, hauntology*, the wholly other (*le tout autre*) and so on). The
ceaseless movement of this renaming, as Spivak rightly points out
in her Preface, itself enacts the refusal to assign priority to any
master-word, any master trope.

Spivak's translation in 1976 marks an important opening of the
whole epoch that is the history of the reception of so-called poststructuralism in the anglophone world, and these two narratives –
the internal logic or unfolding of Derrida's writings in French over
four decades, and the history of deconstruction in the anglophone
world, in which Derrida himself played a very active and central role –
will be inextricably intertwined. This translation is also the text that
kick-starts Spivak's own career, and throughout her own particular
brand of deconstruction/postcolonialism/Marxism/feminism she will
constantly circle back to this opening page, with its foregrounding
of the inherently ethnocentric, colonizing power of language as logocentrism (an implicit theme that Derrida himself will take up most
explicitly in *Monolingualism of the Other*), as a kind of touchstone
for her own work – perhaps in this respect it is even for her 'the most
original and powerful' of all Derrida's insights, which has become
a sort of founding statement of the 'ethico-political' underpinning of

deconstruction, not only for Spivak, but also for many other critics, particularly in postcolonial contexts.

Yet, as Paul de Man showed so brilliantly in his reading of *Grammatology*, 'The Rhetoric of Blindness', if what Derrida names 'logocentrism' is only possible as a dissimulation of an (impossible) origin, it becomes a story precisely of blindness and insight, the extent to which the language of the narrative is aware of its own 'logocentric fallacy'. De Man argues that Rousseau's texts are in fact absolutely wide-eyed and extraordinarily insightful about their own inevitably rhetorical structures, and his writings thus form exemplary narratives about language, what de Man will later name 'allegories'. De Man is not interested in using Rousseau to trump Derrida, but the thrust of his argument is that Derrida's text exactly resembles Rousseau's 'Essay on the Origin of Languages', insofar as it also narrates the logocentric fallacy of privileging voice over writing as the *fiction* of a consecutive, historical process. Here is de Man: 'Throughout, Derrida uses Heidegger and Nietzsche's fiction of metaphysics as a *period* in Western thought in order to dramatize, to give tension and suspense to the argument, exactly as Rousseau gave tension and suspense to the story of language by making them pseudo-historical' ('Rhetoric of Blindness' 137).

Could one say likewise that Spivak's Preface to her translation of *De la grammatologie,* for all of its erudite references to Derrida up to and including *Glas* (1974) and the lectures on Ponge and Heidegger at Yale in 1975, and despite its theoretical sophistication and its apparent deconstructive self-awareness of the impossible nature of prefaces, seems to fall into this very trap of telling the 'story' of grammatology in terms of historical periodization, from Plato through to Hegel and Husserl, with Heidegger, Freud and Nietzsche cast as 'proto-grammatologues' (*OG* 1).

This long story of Spivak as a reader of Derrida I have sketched out in more detail elsewhere (*Deconstruction and the Postcolonial* 40–61), but I would like to look at another critic, Robert Young, who like Spivak references this one line in *Of Grammatology* in order to underpin the claims made in his own particular version of a historical narrative. In an article on deconstruction's relationship to postcolonial theory written for the volume *Deconstructions: A User's Guide* (2000), Young reaffirms the argument he first advanced in his 1990 book *White Mythologies,* namely that Jacques Derrida's work has always challenged the ethico-political tensions at the heart of colonialist ideology. Young resituates Derrida's work within a postcolonial theoretical framework (and, from the outset, an anti-colonial one) by reminding us that Derrida's long, meticulous analysis of the discursive privileging of speech over writing in the Western metaphysical tradition is relayed through a critique of *ethnocentrism*, more precisely of ethnocentrism as a kind of Eurologocentrism. Young's earlier arguments demonstrating the mutual interests shared by deconstruction and postcolonial theory are vindicated, according to him, by the publication in the intervening decade of texts which are both more explicitly autobiographical (*Monolingualism of the Other*, 'Circumfession' and *Archive Fever*, among others) and more overtly ethico-political in terms of their themes (*Specters of Marx*, *Of Hospitality*, and *On Cosmopolitanism and Forgiveness*, for example). For Young, then, Derrida's grammatological notion of *writing* is co-extensive or congruent with his persistent and enduring condemnation of forms of *actual* violence, beginning with his own experiences of racism and exclusion as a Francophone Maghrebian Jew in colonial Algeria. This leads Young to conclude that deconstruction has 'itself been a form of cultural decolonization' ('Deconstruction and the Postcolonial' 199), a statement that is then confidently expanded into a series of more sweeping propositions. Young suggests that Derrida effectively took Sartre's critique of totalitarian politics, in North Africa and elsewhere, and extended it to a generalized conceptual critique of all forms of 'totalization'. It was, as he says, 'the deconstruction of the idea of totality borne out of resistance to totalizing regimes of late colonial states' (192). Once Derrida moved to metropolitan France from Algeria, his early experiences were translated, according to Young, into a permanent and continuous political subversiveness: 'Derrida, neither French nor Algerian, always anti-nationalist and cosmopolitan, critical of Western ethnocentrism from *Of Grammatology*'s very first page, preoccupied with justice and injustice, developed deconstruction as a procedure for intellectual and cultural decolonization within the metropolis' (193). We are then provided with a long list of illustrative examples, starting with the notion that the deconstruction of centrism, or of *logos*, only makes sense in the context of the centralization of the French administrative system (194), and thus the concept of 'erasure' [in the famous phrase *sous rature*, 'under erasure'] echoes General Bugead's tactics of suppression of the Algerian uprising (195), leading finally to the statement that Derrida's ideas have been taken up by a large number of post-colonial migrant and immigrant groups (208).

There is a danger, though, that rather than offering watertight evidence to support the central proposition of his argument, Young's long list of 'proofs' produces an internal tension of its own. While on the one hand he is contesting the tradition of a certain 'grand narrative' of intellectual history, on the other it appears that he is constructing an *alternative* grand narrative, which produces a homogenous unity that goes against the grain of a deconstructive reading. His 'isomorphic' mapping of deconstruction onto postcolonial concerns also implies a causal flow from historical context to theoretical text (which can be retrospectively 'excavated'). What is more interesting is that Young appears to elide the very manoeuvres of Derrida's work that he is at the same time celebrating. This is more than a matter of misunderstanding, given that the idea of being able to 'make sense fully' is precisely the sort of metaphysical ideal that Derrida consistently uncovers as an illusion, albeit an unavoidable one.

None of this is to deny that Young is a fine reader of Derrida's work, and certainly a far better one than most postcolonial critics, but one might at least question the kind of discursive isomorphism between deconstruction and various forms of cultural or ideological decolonization that Young is proposing, since deconstruction can never, as Derrida himself remarked on numerous occasions, cohere into anything one might conventionally understand as theory or critique. It is rather, to borrow Paul de Man's phrase, an endless 'resistance to theory', that is nonetheless irresistible, because it conditions and constitutes the terms in which we can even think about theory. One way of phrasing it might be to say that Young, in proposing empirical or experiential grounds where one could locate the 'origins' of deconstruction, is repeating the rhetorical manoeuvre that a thinker such as Lévi-Strauss performs (as Derrida will go on to demonstrate later on in *Of Grammatology*), namely the reduction of the logically anterior 'arche-violence' of writing, in the strong theoretical sense of the term, to historically or empirically determinate, local manifestations of violence. Derrida's point about originary violence is that one has to go further 'upstream' in the decision chain, and this has implications for everything else further downstream. Indeed, if there is any isomorphism in these closely interlinked narratives – Spivak and Young reading Derrida, Derrida reading Rousseau or Derrida reading Heidegger, reading Husserl – it is that they are all allegories of the necessity of misreading. To put it another way, we are always within grammatology: we have perhaps never been without *Grammatology*.

SEAN GASTON, EVEN LEIBNIZ (*OG* 3; *DG* 11–12)

Derrida uses Leibniz to distinguish a logocentric language based on sight from a logocentric language founded on hearing (oneself speak). In the Exergue, he writes: '*the history of metaphysics* which, despite all the differences, and not only from Plato to Hegel (even including Leibniz) but also, outside of these apparent limits, from the pre-Socratics to Heidegger, has always assigned the origin of truth in general to the logos' (*OG* 3; *DG* 11–12, trans. mod.). Derrida gives Leibniz this distinction of a parenthetical addition in the logocentric history of metaphysics because of the *characteristica universalis*, Leibniz's notion of a universal language based on a system of characters or non-phonetic signs.

As Derrida notes, Hegel rejects Leibniz's theory of universal language because it threatens the logos and its connection to 'the origin of truth in general' by advocating a writing that generalizes – and sets aside – both the sensible and the intellectual: 'When he [Hegel] criticizes the Leibnizian characteristic, the formalism of the understanding and mathematical symbolism, he makes the same gesture: denouncing the being-outside-of-itself of the logos in sensible or intellectual abstraction' (*OG* 24; *DG* 39, trans. mod.). For Hegel, Leibniz's work has the potential to interrupt or disorder one of the key discriminations or self-evident oppositions of the history of metaphysics. This might lead one to think of Leibniz as a way of resisting the Hegelian theory of language. But Derrida warns against the confident assertion of such a radical alternative. Even Leibniz cannot provide the pure exit from metaphysics.

According to Hegel, unlike the alphabet, Leibniz's universal language fails to efface itself before the voice (*OG* 25). Leibniz's non-phonetic language retains and relies on a privileging of the visible and space and resists the *Aufhebung* of writing (*OG* 39). At the same time, Derrida argues, this non-phonetic gesture is based on a profound *ahistoricism*. For Leibniz, 'what liberates Chinese script from the voice is also that which, arbitrarily and by the artifice of invention, wrenches it from history and gives it to philosophy [*la rend propre à la philosophie*]' (*OG* 76; *DG* 113). Derrida's reading of Leibniz raises the challenge of a non-phonetic writing that does not succumb to an ahistoricism.

Leibniz's 'ethnocentric metaphysics' is apparent, Derrida argues, in his idealized use of Chinese writing as a writing that does not refer back to the voice and announces 'its independence with regard to history' (*OG* 79). Chinese writing is a writing of the mind: it has no body and no history. As a 'sort of European hallucination', it promises a writing *for* philosophy: a transparent or diaphanous writing (*OG* 80). For Derrida, this use of the non-European to dream of an ideal writing is also connected to an idealized Western science of perfect calculation (the *epistēmē*). In dreaming of a language without voice, without body and without history, Leibniz thinks of universal writing as a calculating machine. The *characteristic* will stabilize reasoning, mirroring an objectivity that will identify and redeem what we – as philosophers – lack (*OG* 78). It will redeem what is still lacking in philosophy itself. It will contribute to the completion of philosophy.

This 'technicism', or the attempt to colonize *tekhnē* in the late seventeenth century, also reiterates an 'infinitist theology' (*OG* 79). Despite his non-phonetic gesture, even Leibniz is part of the history of metaphysics because he founds this ahistorical, technicist non-phoneticism on a fundamental harmony with the logos. Derrida writes: 'That is why, appearances to the contrary, and in spite of all the seduction that it can legitimately exercise on our epoch, the Leibnizian project of a universal characteristic that is not essentially phonetic does not interrupt logocentrism in any way. On the contrary, universal logic confirms logocentrism, is produced within it with its help, exactly like the Hegelian critique to which it will be subjected' (*OG* 78–9). As Hegel's other, Leibniz should not be mistaken for a figure of alterity or resistance.

CHRISTOPHER JOHNSON, THE CYBERNETIC IMAGINARY (*OG* 6–10; *DG* 15–21)

[L]e biologiste parle aujourd'hui d'écriture et de *pro-gramme* à propos des processus les plus élémentaires de l'information dans

> la cellule vivante. Enfin, qu'il ait ou non des limites essentielles, tout le champ couvert par le *programme* cybernétique sera champ d'écriture. (*DG* 19; *OG* 9)

While there is no explicit reference to structuralism in the first chapter of *Grammatology*, this chapter begins with a critique of its pervasive influence in 1960s France. The extension of the structural-linguistic model to a wide range of disciplines and discourses has resulted, Derrida argues, in a generalized 'inflation' and hence 'devaluation' of the word 'language' (*OG* 6). At the same time, he notes a subtle displacement within the linguistic paradigm itself. Whereas for logocentrism writing is systematically part of language, a secondary feature or *supplement* of speech, in the transition to grammatology language becomes part of a more generalized 'writing' (*OG* 6–7). The different types of human activity which under structuralism were described in terms of a 'language' are therefore now described as a form of 'writing': 'All this to describe not only the system of notation secondarily connected with these activities but the essence and the content of these activities themselves' (*OG* 9).

It could be argued that the transition from 'language' to 'writing' was already implicit within structuralism itself. The chapter's first section, 'The Program', situates the emergence of grammatology in the wider context of cybernetics, a movement or discipline which exercised its own, peculiar field of influence from the 1950s through to the early 1970s. Structuralism in fact combined models of interpretation drawn from linguistics with concepts of a higher level of abstraction taken from cybernetics: communication, control, feedback, program, code, information, message. However, while the discourse of structuralism tended to gravitate towards the lexical field of coding, communication, information and message, for grammatology it is the concept of 'program' which approximates most closely to the structuring principle of 'writing':

> It is also in this sense that the contemporary biologist speaks of writing and *pro-gram* in relation to the most elementary processes of information within the living cell. And finally, whether it has essential limits or not, the entire field covered by the cybernetic *program* would be the field of writing. (*OG* 9)

The reference to biology is an important one. Watson and Crick's discovery of the structure of DNA in 1953, followed by the research of French biologists Jacob and Monod on RNA 'messenger', were directly influenced by developments in information theory and cybernetics. In their turn, these scientific advances seemed to confirm the universalistic aspirations of cybernetics, articulated in Wiener's programmatic text of 1948. Derrida continues with a qualified acknowledgement of the convergence of grammatology and cybernetics:

> If the theory of cybernetics is by itself to oust all metaphysical concepts – including the concepts of soul, of life, of value, of choice, of memory – which until recently served to separate the machine from man, it must conserve the notion of writing, trace, *grammè*, or grapheme, until its own historico-metaphysical character is also exposed. (*OG* 9)

This sentence alludes to a wider context of debate in the 1950s and 1960s, where the self-correcting, self-regulating 'thinking machines' described by cybernetics were raising questions about the uniqueness of human consciousness and the life processes that supported it, and redrawing the traditional boundaries between human and machine, life and non-life. In this sense, it could be said that cybernetics performed a kind of revealing function essential to the emergence of grammatology. However, if grammatology and cybernetics might be described as philosophical fellow travellers, for Derrida the language of cybernetics has not entirely disengaged itself from the language of metaphysics, as he qualifies in a note:

> Wiener, for example, while abandoning 'semantics', and the opposition, judged by him as too crude and too general, between animate [*le vivant*] and inanimate [*le non-vivant*], etc. nevertheless continues to use expressions like 'organs of sense' [*organes des sens*], 'motor organs' [*organes moteurs*], etc. to qualify the parts of the machine. (*OG* 324 n. 3; *DG* 19 n. 3)

The preoccupation of cybernetics with processes of control and communication in living and non-living systems, the animal and the machine, 'deconstructs' the opposition between human and machine, life and non-life, etc. But according to Derrida, cybernetics continues to use what may be termed a 'zoo-morphic' language in its conceptualization of the machine. The role of grammatology as a 'positive' science is precisely to maintain this kind of critical distance from the different scientific discourses that support it. As a footnote to Derrida's footnote, it might be said that we are perhaps also dealing here with an effect of translation between English and French, Wiener and Derrida – and, if one includes the English quotation above, between Wiener, Derrida and Spivak, Derrida's translator. If one looks at texts such as *Cybernetics* (1948) and *The Human Use of Human Beings* (1950), the texts to which Derrida must be referring here, Wiener's vocabulary is in practice less systematic than the above quotation might suggest. While the term 'sense organ' does indeed figure in his descriptions of both human (animal) and machine behaviour, it is normally correlated not with the term 'motor organ' but 'effector', a more neutral, hybrid term that belongs to both engineering and biology. This is not to say that Derrida's caution regarding the language of science is not valid with respect to cybernetics, rather that the question of the language of science and the language of metaphysics can also be complicated by the question of translation between languages.

JULIAN WOLFREYS, OF DARK SENTENCES AND GNOMES[1] (*OG* 7; *DG* 16)

Where does one begin in *Of Grammatology*? There must be a kind of 'reading experiment', a process of construal through the various folds and turns of the text, which wagers everything on the possibility that something can be invented. What will I find, this time? Where will it lead? Perhaps nowhere, or to a place where I return to myself, though different, touched by a difference. I am sentenced to a reading, with which I will never have done, as I follow, sentence by sentence, sentence after sentence, feeling almost blindly through a labyrinth which promises to have already opened onto an abyss. Way of thinking, opinion, an authoritative decision or judgement: the 'correctly ordered series of signs' find themselves always already in deconstruction, and it is this, which, in directing reading, gives us to think, and so, perhaps, to read.

A phrase to which I find myself returning repeatedly is ' "signifier of the signifier" ' ('signifiant du signifiant') (*OG* 7; *DG* 16) near the beginning of *Of Grammatology*, and the sentence of which it is a part. This phrase though small, orders disorder from within the sentence. It is idiomatic, perhaps axiomatic, in that, performatively, it stages not only its own radical instability, an instability, as I shall continue to explore below, arising out of, even as it constitutes and so projects, an undecidability; additionally, it also gives expression and place to the 'truth', if you will, of Derrida's radically expanded conception of 'writing', summed up by Sarah Kofman, in the observation that 'l'écriture est la différence, l'espacement originaire de soi avec soi' ('writing is difference, the originary spacing of itself by itself') (Kofman 20). It marks that which is, simultaneously, *finite* and *endless*, signalling, countersigning perhaps, as one phrase has it, the end of the book and the beginning of writing. Always already underway, always already interrupting, folding back, enfolding, unfolding and cutting into, even as it erupts out of, itself, 'signifiant du signifiant' marks that which *just is* writing, the articulation of disarticulation: '[t]issu de différences, le texte est toujours hétérogène. Sans identité propre, ouvert sur son dehors' ('a tissue of differences, the text is always heterogeneous. Without proper identity, open on its outside') (Kofman 16).

The work of doubling and iterability informs the phrase, but also disturbs logical or grammatical order, as well as sense, and could take up some time here. Doubled in its appearance, the phrase – operating in the manner of an idiom or axiom – maintains its doubling; doubling itself as it itself becomes redoubled before our eyes, it threatens to engulf or overwhelm, in a gesture which I would like to read as simultaneously enfolding and opening. I find myself 'adrift in the threat of limitlessness', and in this my experience doubles that of the simple, though enigmatic form. However, there is an initial sense of paradox. For, while limitlessness, or its threat, leaves both reader and idiom 'all at sea', as it were, the expression remains within itself, folding back on itself. Simultaneously, then, it finds 'itself recaptured within that play' that also promises the erasure of limits, forcing reading to 'economize on the abyss', as Derrida has it elsewhere ('Parergon' 37); and so, in this recuperation, it appears 'brought back to its own finitude at the very moment when its limits seem to disappear' ('inflation', I am tempted to say, in a partial citation, and in an iterable gesture, 'absolute inflation, inflation itself' (*OG* 6)).

Its doubling thus reduplicated, the perhaps axiomatic expression becomes replayed in a single page, and also ironized through the introduction of quotation marks, in the sentence where it appears, following the observation that '[i]n all senses of the word, [and the word is writing, not *logos*] writing thus *comprehends* language' (*OG* 7). Here is the sentence:

> Not that the word 'writing' has ceased to designate the signifier of the signifier [this is already the second appearance of the phrase, the first shortly before the line I am quoting, it being given in italics, its graphic and material condition emphasised], but it appears, strange as it may seem, that 'signifier of the signifier' *no longer* defines accidental doubling and fallen secondarity. (*OG* 7, emphasis added)

There has been a graphic play on and of the words in their given form leading up to this particular sentence, thus:

> By a hardly perceptible necessity, it seems as though the concept of writing – [. . .] no longer designating the exterior surface, the insubstantial double of a major signifier, *the signifier of the signifier* – is beginning to go beyond the extension of writing. (*OG* 6–7)

So, from '*the signifier of the signifier*' (italics) to 'signifier of the signifier' (without quotation marks, no italics, shortly to be cited in the sentence that frames it), and, thence, to '"signifier of the signifier"' (in quotation marks, in that sentence from which I have drawn the phrase in order to begin), none of the differences of which can be heard, save for the abandonment of that first definite article. In this movement, in that motion being mapped, taking place from place to place and so reiterating as there is displacement, this elegant and enigmatic phrase stages in miniature 'the end of the book and the beginning of writing'. Everything – and all the rest – is performed, as there remains to be read that 'beginning to go beyond the extension of writing'.

With a degree of circumspection all too necessary here, Derrida proposes a transformation in the signification of the concept of writing, which, we should recall, is observed in 1967. The historical moment of inscription is worth noting, albeit in passing, given the sudden coming-to-appear, and frequency, of 'aujourd'hui' in the Exergue, a frequency a little downplayed by Gayatri Spivak's omission of the first reference to a today, and the world or planet *today*,

at the end of the first paragraph (*OG* 3); and from here to the following page, 'But *today* something lets itself appear as such, allows it
a kind of takeover without our being able to translate this novelty
into clear-cut notions of mutation, explicitation, accumulation,
revolution, or tradition. These values belong no doubt to the system
whose dislocation is *today* presented as such [. . .] only within a logocentric epoch' (*OG* 4, emphasis added). Of course, *today* appears
and is always already problematized, erupting within any present
moment. Which today is spoken (of) here? *Today* is a word that
at one and the same time programmes closure, the finite, and opening, the infinite. Its apparent or, let us say, its surface certitude,
its *cerfinitude*, pro-grammes its own openness to the arrival of
countless future *todays.*

What would constitute the *today* that causes Derrida to pause with
intense reflective concern about what is taking place, what is coming
to take place within an epoch which, presumably, encompasses that
today even as, in not being specified, singular and yet without date,
today is the trace of something excessive, overflowing the limits of
(the thinking of) an epoch, or any thinking that is implied by the
notion of epochality?

In that sentence where *signifier of the signifier* appears, italicized,
it does so no longer as the equivalent of the concept of writing
conventionally and traditionally received or designated. Thus, *today*,
it remains to be read, as the phrase *par excellence,* and 'by a hardly
perceptible necessity [. . .] to go beyond the extension of language'
(*OG* 6–7). In clearing the ground through the accumulation and signification of negation, in a supplementary multiplication, expansion,
explication *and* slippage (as if we were, in fact, still the witnesses, as
well as the heirs, of the generative effects of an insubstantial double),
Derrida engages in the construction of a sentence in which writing
appears to begin to go beyond mere extension, 'accidental doubling
and fallen secondarity' (*OG* 7). What goes 'beyond' is, in practice and
in effect, that which in the programme of writing finds itself remarked
in this 'today', and in every 'today' where one comes to read. The
sense of an extension beyond also does double work, for, on the one
hand, it signifies the extension that writing just is in any logocentric
system, the extension or prosthesis of voice and presence, while, on
the other hand, Derrida's supplementary iteration extends writing or
demonstrates writing extending itself beyond itself in a performative
gesture of its own operation and excessive reduplication, without

recuperation into a final signified, a presence or some anterior presence or metaphysical concept. Thus begin the destabilizing effects of a writing which, no longer just the signifier of some (transcendental or metaphysical) signifier, via the ruse or illusion of presence, comes into its own, through the iterable and graphic morphology – graphemorphology or grammamorphology – of the phrase 'signifier of the signifier'.

But, before I say any more about this operation, which in its performative play both invites commentary and hints at the exhaustion of that commentary without its having reached an end, this is what follows:

> 'Signifier of the signifier' describes on the contrary the movement of language: in its origin, to be sure, but one can already suspect that an origin whose structure can be expressed as 'signifier of the signifier' conceals and erases itself in its own production. There the signified always already functions as a signifier. (*OG* 7)

The question of that which is questioned implicitly under the sign of an 'origin' in this sentence aside (for the moment at least), it is of course both obvious and important that one reiterates a structural matter here, a matter which, while being initially or provisionally structural, is not simply, if ever, merely formal, a retreat into formalism, or symptomatic of any other such misreading.

Clearly, 'signifier[1]', that is to say, the first mark on the page in the quasi-idiom 'signifier[1] of the signifier[2]', or let us call it, for argument's sake, 'A' is, on the one hand, that which signifies 'signifier[2]', or, provisionally, B. On the other hand, A is also that which is being signified by B, signifier[1] being the signified of signifier[2], as if the phrase operated according to the logic of the double genitive. In effect, one could substitute the first for the second, supposing each to be so designated, and the work of expression remains apparently the same. So A signifies B but A is, momentarily in the two-way passage, the signified of B. The logic of the sentence does nothing to resolve the installation of such destabilization. It cannot, for the destabilization or explication – that motion by which the idiom unfolds itself, expanding beyond itself, while remaining in its own bounds – is always already there, and is that on which the most fundamental semantic coherence is dependent. Meaning is thus structured around the most disquieting and radical undecidability.

Indeed, 'signifier of the signifier', as formal phrase, only serves to promote that which is, simultaneously, adrift and recaptured, limitless and finite. If, instead of referring to A and B, we refer to A^1 and A^2, this hardly helps, if one requires help in the sense of a reduction or simplification of the ineluctable motion that is at work. What might be done however is to pursue a certain mathematical work within language, that frees language from the assumptions of its representational subordination, while also reminding us of the valency of writing, and why, within the history of metaphysics, writing is read as threat, as dead, exterior and so on. Logic cannot save us either, for in what might look like a parody of representation or a parodic meditation *chez* Badiou, mathematical logic only tends to the 'end' of proving – as if such a thing were possible – an arche-originary deconstruction as that which *is* writing in the expanded Derridean sense, and as that which haunts writing as the concept put to work in the service of metaphysics and logocentrism.[2] Writing, far from being the double or instance of the fallen, of a 'having always already fallen', by which Being is re-marked as a being-there, extends itself, not *tomorrow and tomorrow and tomorrow* but 'today' and 'today' and 'today' . . .

But this is only a preliminary step, admittedly one by which we appear to travel not at all. If there is any meagre merit here it is that, for me at least, the performative work of the phrase inaugurates a double gesture of ravelling, of pulling at a thread, which one might pursue throughout *Grammatology* (see, for example, though to remark the caution that Derrida issues regarding the problem of exemplarity early on, pages 17, 21, 23, 30, 36, etc.), undoing particular nodal points in a matrix, even as we weave a particular shape. Returning to the phrase, as will be equally obvious, language, that is to say spoken language and the privilege given that through phonocentric and logocentric assumptions, which seeks in what Derrida calls 'our epoch' to displace and debase writing, cannot escape that which it remarks – in short, saying aloud 'the signifier of the signifier' or 'signifier of the signifier' does not solve the 'problem' of which is which, which signifier signifies which signifier and is the supplement of the other, or indeed the other's supplement, the other as supplement, supplement of the other. (In this, I would suggest, albeit with the benefit of hindsight, we might read an anticipation of the inscription of a much later phrase: *tout autre est tout autre*.) Every time I read the phrase aloud, every time I give voice to the phrase, I only serve to re-introduce writing, the structure and play of which comprehends language, grasping, encompassing, bringing together language in its own matrix, a matrix which reforms itself around the axis of the speaking subject, and constituting that subject in the process, to the finitude of a limitless matrix 'at the very moment when the limits seem [about] to disappear'. Thus, 'origin', which in the first sentence cited refers not to an absolute origin, or the possibility of thinking such a thing, but instead, an iterable 'origin' that appears every time there is language. Or to put this slightly differently, the axis that I name here 'origin' (an origin that takes place through the articulation I make and *every time I do so*) is constituted, comprehended, in and through the reformulation of the phrase expressed as 'signifier of the signifier'.

Clearly, there is a quite powerful and subtle performative at work in the opening, which one might trace back to the preface or 'avertissement' and the, for me, interesting phrase 'theoretical matrix' (*une matrice théorique*), from the first sentence (*OG* lxxxix). As Derrida remarks, tracing such a matrix 'indicates certain significant historical moments', and thus extends – something so often missed – beyond language, beyond 'merely' formal or semantic concerns. Or, to say this differently, there is no formalism that is not, properly apprehended, implicated within and also announcing a radical materiality or historicity. As Derrida observes in a few brief sentences that, for more than forty years, appear to remain by many as yet unread, 'I should mention that I have concerned myself with a *structural figure* as much as a *historical totality*. I have attempted to relate these two seemingly necessary approaches, thus repeating the question of the text, its historical status, its proper time and space. The age already in the *past* is in fact constituted in every respect as a *text*, in a sense of these words that I shall have to establish' (*OG* lxxxix–xc). As we all know there are both immediate and supplementary readings, transparent readings and strong readings to be mined or invented. The phrase 'theoretical matrix' is evidence of that, for, on the one hand, the 'theoretical matrix' may well be taken or mis-taken as one which Derrida will propose or draw (*dessiner*). On the other hand, while Derrida is about to embark on the constitution of a matrix, or at the very least, the invention of one, it is a matrix already in place, to be traced, generated by a constellation of theoretical models and paradigms.

The gathering – or perhaps 'ravelling' is the better word, the *bon mot* or *mot juste*, given the simultaneity of knitting up and undoing that it doubly signifies – Derrida undertakes, maps an epoch, which remains ours (today), and with which we are not yet done (the todays to come). At the same time, while Derrida suggests that the critical concepts belong to the matrix, this is not, he cautions, to imply that these are examples, for the notion of the example leads one to think of relation. The example is exemplary of that which, greater than itself, can be deduced or adduced from it. There may be a non-synonymous relation, a 'relation without relation', but that is as much, if not more, a generation that is ours rather than being that which we can assign to another's proper name, or historical moment, as in the phrase 'the "age" of Hegel'. As Derrida cautions, an age already in the past is 'in fact constituted in every respect as a *text*'; that is to say, a matrix is constituted through the assemblage or bricolage of reading, as it constitutes, shapes and perhaps, 'gives birth to' the reading. A certain 'significant historical moment' is given to be read in a today to come (in all the todays in which I begin, again and again, to attempt a reading of *Of Grammatology*), which 'to come' is always already anticipated and inscribed *in extenso* in the 'today' that Derrida undertakes to trace, and so re-mark, the theoretical matrix, with each of its historical moments, which has given birth to *Of Grammatology*.

In the 'avertissement' then, or 'preface', neither inside nor outside the book as such, yet forming and informing, the matrix (*matrice*), the mother or womb, *khora* perhaps, registering, forming, giving shape to philosophy, history, linguistics. Not a philosopher herself, but mother to philosophers, engendering a demand that 'reading should free itself, at least in its axis, from the classical categories of history [. . .] and perhaps above all, from the categories of the history of philosophy' (*OG* lxxxix).

It's all a matter of decision. The written being or being written? Signifier of the signifier indeed . . . From this to pages 17 ('it is non-self-presence that will be denounced', 'On the one hand [. . .] On the other hand'), 20 ('the logos *of* being [. . .] is the first and last resource of the sign, of the difference between *signans* and *signatum*'), 21 ('On the one hand, if modern linguistics remains completely enclosed within a classical conceptuality, if especially it naively uses the word *being* and all that it presupposes, that which, within this linguistics, deconstructs the unity of the word in general can no longer, according to the model of the Heideggerian question [. . .] be circumscribed as ontic science or regional ontology'), 22 ('It is at once contained within it and transgresses it. But it is impossible to separate the two [. . .] being escapes the movement of the sign'), 23 ('Heidegger occasionally reminds us that "being", as it is fixed [. . .] within linguistics and Western philosophy [. . .] is still rooted in a system of languages and an historically determined "significance" [. . .]. To question the origin of that domination does not amount to hypostatizing a transcendental signified, but to a questioning of what constitutes our history'), and so on, reading an irregular sequence and extension, to the question of Being, the dismantling of the separation between linguistics and ontology, and the radical restaging of the question of Being (Heidegger), to the de-sedimentation of being as signifier, not signified, the moment of which is perceived as the work of the trace and writing through differance. . . . If problems, onto-phenomenological problems to do with writing, historicity, and so on, are, in a certain manner, always oriented towards, but disorientated by 'problems of definition and beginning' (*OG* 28), then a return to the phrase 'signifier of the signifier' and a turn around this phrase, which itself turns and returns, though never to the same place, illustrates, or better yet, illuminates, for us, how we are always already in this problem, we are the problem and the question, subject to it, as subjects of its motion, the movement of its inscription and iterability. Inscribed within a theoretical matrix that it remains given to us to read, we remain to come to beginning a reading of *Of Grammatology* today. Or to give the last word to Derrida, last word as inaugural opening and invitation to read: 'In as much as it de-limits onto-theology, the metaphysics of presence and logocentrism, this last writing is also a first writing' (*OG* 23).

FORBES MORLOCK, DECONSTRUCTION –
A LITTLE NOTE (*OG* 10; *DG* 21)

Sarah Wood jokes about the future Critical Edition of the Collected Works of Jacques Derrida – a fantasy, an impossible work, but also the fulfilment of our desires that his corpus should be complete, without supplement, that its texts should all be known (and no longer need reading). Someone else, in an introduction to an early volume of this edition, will provide the definitive account (history and definition) of deconstruction. Until such time . . .

One of the delights of returning to the article 'De la grammatologie', published in two parts in *Critique* at the end of 1965 and beginning of 1966 (and significantly altered in its expansion into Part I of *Of Grammatology*), is de-sedimenting the fixities now consolidated in writing about Derrida. Another is (re)visiting the excitement of the moment of his writing: much later Derrida will reflect on this writing as a moment for him like no other – he even dates it: summer 1965 (Derrida and Dick, *Derrida*, Special Features/Derrida Interviews/ Eureka). Others will write in this book of preference, and there is something to be preferred in the early writing of this moment: it is less freighted with scholarly reading, its formulations are more open, and one or two things get said, almost naively, that later (and ever after) are left unspoken.

Here, on this page of *Of Grammatology*, the hesitant stumbling for words, the beautiful stumbling onto the word de-construction, is exactly as it is in the article in *Critique* (*OG* 10; *DG* 21; 'De la grammatologie I' 1023). But it is not always thus. In two or three places the article's 'dé-construction' is the book's 'déconstruction' (*OG* 19, 73, 329 n. 38; *DG* 33, 107; 'De la grammatologie I' 1028; 'De la grammatologie II' 40 n. 15). Three times what is for us (in the French) 'déconstruction' was once only 'destruction' – including 'what we have called above [but where?] the "destruction" of the transcendental signified' and 'the "destruction" of the history of philosophy' (*OG* 49, 86; *DG* 71, 128; 'De la grammatologie II' 26 n. 4, 48; cf. *OG* 83; *DG* 124; 'De la grammatologie II' 45). Heideggerians and historians of philosophy can trace the line of 'deconstruction's' development as a word and a thought. The sometime presence of a hyphen, the silent vanishing of quotation marks, the appearance (in the French) of an accent, the awkward condensation of a coinage . . . in short, the shifting passage between 'destruction' and 'deconstruction' reminds us, rather, of the little earthquakes of writing.

MICHAEL SYROTINSKI, FROM ETYMOLOGY (*ETUMOS LOGOS*) TO TRANSLATION, VIA BADIOU AND PAULHAN (*OG* 10–18; *DG* 21–31)

How does one approach the history of *logos* without falling into the logocentrism which determines the history of Western metaphysics, even if it is a necessary fiction, and even if a grammatological opening can gesture towards its closure (which is not to say its end)? Derrida's response to this question is clearly already profoundly indebted to Heidegger's engagement with Husserlian phenomenology, and as Derrida himself points out, the book called *Of Grammatology* is also indissociable from his early reading of Husserl, *Speech and Phenomena*. Indeed, one might say that Heidegger's attempt to work back to the founding conditions of possibility of phenomenology, and the 'destructive' task he sets for philosophical thinking, provides the model for Derrida's own method of reading, via the deconstruction of Western metaphysics (which for him would now include Heidegger). In this respect, *Of Grammatology* is perhaps the key text of the post-war reception and 'translation' of Heidegger in France. In a similar manner to Heidegger in the introduction to *Being and Time*, Derrida lays the ground for his own method, which he will term *grammatology*, a 'science of writing' that will tease apart the basic conceptual structures and underlying logocentric assumptions of all the other '-logies' he will bring into play: metaphysical ontology (*OG* 10), medieval theology (*OG* 11), – as well as the neologism connoting their common ground, metaphysico-theology (*OG* 13) – anthropology (*OG* 11), semiology (*OG* 13) and historical genealogy (*OG* 14). Derrida's opening will thus be a double gesture: on the one hand, he will go on to demonstrate how each of these various epistemologies are part of an unbroken genealogical chain that is traceable back to *logos*, with the semiological distinction between signified and signifier, as well as the presumed priority of the former over the latter, merely its most recent manifestation and consolidation; on the other hand, he will go on to deconstruct the claims upon which they are founded, by showing how each in fact cannot avoid having at its very origin (say, speech) the very term it has located as a secondary, supplemental derivation of that origin (say, writing).

If Heidegger takes us back to *logos* through a similar historical genealogy of Western metaphysics to the one Derrida will offer us, his poeticizing method requires an extraordinarily intimate attention to etymology, the 'science' of the often obscure genealogy of the linguistic sign, which is formulated as the story of the slow erosion over time of its original meaning. Heidegger's intent is not, of course, to give us a more 'truthful' account of *logos*, but is rather to rethink the very idea of 'truth' in its historical alignment with *logos*, thereby bringing to light, or uncovering the truth (*a-letheia*) of the Being of phenomeno-logy. To this extent, its translation into Latin as *ratio* (reason), like the translation of *aletheia* into *veritas*, was for

Heidegger symptomatic of the closing down or occlusion of the pre-Socratic understanding of *logos*, and its subsequent theological, metaphysical and indeed political (imperial) transformations.

One might suspect Derrida's own etymological tracing of *logos* as presence and speech to be part of this process of semantic homogenization. As more recent studies in the etymology and translation history of *logos* have reminded us, it was an extraordinarily complex, heterogeneous and polysemic term in Greek (*Vocabulaire européen des philosophies* 727–41). A non-exhaustive list of meanings would include the following: *discourse, language, speech, rationality, reason, reasoning, intelligence, foundation, principle, proportion, count, account, recount, thesis, tell, tale, tally, argument, explanation, statement, proposition, phrase, definition* (*Vocabulaire* 727). Although this has posed a vast set of intractable problems for translators from the Greek down the ages, this almost infinite dissemination of meanings does not invalidate Heidegger's ontological emphasis, or Derrida's phonocentric emphasis, but rather lends weight to their respective arguments. In both cases, the point they are making is that the gathering together (one of the core meanings of the Greek *legein* from which *logos* is derived) into one term of this infinitely scattered series of meanings *is* the very operation of *logos*. We might even, in attending to its very diverse semantic history, draw out more explicitly than Derrida does in *Of Grammatology* the inherently supplemental nature of this scattering, which often suggests the process of writing or deliberate inscription (the connotations that link counting-accounting-recounting, with telling-tallying, for example). One could, then, read Derrida's deconstructive repetition of Heidegger's ontological rethinking of phenomenology, his re-invention of grammatology as a 'writing science' (along with all the quasi-transcendental neologisms he will later invent) as perhaps the first attempt to ground a non-metaphysical philosophizing within the French language, in a gesture that translates Heidegger's re-covering of the Greek origins of philosophy within the German language.

Alain Badiou in his article *Français* in the *Vocabulaire européen des philosophies* gives us another take on the 'History of Western Metaphysics', and in particular the Cartesian moment of inauguration of contemporary (particularly French) philosophy. According to Badiou, Descartes's decision to rewrite *cogito* as *je pense* (I think), rather than challenging the hegemonic superiority of Latin through a national-linguistic re-appropriation of the privilege of writing and teaching philosophy (as was the case with Greek philosophy before him, and as will be the case with the German metaphysical tradition after him), in fact *has nothing to do with language*, but claims for itself a paradoxical universalism: 'the privilege accorded to French has nothing to do with any intrinsic quality of the language, but with the possibility of a universal and democratic orientation of philosophy' (465). Indeed, as Badiou says, referring to Jean Paulhan's little-known but intriguing essay on etymology, 'Alain, ou la preuve par l'étymologie' ('Alain, Or Proof By Etymology'), 'France has always scorned what Paulhan called "proof by etymology"' (468). Cartesian universalism, as Badiou sees it, is a radical departure from the etymologizing tradition that for him characterizes German philosophy, not only insofar as this rupture severs language from any essential, natural relationship to national community, but also because it brings about a radical shift to privileging the *syntax* of language, its form, over its *substance*, its nouns or substantives (*substantifs*), and thus the very ground of the subject as *subjectum* that Heidegger traces modern subjectivity back to: 'In spite of the most vehement imported attempts, nothing has ever been able to bend philosophy in France to this German hard labour which opens up words, traces them back to their indo-European roots, enjoins them to speak Being and Community' (468).

His thesis locating the Cartesian moment as the foundation of a paradoxical universalism suggests, then, a radical break with a certain faith in etymologism, an idea he draws from Paulhan's text on etymology. In this text, Paulhan questions the claims etymology makes to be able to recover, through an archaeological process of reconstruction, an original, authentic meaning beneath the sedimented layers of its successive transformations and translations, an argument Badiou extends to the use of etymology as a paradigm for philosophical genealogy more generally. Paulhan's text takes as its main target the French philosopher of language Alain's belief that earlier languages must have expressed more closely an original meaning, which *must* have been motivated and not arbitrary (this short text of Paulhan might thus be read as his own version of Derrida's reading of Rousseau). Paulhan, however, argues that etymology as the search for the origin, or the truth in language (the *etymon* of/in etymology), often turns out to be about as reliable as a play on words, or paronomasis (his word is *calembour*), that can never give us access to truth, but merely to more and more language: 'What is more, the name itself tells us this: *etymology* is *etumos logos*, or true meaning. Etymology is thus its own advertisement, and refers back to etymology' (265). Ironically, false (or what are often called 'folk') etymologies teach us more, it would seem, about the underlying meaning of a word than so-called true etymologies (and Paulhan's text gives several witty examples). The epistemological aporia we are confronted with is thus the following: how can we know true from false etymology, when the very terms which allow us to make such a determination are themselves indissociable from this very history, and philosophical genealogy? Underlying this playfulness, then, is a very serious question. Regardless of whether such etymologies are mistaken or not, they have had actual historical effects, and Paulhan explicitly includes Heidegger among the list of philosophers who look to etymology for 'proof' of their theories: 'The metaphysics of Heidegger, among others, is entirely etymologizing' (267 n. 2). It leaves us with a more radical undecidability, in which it becomes impossible to tell whether a particular etymological genealogy (say, of *logos*) is a historical fact, or simply a series of linguistic puns, or accidents of language.

Maurice Blanchot, in the section of *The Writing of the Disaster* in which he discusses Heidegger's etymologism, explicitly refers to Paulhan's text, and reflects at length on this very point: 'the etymological series reconstitutes the becoming of language as a kind of historical *nature*' (97). This historicism is described a little later as 'the necessity of some provenance, of successive continuity, the logic of homogeneity, the revelation of sheer chance as destiny' (97). Blanchot explicitly alludes to Paulhan's text at this point as he questions the privilege accorded to etymology in Heidegger's 'return to the Greeks'. What Paulhan does in his text is to reformulate philosophical genealogy as a linguistic drama, such that we could read the history of *logos*, for example, as a kind of allegory of translation, which radically questions the natural relationship of language to truth, national or otherwise. Paulhan's critique of etymologism does not lead him, like Badiou, out of the French language to a philosophy of universal 'truth', but to a radical rethinking of the very politics of language as such. By extension it also questions the supposed natural relationship of language to any philosophical nationalism, but reinscribes it as a question of translation, or more precisely of untranslatability, a theme which Derrida will of course pick up and develop at great length in many other texts and contexts.

MICHAEL NAAS, PNEUMATOLOGY, *PNEUMA, SOUFFLE,* BREATH (*OG* 17; *DG* 29)

The term *pneumatology* (or *pneumatological*) is used but once in *Of Grammatology*, but since it is used in a line that explicitly contrasts it with *grammatology* (or *grammatological*) it might be shown to play an organizing role in Derrida's overall argument. He thus writes near the beginning of the book: 'Natural writing is immediately united to the voice and to breath. Its nature is not grammatological but pneumatological. It is hieratic [. . .]' (*OG* 17).

What, then, is the *pneumatological* and how is it related in the above passage to 'natural writing'? A combination of the Greek words *pneuma* (meaning breath or animating spirit) and *logos* (meaning speech, language, study, science), the *pneumatological* suggests the close relationship in Western thought between language in general and speech or voice (the *phonological*) in their connection with the breath. One of the central theses of *Of Grammatology* is that the very concept of language privileges this relationship to voice, sound, breath and speech *as opposed to* writing (*OG* 7; for *souffle*, see *OG* 18, 308; *DG* 31, 434). By following this close identification of breath (*souffle*) with language (*logos*) and voice (*phonē*) from Plato right up through Rousseau, Hegel and Saussure, Derrida demonstrates that the Western tradition is not only *logo*centric but *phono*centric, that is, it favours speech over writing but then also, within writing, phonetic over non-phonetic writing. Because phonetic writing *seems* at least to provide a more direct access to meaning, to the signified, because the phonetic signifier seems to efface itself before the concept or the signified, philosophers such as Hegel have favoured speech over writing and then phonetic over non-phonetic writing because of the former's relation to breath: 'The nonphonetic moment menaces the history and the life of the spirit as self-presence in the breath [*souffle*]' (*OG* 26; *DG* 41). (These connections are developed further by Derrida in *Speech and Phenomena* and 'La parole soufflée', to which he refers in *Of Grammatology* (*OG* 325 n. 15, 332 n. 31).)

Now, if it is essentially speech and not writing that is related to the breath and the life of the spirit, then why does Derrida say that it is 'natural *writing*' (my emphasis) that is 'immediately united to the voice and to breath'? The key word here is *natural*. By means of what might seem to be a merely metaphorical use of the notion of writing, there would be a 'natural writing' related to the voice, to breath and the living spirit, and a non-natural, artificial writing, writing in the literal and more common sense of the term, related to the external body and the dead letter. It is this latter that Derrida is speaking of when he writes: 'Writing, the letter, the sensible inscription, has always been considered by Western tradition as the body and matter external to the spirit, to breath [*souffle*], to speech [*verbe*], and to the logos' (*OG* 35; *DG* 52). Added here to the configuration we have seen thus far opposing the letter, the body, the external, and so on to spirit, the breath, and the internal is the notion of the *verbe* – a quasi-synonym of *parole* or speech but one that brings along with it a distinctly theological association. Indeed the traditional French translation of John 1.1 runs: *Au commencement était le Verbe* (In the beginning was the Word). This addition helps explain Derrida's use of the term 'hieratic' in the passage cited at the outset, which continues: 'It [natural writing] is hieratic, very close to the interior holy voice of the *Profession of Faith*, to the voice one hears upon retreating into oneself: full and truthful presence of the divine voice in our inner sense' (*OG* 17). Derrida is here already anticipating his reading of Rousseau in the second part of *Of Grammatology*, his interpretation of Rousseau's own privileging of speech over writing but also his characterization of speech as a kind of natural writing that would be identified with what is most interior, that is, with a sort of *divine voice* within us. Hence Derrida speaks much later in *Of Grammatology* in the context of his reading of Rousseau of 'this exemplary model of a pure breath (*pneuma*) and of an intact life [*une vie inentamée*], of a song and an inarticulate language, of speech without spacing' (*OG* 249; *DG* 353). For Rousseau, 'natural expression' would thus be related to the breath, but insofar as it is 'inarticulate' it can hardly be called 'expression' in any recognizable sense of the term. Indeed, for Derrida, the very idea of an inarticulate language, of a speech without spacing, is not simply a contradiction in terms but a phantasm or illusion (*leurre*) of a language before language, of a divine logos that is pure and uncontaminated by space and by difference, that is, by writing.

While *pneuma* is thus used in Greek philosophy to describe a living breath that is close to speech and voice and that is threatened in its life by writing, Derrida invokes throughout *Of Grammatology* but particularly in his reading of Rousseau and related figures a theological tradition where *pneuma* refers to the animating principle within mankind, a living spirit given to him by God. Luther, for example, defines *pneuma* as the 'highest, deepest, and noblest part of man, which qualifies him to lay hold of incomprehensible, invisible, eternal things; in short, it is the house where Faith and God's words are at home' (*Luther's Works* 21: 303). Accordingly, a pneumatology is always a theology, where a certain concept of the divine logos is thought in terms of an eternal present and a divine voice (*OG* 73). We now see why Derrida would claim that natural writing has to be considered pneumatological rather than grammatological. Assuming for the moment that the latter can ever really be thought at the limits of a Greek notion of science as episteme and as logos (something Derrida himself questions when he writes, 'Grammato*logy*, this thought, would still be walled in within presence' (*OG* 93)), grammatology would in effect announce the end or the closure of a certain Greco-Christian pneumatology, that is, the closure of an epoch where what is privileged is language's seemingly natural relationship to speech, voice, the verb, the living breath and so on, as opposed to writing.

This brings us to a final, related term in *Of Grammatology*, one that is even more difficult to render in English – *essoufflement*, or the related words *essouffler, s'essouffler*. In a first moment, this series of words is but the flipside of the configuration we have seen: if writing is what threatens life itself, what compromises or broaches the breath of voice and of speech (*OG* 25), then it could be said that writing is what leaves language breathless, what exhausts speech, what knocks the breath, and thus the life, right out of it: 'Writing in the common sense is the dead letter, it is the carrier of death. It exhausts [*essouffle*] life' (*OG* 17; *DG* 29). As a reflexive, the verb *s'essouffler* thus means to become exhausted, and it is used in at least one instance to apply to the entire tradition. Derrida says early on in *Of Grammatology* that the 'adventure' of a history that relates certain developments of technology (including and especially writing) to a logocentric metaphysics is today, after three millennia, approaching its *essoufflement*, that is, its *exhaustion*, the point where it runs out of *souffle*, out of breath (*OG* 8; *DG* 18). In other words, the epoch of a logocentric metaphysics where language in general has been related to interior breath rather than to exterior writing, to *logos* rather than to *gramme*, is today approaching an end or running out of breath. It is this *essoufflement* of an epoch of breath, of *souffle*, that has made it possible to consider writing as a more general category than speech and, thus, to think a *gramma*tology rather than a *pneuma*tology.

SARAH WOOD, GOOD WRITING (*OG* 18; *DG* 31)

First some marks to act as a warm-up or sound-check: . . . *i* . . . *e* . . . *l* . . . *eu*. Around them: the page, some points indicating ellipsis, silence. A certain lack of immediate context. But a scene constitutes itself here nonetheless.

There's something similar in what follows here: a reading of sections from pages 18, 88 and 226–7 of *Of Grammatology*. Singled out by certain passages before entirely knowing how they may be related, I feel touched by unbookishness and worked on by what Derrida calls the 'aphoristic energy' of writing (*OG* 18). Without my making it happen, what happens, happens as pictures and scenes.

. . . *i* . . . *e* . . . *l* . . . *eu*. These letters are not fragments of signifiers. I hesitate to call them letters or phonemes or graphemes. The notion of linguistic form doesn't apply here because the unity and wholeness of the text generally presupposed by classical notions of close reading (Wimsatt, for example) is put into question by *Of Grammatology*. Derrida writes that the 'totality of the signifier cannot be a totality, unless a totality constituted by the signified pre-exists it, supervises its inscriptions and its signs' (*OG* 18). This funny collection of stray vocables is outside language. It is not supervised by a pre-existing signified. The repetition of marks becomes legible only in a way that transforms reading. I can offer no generalized logic for the process. It is a matter of failing to learn to read. Letters become objects of attention without help from 'the encyclopaedic protection of theology', by being *invested*. (Or to speak more technically and psychoanalytically they are 'cathected': 'investissement' can mean either 'investment' or 'cathexis' (*OG* 88; *DG* 134).) We'll be hearing more from psychoanalysis in a moment. But the 'good writing' that Derrida discusses on 18 and the pages leading up to it, tries to ignore the law of writing, which is that it advances blindly. As Cixous puts it in an interview with Derrida: 'one can only write in the direction of that which does not let itself be written and which one must try to write. What I *can* write is already written, it is no longer of interest' (Cixous, 'From the Word to Life' 9). Writing, Derrida teaches us, need not be 'good' (*OG* 18). It need not be already understood. The French phrase he uses to describe 'la bonne écriture' is 'toujours été comprise': it has 'always been *comprehended*' or more concretely 'held' (*DG* 30). Such writing can be anticipated. It does not surprise. Derrida has said that he:

> began by trying to have my philosophical work legitimized by the academic institution. Before taking a certain number of liberties with writing, it was necessary that I first be accorded a certain amount of credit. Before this, I betrayed the norms only in a prudent, cunning and quasi-clandestine manner. Though this didn't escape everyone. (Derrida, 'From the Word to Life' 4)

Of Grammatology treads a line between being a work that can be read theologically, conceptually or by the procedures of 'close reading' and being a manifestation of writing, a book whose writing participates in 'the destruction of the book' that Derrida mentions on page 18 as being 'now underway in all domains'. Reading *Of Grammatology* we encounter the necessary violence that 'denudes the surface of the text'.

IAN MACLACHLAN, THE IDEA OF THE BOOK (*OG* 18; *DG* 30)

In the various early essays that would form parts of two of the three books published in 1967 (that is, *Writing and Difference* and the first part of *Of Grammatology*), Derrida addresses the idea of the book on a number of occasions, and he does so again in an interview held in December of that year where, invited to reflect on the relations between the three books he has just published, he declares that '[i]n what you call my books, what is first of all put in question is the unity of the book and the unity "book" considered as a perfect totality, with all the implications of such a concept' (Derrida, 'Implications' 3). Developing on this claim, Derrida suggests that what holds open the closure of the book in relation to the three publications in question is a distinctive practice of reading and writing, an 'operation' (suspended in quotation marks) 'whose unfinished movement assigns itself no absolute beginning, and which, although it is entirely consumed by the reading of other texts, in a certain fashion refers only to its own writing' ('Implications' 3). There is a hint about the strangeness of this 'operation', and about the reason why one of its peculiar effects would be to hold open the book as a totality, in the notion that it might, on the one hand, be *entirely* given over to reading while, on the other, being exclusively concerned, in a gesture beyond or other than its entirety, with its own writing.

In response to his interviewer's question about effective points of entry for the reader of these constitutively open publications without determinate beginning or end, Derrida offers some possible configurations of the mobile architecture of his work: 'One can take *Of Grammatology* as a long essay articulated in two parts (whose juncture is not empirical, but theoretical, systematic) *into the middle* of which one could staple *Writing and Difference*' ('Implications' 4). What Alan Bass translates here as a 'juncture' is a *soudure* in the French text ('Implications' [French] 12), the soldering (etymologically, a strengthening) of a joint, which we might read in relation to the 'hinge' (*brisure*) that both separates and joins, given as the title of the third section of Chapter 3 of *Grammatology*. We might also wonder what makes a soldered joint theoretical and systematic, rather than empirical. The question seems more significant, not just when the reader is invited to 'staple' or bind (*brocher*, in the French) *Writing and Difference* into this juncture of the other text, but when the inverse operation is also invited, on grounds that are apparently at once theoretical and empirical: 'Inversely, one could insert *Of Grammatology into the middle* of *Writing and Difference*, since six of the texts in that work preceded – *de facto* and *de jure* – the publication in *Critique* (two years ago) of the articles that announced *Of Grammatology*' (4). The complexity of the variable configuration of these books is compounded when Derrida reaches the provisional conclusion, with the help of a curious figure in which the spatial is, as it were, soldered to the temporal: 'that two "volumes" are to be inscribed one *in the middle of* the other is due, you will agree, to a strange geometry, of which these texts are doubtless the contemporaries' (4). Reminded about *Speech and Phenomena* ('I forgot'), Derrida remarks that it is 'perhaps the essay which I like the most', a preference that is surprisingly manifested not just by being forgotten but by the idea of binding it 'as a long note to one or the other of the other two works' (4), notwithstanding the fact that 'in a classical philosophical architecture, *Speech* . . . [*sic*] would come first' (5). After a further elaboration linking *Speech and Phenomena* to his introduction of his 1962 translation of Husserl's *Origin of Geometry* (of which it might be read as 'the other side (recto or verso, as you

wish)'), Derrida's interviewer is left to observe plaintively, 'I asked
you where to begin, and you have led me into a labyrinth' (5).

In light of these multiple configurations, it is therefore with some
caution that I approach what is ostensibly the immediate context
of the paragraph in *Of Grammatology* where Derrida addresses
most directly that 'end of the book' that provides part of the title
of Chapter 1, 'The End of the Book and the Beginning of Writing'
(*OG* 18). The preceding pages have referred to a variety of sources to
outline the complicity between an essentially theological conception
of the book and a natural, divine, living writing, one which is not
external, literal inscription – 'not grammatological but pneumatological' (*OG* 17). Drawing specifically on a passage from Rousseau's
Émile in order to establish this polarization of writing, Derrida has
referred to it as 'a good and a bad writing' (*OG* 17), and it is that
formulation that is operative when he diagnoses the 'comprehension'
(both containment and hermeneutic saturation) of 'good' writing
within the theological model of the book, or Rousseau's 'book of
Nature':

> The good writing has therefore always been *comprehended.*
> Comprehended as that which had to be comprehended: within
> a nature or a natural law, created or not, but first thought within
> an eternal presence. Comprehended, therefore, within a totality,
> and enveloped in a volume or a book. The idea of the book is
> the idea of a totality, finite or infinite, of the signifier; this totality
> of the signifier cannot be a totality unless a constituted totality of
> the signified preexists it, supervises its inscription and its signs,
> and is independent of it in its ideality. (*OG* 18, trans. mod.)

As it happens, the passage itself has undergone a modification in
its transition from journal article to its place here in the book *Of
Grammatology*. In the December 1965 issue of *Critique*, a version of
the preceding survey of writing and the book that culminates in the
discussion of 'a good and a bad writing' inspired by Rousseau appears
instead as a long footnote. Furthermore, the equivalent paragraph in
Critique begins with the reference to the '[i]dea of the book', lacking
the first three sentences on the 'comprehension' of 'good writing'
('De la grammatologie I' 1025–7). One of the effects of this earlier
disposition is to place the summary about the 'idea of the book' as

a 'totality of the signifier' immediately after a discussion that draws out the reliance of a supposedly prior 'good writing' in a *metaphorical* sense on the *proper* sense of writing as finite, material inscription, that is, on a supposedly secondary 'bad writing', the point of this diagnosis, Derrida insists, being not to invert the proper and the figurative senses of writing, 'but to determine the "proper" sense of writing as metaphoricity itself' ('De la grammatologie I' 1027; *OG* 15).

But what is 'metaphoricity itself'? Perhaps it names nothing other than the possibility of *carrying over* – from article to book, within or across volumes, or more generally from one place to another, whether that place is literal or metaphorical, by means of joints, hinges or bindings that might be theoretical, empirical, or on the way from one to the other. This is the carrying over of a 'ference' that passes through *différance*, a transport of words, as Derrida notes in another context, that 'are *carried* [*portés*], both *exported* and *deported*, by the movement of *ference* (transference, reference, difference)' (*On the Name* 58). This movement of words is what eludes the comprehension of the book, ruinously compromising the independence of the ideal 'totality of the signified' that should underwrite the book's 'totality of the signifier'.

That this movement of words should spill over the confines of the book is doubtless no surprise, but what may be much less obvious is that it is also to be read *within* the book, the closure of which, Derrida insists on several occasions, is not its definitive end (e.g. 'Implications' 13–14, which refers in turn to the distinction between 'closure' and 'end' proposed in *OG* 4). At the close of another 1967 volume, in 'Ellipsis', the only essay written specially for *Writing and Difference*, Derrida begins with a backward glance over the preceding essays: 'Here or there we have discerned writing: an asymmetrical division or distribution [*partage*] marked out on the one hand the closure of the book, and on the other the opening of the text' ('Ellipsis' 294; 'Ellipse' 429, trans. mod.). My cumbersome modification of Alan Bass's translation signals that Derrida's 'partage' may mark what both divides and draws together, the opening of the text not simply exceeding once and for all the closure of the book, as Derrida soon goes on to suggest: 'And yet did we not know that the closure of the book was not a simple limit among others? And that only in the book, coming back to it unceasingly, drawing all our resources from it, could we indefinitely designate the writing beyond the book?' ('Ellipsis' 294).

PEGGY KAMUF, A CERTAIN WAY OF INHABITING
(*OG* 24; *DG* 39)

The movements of deconstruction do not shake up structures from the outside. They are possible and effective, their aim is accurate only if they inhabit [*en habitant*] these structures. Only if they inhabit them *in a certain way* – for one is always inhabiting and even more so when one does not suspect it. Necessarily operating from within, borrowing from the old structure all the strategic and economic resources of subversion, borrowing them structurally, that is, without being able to isolate their elements and atoms, the enterprise of deconstruction always falls prey [*est emportée*] in a certain way to its own work. This is what is eagerly pointed out by whoever has begun the same work in another area of the same habitation. No exercise is more wide-spread today and it should be possible to formalize its rules. (*OG* 24; *DG* 39, trans. mod.)

Deconstruction inhabits, in a certain way. It is within structures that it shakes up and deconstructs from inside, a certain inside, which nevertheless opens to some outside. Deconstruction is a way of inhabiting structures that turns them inside out or upside down, like an uncanny guest who displaces all the host's property. This figure of habitation, inhabitation seems to have been called up here by some resistance to thinking about deconstruction's strategic aims and actions in such domestic or familiar terms. In evoking an accurate aim, Derrida, one understands, is taking aim at the prevailing assumption that any effective action against these structures – of historical oppression, sexual repression, political, cultural and anthropocentric suppression – must first make sure it is standing outside the master's house. In the remark that 'one is always inhabiting and even more so when one does not suspect it', there is perhaps the echo of a pointed retort to some contemporaries, Foucault among them but also certain Marxists, who sought to dismiss Derrida's undertaking as a repetition contaminated and brought down by – or fallen prey to – the very structures it is taking apart. But the complaint that deconstruction is not effectually or sufficiently oppositional has continued pretty much unabated since then, such that the retort fashioned here in *Of Grammatology* has remained no less to the point more than forty years later. For one is still always inhabiting and never more so than when one doesn't suspect it.

There is, then, a manner of provocation launched here by way of the figure or the notion – not exactly a concept – of *habitation* and the action, if you will, of *inhabiting*, which is precisely not an action when it is undergone as a given state 'and even more so when one does not suspect it'. By emphasizing that deconstructive movements inhabit *in a certain way*, however, Derrida is announcing something like an *awakening* of the action that habitually slumbers passively unaware in this state called habitation or inhabiting. If indeed everyone always inhabits – and who could deny that? – then the question is *how* one inhabits there where one finds oneself and that *in which* one is already inscribed. For, that habitation is indeed another name for inscription and thus for differance is what we will have come to understand many pages later in *Of Grammatology* (*infra* Kamuf, 114–15, 221–3).

CHAPTER 2

LINGUISTICS AND GRAMMATOLOGY

J. HILLIS MILLER, EXERGUE (*OG* 27–73; *DG* 42–108)

Reading *De la grammatologie* again after many years (my *For Derrida* concentrates on Derrida's later writings), I have been struck by the continuity between early and late Derrida. *Of Grammatology* contains in one way or another, though not of course predictably, the programme for everything Derrida subsequently wrote. A full reading of *De la grammatologie* and its relation to Derrida's later writings would be a more or less interminable task. In order to keep within some bounds, I shall focus on Chapter 2 of Part 1 and, within that, on Derrida's use there of several 'antithetical' words, quasi-puns, *calembours* ('différance', 'brisure', 'jeu' and 'trace'), as a fundamental part of what might be called the 'rhetoric' of Derrida's argumentation. Freud, in 'The Uncanny' ('Das Unheimliche'), showed that the German word 'unheimlich' has two antithetical meanings. It names something strange that is at the same time familiar. 'Jeu', 'brisure', 'trace' and 'différance', I claim, are antithetical words in this sense, though not all in the same way. Their use is essential to the rhetorical strategies of *De la grammatologie*.

So what's the problem? Why did Derrida need to use such extravagant linguistic contortions to say what he was trying to say? His goal in *De la grammatologie* is clear enough. Derrida wants to reverse the priority of spoken language over written language and to claim that 'archi-écriture comme espacement' or 'écriture avant la lettre', far from being secondary and derived, has always already been there (*DG* 99, 9). Arche-writing is the invisible generator, the 'trace', that has magically created all our ordinary and illusory assumptions about language, linguistics, subjectivity, the subject, consciousness, the unconscious, science (as in 'the science of linguistics'), inside-outside distinctions, time, space, history, the transcendental patron, what is called 'God'. Deconstructing these performs a wholesale demolition. 'Exit the whole shebang', in Wallace Stevens's phrase. Of course what has been deconstructed remains still there, apparently as solid as ever. Performing this reversal, though Derrida says it is not at all just a reversal, means deconstructing, piece by piece, what he calls 'Western metaphysics', or 'logocentrism', or 'ontotheology'. This deconstruction has as one of its strategies working through logocentric assumptions in Husserl, Heidegger et al., to the very end, until they are 'seriously *exhausted*' (*OG* 50).

Well, why not just do that in straightforward philosophical language, in 'plain French vanilla'? Why all the linguistic hi-jinks that have offended so many readers? The answer is that logocentrism is inscribed ineluctably within all our Western languages. As soon as you open your mouth or put pen to paper you are imperturbably repeating logocentric assumptions, as in my words 'reversal' and 'generator' above, or in the assumption that words written earlier are somehow 'above' words written later. Hence Derrida's linguistic contortions, the extravagant rhetoric that is the focus of this essay. Derrida is trying to say something that cannot be said. Or it can be said only with great difficulty, that is, by twisting words away from their normal usage.

That twisting takes several forms. One is a straightforward demonstration by way of citation and slightly ironic paraphrase that a presumably coherent scholar, such as Saussure in the *Cours de linguistique générale*, necessarily contradicts himself and, in some statements, for example, gives written language priority over spoken language. Saussure is the main target of Chapter 2 (along with Husserl's phenomenology). This subordination of spoken to written language happens in spite of Saussure's firm repeated assertions elsewhere in the *Cours* that spoken language came first. Written phonetic language is the mere copy or image of spoken language in a different medium. Derrida shows that Saussure's own language is contorted. It is contorted by the traces within it of the 'arche-trace'.

Another form of twisting is the relative lack of logical development in the chapter. Derrida keeps saying the same things over and over in slightly different formulations. He uses the same relatively restricted, though always proliferating, vocabulary, in potentially endless permutations and combinations, as if he doubts whether he has said what he wants to say, or has communicated what he wants to say to the reader. He repeats himself, it might seem, in the hope that he might, sooner or later, 'get it right', get those few words in just the right 'Open Sesame!' combination, so the reader will say, 'Ah ha! I get it now'.

The key words of Chapter 2 are each used to define the others in these formulations. This creates an endless round robin or circular game in which no one word is the solid ground for all the others. 'Différance' is defined by 'espacement', which is defined by 'trace', which is defined by 'jeu', which is defined by 'écriture', which is defined by 'différance' and so on, round and round. This formulation is incorrect, however, since each of the words can be, and is, defined by its connections to any and all of the others, in an inextricable crisscross. Nor is the list ever complete or finite. It is always n-1, with yet another word missing or yet to be added. The circle is never completed. This structure might be called 'rhizomatic', after Deleuze and Guattari's usage in *A Thousand Plateaus*, except that a rhizome is, after all, an organic model, whatever Deleuze and Guattari say about 'machinal assemblages' as characterizing rhizomes. Derrida's models are explicitly inorganic and inhuman. Moreover, Derrida's way with words is quite different from that of Deleuze and Guattari. He never, so far as I remember, uses the word 'rhizome', though it may be there somewhere.

Another linguistic ploy employed by Derrida is to use openly logocentric words, like 'est' or 'étant' ('is', 'entity'), words that belong to logocentrism from Plato and Aristotle down to Heidegger, 'under erasure', 'sous rature', sometimes by actually crossing them out on the page, sometimes by just saying they are under erasure, as when he says of 'passé' (past) that it is 'another name to erase' (*OG* 66). By 'under erasure', I suppose, Derrida means he is using them without using them, but of course that is extremely difficult, perhaps impossible. To say or write 'is' is to say or write 'is', and we hear the word behind its erasure, as in 'le dehors est le dedans' ('the outside is the inside'), where the 'est' is crossed out (*OG* 44; *DG* 65).

Sometimes the contortions are grammatical, as in sentences that take away with one hand what they give with the other, as when Derrida speaks of 'a past that can no longer be understood in the form of a modified presence, as a present-past' (*OG* 66). It's a past that is not a past, a 'passé absolu', whatever, exactly, *that* means.

That leaves as examples of linguistic twisting my special topic here, Derrida's use of antithetical words, 'jeu', 'brisure', 'trace' and 'différance'. Even here, however, one must distinguish.

'Différance', notoriously, is a neologism, not a real word in French dictionaries. In this it is like later Derridean words such as 'destinerrance'. Derrida has made up 'différance' by writing it with an 'a' rather than an 'e'. He is, moreover, exploiting the fact that the difference between 'différence' and 'différance' cannot be heard when the two words are spoken. The difference is visible only in the words' differing 'écriture', or writing down. Having manufactured this word, Derrida can then go on to use it as an antithetical word that says 'differ' and 'defer' at once.

I shall now discuss 'brisure', 'jeu' and 'trace' in more detail, each yet a different form of antithetical word. I shall go from less enigmatic to more and more enigmatic, with a close look at places where Derrida uses these words in Chapter 2.

J. HILLIS MILLER, *BRISURE* (OG 65–73; DG 96–108)

You have, I suppose, dreamt of finding a single word for designating difference and articulation. I have perhaps located it by chance in Robert['s Dictionary] if I play [jouer] on the word, or rather indicate its double meaning. The word is brisure *[joint, break, hinge] [. . .]* – Roger Laporte (letter).

(*OG* 65; *DG* 96)

'The hinge [*brisure*] marks the impossibility that a sign, the unity of a signifier and a signified, be produced [*se produire*] within the plenitude of a present and an absolute presence' (*OG* 69; *DG* 102). Derrida's citation from Laporte's letter is the epigraph of the third and final section of Chapter 2, entitled 'The Hinge' ('La brisure'). The word itself is used only once in 'The Hinge', in the sentence I have just cited. Nevertheless, the shadowy presence of this word presides over the whole section. 'Brisure' is a genuine antithetical word, like 'Umheimliche'. 'Brisure' means, at one and the same time, two opposed things: a hinge or joint that connects two separate things, and a break that divides two separate things. In both cases, the word 'brisure' names something that comes between, as both separator and connector.

41

Why does Derrida need this word? The citation from his own words gives the answer. Derrida picks up and radicalizes the Saussurean notion that the meaning of a word lies not in the word itself but in its difference from other words. That difference is invisible. It is the blank between signs. You cannot hear, see, feel, touch or taste, or otherwise sense it. It appears in its disappearance. The difference is in the temporal or spatial interval between signs, the break that connects. That evasive interval is connected by Derrida not only to other key words in this section, *différance, jeu, espacement* and *trace*, all of which are 'brisures', but also, more specifically to another related antithetical word, 'articulation'. No language exists without articulation. Incomprehensible speech is called 'inarticulate'. 'Articulus' in Latin, as Saussure says in a passage Derrida cites, noting that it contradicts what Saussure elsewhere says, 'means a member, part, or subdivision of a sequence; applied to speech [*langage*], articulation designates either the subdivision of a spoken chain into syllables or the subdivision of the chain of meanings into significant units' (*OG* 66). Articulation is division, but it is also the connection that makes detached signs in a spatial or temporal string generate meaning. One bone is articulated to another in a body. 'Disarticulation' names a dislocation putting a shoulder or knee 'out of joint'.

That returns us to 'brisure' as joint that disjoints, in a miniature version of the always incomplete round robin already mentioned that defines each enigmatic double word in terms of other enigmatic double words. The first sentences after the citation about 'brisure' from Laporte's letter focus on the word 'articulation'. That word has to be heard as saying at one and the same time 'connection' and 'disconnection'. The passage is a tissue woven of key words in Derrida's deconstruction of logocentrism, each of which must be felt to vibrate with its multiple contradictory meanings. The clothespins of quotation marks around 'same', 'visual', 'tactile' and so on indicate that the words are put in question, their everyday meanings suspended or 'under erasure' ('sous rature'). It is the experience of a same that is not the same by a body proper that is the same and not the same, and so on for the other words. The reader will see the extraordinary linguistic twisting or contortion Derrida must go through to try to say something that does not want to be said in ordinary language, though it is present as a 'deconstructive' possibility in ordinary language, if you turn that language away from what it wants to say to make it say something other. This is the

extraordinary feat that all Derrida's writing accomplishes, year after
year and book after book:

> Origin of the experience of space and time, this writing of difference,
> this fabric of the trace, permits the difference between space and
> time to be articulated, to appear as such, in the unity of an experi-
> ence (of a 'same' lived out of a 'same' body proper [*corps propre*]).
> This articulation therefore permits a graphic ('visual' or 'tactile',
> 'spatial') chain to be adapted, on occasion in a linear fashion, to
> a spoken ('phonic', 'temporal') chain. It is from the primary
> possibility of this articulation that one must begin. Difference is
> articulation. (*OG* 65–6)

This extravagant verbal merry-go-round may now allow a glimpse
of what Derrida means in what he says about signs in the sentence
using the word 'brisure' that is my ostensible focus in this section.
The fact that meaning is generated from the joints between words
that are also breaks between them, disarticulated articulations, means
that our usual assumption that a word is a sign referring to its meaning in the plenitude of the presence of the present, 'the unity of a
signifier and a signified', is in error. Meaning is generated rather out
of an infinite play of sign to sign relations, with never a grounding in
anything outside the play of signs. No present or presence as such
exists, ever did exist, or ever will exist, only an endless difference and
deferral that Derrida names 'la différance', with an 'a'. He 'defines'
this word on the back cover of *L'écriture et la différence*: 'Ce qui s'écrit
ici *différance* marque l'étrange mouvement, l'unité irréductiblement
impure d'un *différer* (détour, délai, délégation, division, inégalité,
espacement) dont *l'économie* excède les ressources déclarées du
logos classique'. ('What is written here as *différance* marks the strange
movement, the irreducibly impure unity of a *deferring* (detour, delay,
delegation, division, inequality, spacing) the *economy* of which exceeds
the declared resources of the classical *logos* [reason]'.)

J. HILLIS MILLER, *JEU* (*OG* 7, 48, 50; *DG* 7, 70, 73)

It is therefore *the game of the world* [*le* jeu du monde] that must be
first thought; before attempting to understand all the forms of
play [*jeu*] in the world. (*OG* 50; *DG* 73)

It is time now to play a game of *jeu*. Playing with 'jeu' is harder than handling 'brisure'. This is partly because 'jeu' is not exactly an antithetical word. 'Jeu' is a bit more complex in its multiple meanings. The word is also used much more often in Chapter 2 than is 'brisure'. A word's meaning is defined by its use, that is, by its placement in a sequence of words. Dictionary meanings are only an abstract approximation. This means that what a given word means in a given text can only be determined by a hard look at those uses. In the case of 'jeu' that would take a long time and a lot of words, since the word appears often in Chapter 2, as well as in such other places as the paper Derrida gave at the Hopkins symposium: 'La structure, le signe et le jeu dans le discours des sciences humaines' ('Structure, Sign, and Play in the Discourse of the Human Sciences'). As Gayatri Spivak's perfectly legitimate translations of 'jeu' in my key citation indicates, the word can mean both 'game' and 'play' in the same sentence. In English, 'play' can name a drama enacted on the stage, as 'Spiel' can in German, as in Wagner's 'Singspielen', though 'drame' is the normal French word for a stage play. 'Jeu' can also mean a looseness in connections or articulations as when one says, 'There is play in this steering wheel', or even 'There is play in this word, leading to word play'. Certainly such play exists in ordinary usages of 'jeu', as well as in Derrida's play with those usages.

Well, what does Derrida mean by distinguishing between 'forms of play in the world' and 'the play of the world'? Perforce I must be brief, where an interminable commentary or 'reading' might be in order. I shall limit myself primarily to three passages where the word 'jeu' is especially salient (*OG* 7, 48, 50; *DG* 7, 70, 73). I take these passages as contexts for understanding the sentence I cited initially in this section, my sample for 'close reading'.

We ordinarily think of a game as existing as a separate social entity within the world, along with all sorts of other social behaviour and conventions. A game has arbitrary but fixed rules that are external to the game. Those rules govern the way a given game is played, such as all the rules about bidding in the game of bridge, or such as the rule in basketball that a basket made from a certain distance out earns three points, or such as the complex sets of rules that govern cricket or baseball. What Wittgenstein (not named by Derrida in Chapter 2), called 'language games' are, like other games, intraworldly. They are surrounded by a context that is outside the game. Saussure, cited in a passage from Hjelmslev cited by Derrida, compared language to a game of chess ('jeu d'échecs') (*OG* 57; *DG* 84). Language has grammatical rules outside a particular enunciation and governing it. Grammar determines what can be said, and how, just as the king, queen, pawn, knights and so on in chess each has its own distinctive powers of movement. The difference between a noun and verb consists in the different uses in a sentence each kind of word can have. This is true even though grammarians recognize that nouns can often be used as verbs, and verbs as nouns. They cheerfully call this 'functional shift', often without explicitly recognizing that whether a given word is a noun, a verb, an adjective or an adverb depends on its placement in that string of words we call a sentence. Any word can function as any part of speech, as though any chessman could be knight, bishop, queen, by turns.

Derrida overturns the everyday concept of games. That concept has been crucial among linguists in expressing the notion that writing is a subsidiary game within language: 'Here one must think of writing as a game [*le jeu*] within language' (*OG* 50; *DG* 73). The usual concept of games also supports Plato's denigrations of writing as mere play (*paidia*) as against the serious business (*spoudé*) of spoken language. 'Play' in Plato's usage, however, means something like 'child's play', not a game with complex rules.

For Derrida, on the contrary, as against the whole Western tradition from Plato to Saussure and beyond, the whole world is a game. Nothing exists outside the game, just as there is nothing outside the text. Once more Derrida is twisting a word against the grain to make it say something different from what it ordinarily says, even for linguists and philosophers.

This twisting has devastating consequences both for linguists' theory of signs and for game theory. What is a game that is not grounded on external rules, that makes up the whole world rather than being one event within the world? Derrida notes in a footnote to my initial citation in this section that his phrase 'the game of the world' (le *jeu du monde*) derives from Heidegger's commentaries on Nietzsche and from such related works as Eugen Fink's *Le jeu comme symbole du monde* (*Spiel als Weltsymbol*) (1960). This genealogy gives the reader a clue to essential and mutually defining features of what Derrida means by his 'anasemic' (as Derrida says of Abraham and Torok's word analysis) concept of *jeu*. The word 'anasemic', by the way, is another antithetical word, since the prefix 'ana-', as Nicholas Rand, the translator of Abraham and Torok's *The Wolf Man's Magic Word*, notes, means 'upward', 'according to', 'back', 'backward, reversed', 'again', while '-semic' indicates ' "pertaining to the sign as a unit of meaning" ' (117). An anasemic analysis dissolves a word's unity by working both according to the usual meaning and against it.

I shall identify, in conclusion to this section, three anasemic features of Derrida's use of 'jeu'.

1) The absence of any transcendental signified. If there is nothing outside the game, then no external ground exists, no paternal presence setting the rules of the game. 'One could call *play*', says Derrida, 'the absence of the transcendental signified as limitlessness of play [*illimitation du jeu*], that is to say as the destruction of onto-theology and the metaphysics of presence. [. . .] This *play*, thought as the absence of the transcendental signified, is not a play *in the world*, as it has always been defined, for the purposes of *containing* it, by the philosophical tradition and as the theoreticians of play also consider it' (*OG* 50; *DG* 73); 'No ground [*sol*] of nonsignification – understood as insignificance or an intuition of a present truth – stretches out to give it a foundation [*pour le fonder*] under the play [*jeu*] and the coming into being of signs' (*OG* 48; *DG* 70).

2) 'Limitlessness of play' means that the game of the world is made up of an endless succession of signs, each referring to others, with never an exit or controlling non-sign outside the play of signs. Derrida cites Peirce's definition of a sign, an important source for this part of his argument. For Peirce, a sign is 'anything which determines something else (its interpretant), to refer to an object to which itself refers (its object) in the same way, the interpretant becoming in turn a sign, and so on ad infinitum' (*OG* 50).

3) Since a sign is normally defined as having a referent that is not itself a sign, Derrida's theory of *jeu* is the demolition of ordinary sign theory. This is said most succinctly in a passage in Chapter 1:

There is not a single signified that escapes, even if recaptured [*éventuellement pour y tomber*], the play of signifying references [*au jeu des renvois signifiants*] that constitute language. The advent of writing is the advent of this play; today such a play is coming into its own, effacing the limit starting from which one had thought to regulate the circulation of signs, drawing with it all the reassuring signifieds, reducing all the strongholds, all the out-of-bounds shelters [*tous les abris du hors-jeu*] that watched over the field of language. This, strictly speaking, amounts to destroying the concept of 'sign' and its entire logic. (*OG* 7; *DG* 16)

A final comment: one aspect of what Derrida says about *jeu*, along with the entire rhetorical structure of Chapter 2, is that it turns back on itself to exemplify what it talks about. Do you want to know what alimitless play of signs referring to other signs is like? Read Chapter 2.

J. HILLIS MILLER, TRACE (*OG* 47, 65, 66–7, 70–1; *DG* 69, 95, 97, 102–4)

The trace is in fact the absolute origin of sense in general. Which amounts to saying once again that there is no absolute origin of sense in general. The trace is the differance which opens appearance [*l'apparaître*] and signification. (*OG* 65; *DG* 95)

'Trace' as used by Derrida becomes an antithetical word in a way not too different to what happens to 'jeu' in his hands. The difference, however, is that 'trace' more often gives rise to blankly contradictory formulations, like saying that the trace is 'present-absent', or that it is an origin that is not an origin.

The word 'trace' has a perfectly unambiguous set of meanings in French, or, somewhat differently, in English. 'Trace' means the marks left by an animal or a person who once in the past passed by here, was present here and left footprints or paw prints on the ground. An example is the print of a naked foot in the sand that so strikes Robinson Crusoe with terror. Derrida discusses that footprint at length in his last set of seminars, *La bête et le souverain* (*deuxième année*). The word 'trace' also means to trace out a route on a map beforehand, or to make a tracing on a piece of paper of an already present design. In all these cases, the noun or verb 'trace' designates a mark made by or gesturing towards something pre-existing and non-linguistic that the trace points to, either back in time or forward in time. In its ordinary meaning it is not an antithetical word. Derrida twists the word, 'anasemically', against the grain, against its ordinary, semantic, dictionary meaning, to make it say something else entirely.

Just what does Derrida make the word 'trace' mean? Why does he twist just this word? Here my difficulties begin. I do not think what

Derrida means by the word is at all self-evident or clear, in spite of the fact that everyone knows it is a key Derridean word. The word 'trace' can be traced all through Chapter 2, like a red thread in a tapestry. Read Chapter 2 again for yourself, dear reader. I'll bet you will still find what Derrida means by 'trace' obscure, occulted. Derrida says as much. I can nevertheless perhaps learn something of what Derrida means by the word by seeing how he uses it in a few examples. Perhaps. My reading must, in any case, be extremely truncated. I shall concentrate, though not exclusively, as help in explicating, unfolding, my initial passage using 'trace', on four passages where the word is especially salient (*OG* 47, 65, 66–7, 70–1; *DG* 69, 95, 97, 102–4). I have read and re-read these passages many times. I still find them enigmatic, though what I had discovered already about 'brisure' and 'jeu' has been a help.

The trace is always already there. It is not the result of the marking out of a trace in a world that already exists. The trace is everywhere, like writing, though it would be a mistake to think that the trace is just language, or just writing or just sign-systems in the usual sense of that term as a set of marks referring outside themselves.

This ubiquity of the trace would allow Derrida to say, 'there is nothing outside the trace'. In this the trace is more or less the equivalent of 'arche-writing', as it is of 'differance'. I say 'more or less' because the valences of 'arche-trace' are not quite the same as those of 'arche-writing', nor are those of either quite the same as 'differance'. Else why does Derrida use three different words? Derrida's discourse about the trace depends heavily on negations, on saying what the trace is not. The trace is, for example, not an origin but the occulted origin of the origin. 'The value of the transcendental arche [*archie*]', says Derrida, 'must make its necessity felt before letting itself be erased. The concept of arche-trace must comply with both that necessity and that erasure. It is in fact contradictory and not acceptable within the logic of identity. The trace is not only the disappearance of origin – within the discourse that we sustain and according to the path that we follow it means that the origin did not even disappear, that it was never constituted except reciprocally by a nonorigin, the trace, which thus becomes the origin of the origin' (*OG* 61; *DG* 90). If the trace is nevertheless the 'origin of meaning' this means that 'there is no absolute origin of sense in general', 'no originary trace' (*OG* 61, 65; *DG* 90, 95).

Why is that? It is because what Derrida calls 'trace' is always already occulted, invisible, unlike Friday's footprint in the sand, or unlike the words that I am at this moment typing out on my computer screen.

> *The (pure) trace is differance.* It does not depend on any sensible plenitude, audible or visible, phonic or graphic. It is, on the contrary, the condition of such a plenitude. Although it *does not exist*, although it is never a *being-present* outside of all plenitude, its possibility is by rights anterior to all that one calls sign (signified/signifier, content/expression, etc.), concept or operation, motor or sensory. This differance is therefore not more sensible than intelligible and it permits the articulation of signs among themselves within the same abstract order. (*OG* 62–3; *DG* 92)

No wonder the trace is hard to understand, if understanding means clear-seeing, the interpretation of something that is out in the open, something that can be seen, heard, felt, touched. The trace is the non-presence of the present, which means the trace undoes the metaphysical or logocentric concept of time as made up of a present which is present here and now, a past which was once present and future which will one day be present. Derrida's trace, on the contrary, belongs to a past that is anterior to every present and to every entity (*étant*). It is an 'absolute past': 'That is what authorized us to call trace that which does not let itself be summed up in the simplicity of a present [. . .] if the trace refers to an absolute past, it is because it obliges us to think a past that can no longer be understood in the form of a modified presence, the present-past. Since past has always signified present-past, the absolute past that is retained in the trace no longer rigorously merits the name "past". Another name to erase' (*OG* 66; *DG* 97).

Taking off, as he explicitly affirms, from the use of the word 'trace' by Levinas (in 'La trace de l'autre') and by Heidegger ('Spur' is Heidegger's term), Derrida nevertheless uses the term differently from Levinas or Heidegger, who already differ between themselves. Derrida employs, to explain what he means by 'trace', one of his first uses of a term, 'le tout autre' ('the wholly other') (*OG* 47; *DG* 69), that is of great importance in his later writing. For Derrida the trace refers to the 'wholly other', all right, as it does for Levinas, but Derrida's wholly other is explicitly non-theological, non-metaphysical, non-transcendental. It is generated by the trace rather than generating it, if one can use the word 'generate', under erasure of course:

> The trace, where the relationship with the other is marked, articulates its possibility in the entire field of the entity [*étant*], which metaphysics has defined as the being-present starting from the occulted movement of the trace. The trace must be thought before the entity. But the movement of the trace is necessarily occulted, it produces itself as self-occultation. When the other announces itself as such, it presents itself in the dissimulation of itself. This formulation is not theological, as one might believe somewhat hastily. The 'theological' is a determined moment in the total movement of the trace. (*OG* 47; *DG* 69)

One of the clearest ways, for me at least, to think of what 'trace' means for Derrida, that is to think clearly what is permanently occulted, dissimulated, is to think of it as the space between signs in their 'espacement'. This space is there and not there. It is occulted, like the difference between one sign and another that gives a given sign meaning. Meaning arises magically and spontaneously from that blank space.

Yet another name for the trace is 'death'. Death is present for Derrida, as for Heidegger in a different way, in the midst of life. Death is the dead spot of a trace that is invisible and inaudible, like the presence of a 'trace element' in some rock or earth. Nevertheless that hidden trace is the origin/non-origin of the 'whole shebang' I listed above, all those assumed presences that we so blithely take for granted, subject, object, the presence of the present and so on. 'The outside', says Derrida, ' "spatial" and "objective" exteriority which we believe we know as the most familiar thing in the world, as familiarity itself, would not appear without the grammè, without differance as temporalization, without the nonpresence of the other inscribed within the sense of the present, without the relationship with death as the concrete structure of the living present. [. . .] life without difference, another name for death, historical metonymy where God's name holds death in check [*en respect*]' (*OG* 70–1; *DG* 103, 104).

Why bring in death? I suppose because the trace, like death, is invisible, inaudible, never present as such. On the other hand, the trace 'generates' life, which Derrida here defines not as 'organic' but as a product of differance. As long as you are caught up in the relays of differance, you, and the *vivant*, the living, in general, are still alive. Death is also invoked here in echo of Heidegger's claim that 'Dasein', human 'being there', is fundamentally to be defined as 'Sein zum Tode', being towards death. But Derrida was always 'obsessed with death'. Many of his later writings and seminars focus on death, for example in *The Gift of Death* (*Donner la mort*), down to the last extraordinary seminars on Robinson Crusoe's fear of death when he sees the trace of a naked foot in the sand. To say the trace is death, as Derrida does in *Of Grammatology*, is a splendid example of the way that book foreshadows Derrida's subsequent writings, though that can only be known in hindsight, after reading those later writings.

'Trace', in English, though perhaps not in French, has two strange meanings that differ from the ones I initially gave. 'Traces' are the name of the two straps or chains that connect a horse to the wagon or farm implement, a plow for example, that the horse 'draws'. A trace, even more weirdly, is 'a bar or rod, hinged at either end to another part, that transfers movement from one part of a machine to another' (*American Heritage Dictionary*). The trace is a 'brisure', a hinge, with all the complexities I have found in the French word. The trace is a hinge that connects and disconnects, that articulates, at a breaking point.

'Brisure', 'jeu', 'trace': following these three increasingly complex and in different ways antithetical words through the tangled thicket of Derrida's language in Chapter 2 of *De la grammatologie* is one way to try to come to terms with his language use. Some of his recurrent words are antithetical in themselves, like 'brisure', or, in a different way, 'jeu'. In some cases, such as 'trace', the word has a more or less univocal ordinary meaning, but Derrida uses it in ways that are antithetical to that normal usage. Derrida uses these words to attempt to say what has never been said. I claim that following these words, as they weave in and out of Derrida's discourse, is 'one way to try to come to terms with his language use', but trying does not guarantee success. Nevertheless, one can but try.

NICHOLAS ROYLE, BIZARRE (*OG* 36; *DG* 54–5)

Saussure: 'But the spoken word is so intimately bound to its written *image* that the latter manages to *usurp* the main role' [J.D.'s italics].

Rousseau: 'Writing is nothing but the representation of speech; it is *bizarre* that one gives more care to the determining of the *image* than to the *object*.' Saussure: 'Whoever says that a certain letter must be pronounced in a certain way is mistaking the written *image* of a sound for the sound itself. . . . [One] attribute[s] the oddity [*bizarrerie*] to an exceptional pronunciation.' What is intolerable and fascinating is indeed the intimacy intertwining image and thing, *graph, i.e.*, and phonè, to the point where by a mirroring, inverting, and perverting effect, speech seems in its turn the speculum of writing, which 'manages to usurp the main role'. Representation mingles with what it represents, to the point where one speaks as one writes, one thinks as if the represented were nothing more than the shadow or reflection of the representer. A dangerous promiscuity and a nefarious complicity between the reflection and the reflected which lets itself be seduced narcissistically. In this play of representation, the point of origin becomes ungraspable. There are things like reflecting pools, and images, an infinite reference from one to the other, but no longer a source, a spring. There is no longer a simple origin. For what is reflected is split *in itself* and not only as an addition to itself of its image. The reflection, the image, the double, splits what it doubles. The origin of the speculation becomes a difference. What can look at itself is not one; and the law of the addition of the origin to its representation, of the thing to its image, is that one plus one makes at least three. (*OG* 36; *DG* 54–5)

– You love this passage because it is not a passage. It has already passed out of the book. On the back cover of the so-called original French edition (but not of the English publication), there is the Rousseau quotation: 'Languages were made to be spoken, writing serves only as *supplement* to speech . . . Writing is nothing but the *representation* of speech, it is *bizarre* that one gives more care to the determining of the image than of the object'. (Les langues sont faites pour être parlées, l'écriture ne sert que de *supplément* à la parole . . . L'écriture n'est que la *représentation* de la parole, il est *bizarre* qu'on donne plus de soin à déterminer l'image que l'objet.) And this is followed by Derrida's first words, the immediately succeeding sentence on the back cover constituting in effect his first or final outworking of the book entitled *Of Grammatology*: 'This book is, then, dedicated to the bizarre [*Ce livre est donc voué à la bizarrerie*]'. A dedication to 'oddity' ('bizarrerie'), the experience of what is bizarre, pervades. In the passage itself it is the only word that the translator, Gayatri Spivak, gives parenthetically in the original French, as if to remark or double-mark this oddity, the oddity having already announced itself on the back cover of the French publication. 'Bizarrerie' is possible in English: the *OED* recognizes it as an English word, meaning 'bizarre quality', dating back to the middle of the eighteenth century. But whoever says 'bizarrerie'? It is difficult to get one's mouth around, like a patisserie gone topsy turvy. It is not the sort of thing you'd say in normal conversation.

– Do you call this a normal conversation? People sometimes give the impression that *Of Grammatology* is a rather classical, formal and well-behaved text or series of texts. No: it is bizarre through and through, starting perhaps with its title. It is called 'Of Grammatology' – but no one should suppose for a moment that this book propounds a science of writing. As Derrida later observed, *Of Grammatology* 'never proposed a grammatology, some positive science or discipline bearing that name; on the contrary, [it] went to great lengths to demonstrate the impossibility, the conditions of impossibility, the absurdity, in principle, of any science or any philosophy bearing the name "grammatology". The book that treated *of grammatology* was anything but a grammatology' ('For the Love of Lacan' 52). *Of Grammatology* is a bizarrerie. Its concern with *the bizarre* is a key to its enigma, part and parcel of what Derrida calls his 'final intention in this book', namely 'to *make enigmatic* what one thinks one understands by the words "proximity," "immediacy," "presence"' (*OG* 70, emphasis added).

– Bizarrerie, says Rousseaussure.

– Rousseaussure? Did I pronounce that right? What's your game anyway? Aren't you just messing about with words and letters and trying to lead us astray?

– Us? Who's talking about *us*? The passage in question, I admit, doesn't seem explicitly to have to do with 'playing with words'; but the 'play of representation' to which Derrida refers is not finally separable from what is seductive here. He knows, or his writing shows, that these forms of derangement are endlessly coming on, enabling and haunting what he elsewhere refers to as 'the "regime" of normal hallucination' ('Qual Quelle' 297–8). At the same time he insists on the fact that 'the desire to *restrict* play is irrepressible' (*OG* 59, trans. mod., emphasis added). You see this word, you hear it: Rousseaussure. It is a strange sort of deformation, to be sure, but it gives a hint, perhaps, of the bizarrerie of what is at stake in *Of Grammatology*. It's not so far away from what Derrida, later in the same paragraph, calls the process whereby Saussure 'anagrammatizes' Rousseau (*OG* 37). You can quickly find yourself back to front, as if in a mirror, the 'b' of 'bizarrerie' a 'd' and the letters of Derrida's name like the smile of the Cheshire cat. A busy, dizzy sort of derridelirium. To read *Of Grammatology* requires the most normative attentiveness and traditional respect for grammar, syntax, argument and demonstration, but also another eye and ear, to see or listen to what is going on between the lines, in other spaces. It's bizarre, yes. And it will always have exceeded the book. As he says: 'It is less a question of confiding new writings to the envelope of a book than of finally reading what wrote itself between the lines in the volumes. That is why, beginning to write without the line, one begins to reread past writing according to a different organization of space. [. . .] Because we are beginning to write, to write differently, we must reread differently' (*OG* 86–7).

– You love this passage because, like any in Derrida (and we've already indicated the necessity of questioning that figure of the 'passage', of letting its strangeness overflow, pass through, pass out), it seems to give us a passageway or passport into so many others. You love the abruptness, the violence, but also the irony and humour, the eroticism and lovingness. You love this peremptory kind of manner in which he writes 'Saussure', then a colon, then a quotation, without comment; then 'Rousseau', colon, quotation, without comment; then 'Saussure' again, colon, quotation. It's the sort of quick-fire ascription you associate with other early essays, like 'Force and Signification'. And so here they are in apposition, doubling up, it looks so straightforward. Rousseau and Saussure, side by side. One plus one plus . . .

– And then Derrida's commentary, which is of course not commentary, at least not in the sense of any straightforward exposition and explanation of the quotations. That's what you love, how everything joins up with everything else, the way this passage illustrates what he calls, elsewhere in *Of Grammatology*, the 'task of reading', a task based on the understanding that it is not sufficient merely to 'reproduc[e], by the effaced and respectful doubling of *commentary*, the conscious, voluntary, intentional relationship that the writer institutes in his exchanges with the history to which he belongs thanks to the element of language' (*OG* 158, emphasis added). 'Although it is not commentary', he goes on to make clear, 'our reading must be intrinsic and remain within the text' (159). You have to do something. But you can't do anything you fancy. The task is to bring out the way in which the text is itself but also (and first of all) other than itself, the way that what Rousseau or Saussure is saying is more or other than they might appear to suppose.

– You love the way the passage is doing this. Years prior to any explicit and sustained textual encounter with 'speech act theory' Derrida is showing us how crucial that is to understanding his texts. The words are doing by saying, saying writing. We get quotations from Saussure and Rousseau, then an unfurling of words, lines, sounds and images that are at once faithful to what has been excised from Rousseau and Saussure and doing something bizarrely different. You need a good ear for Derrida. He is not for speed-reading, even if he sets the quotations out on the page like a series of telegrams. He has an exceptionally fine ear in turn, so fine it can bury itself in the ear of the other. He is not only the great philosopher of writing of the twentieth century, but also a 'spectral machine' for speaking, listening and feeling ('Typewriter Ribbon' 160). Tone and affect: you might not think of these as a key component in the passage. With the French text it is easier to pick up, since the footnote appears on the same page. In the bulkier and more cumbersome apparatus of the English edition you have to seek it out in the back section. At the end of the chain of quotations from Saussure and Rousseau, before the onset of Derrida's delirious 'commentary', comes a footnote: 'Let us extend our quotation to bring out the tone and the affect of these theoretical propositions. Saussure *puts the blame on* writing: "Another result is that the less writing represents what it is supposed to represent, the stronger the tendency to use it as a basis becomes. Grammarians never fail to draw attention to the written form. Psychologically, the tendency is easily explained, but its consequences are annoying. Free use of the words 'pronounce' and 'pronunciation' sanctions the abuse and reverses the real, legitimate relationship between writing and language. Whoever says that a certain letter must be pronounced a certain way is mistaking the written image of a sound for the sound itself. For French *oi* to be pronounced *wa*, this spelling would have to exist independently; actually *wa* is written *oi.*" Instead of meditating upon this strange proposition, the *possibility* of such a *text* ("actually *wa* is written *oi*"), Saussure argues: "To attribute the oddity to an exceptional pronunciation of *o* and *i* is also misleading, for this implies that language depends on its written form and that certain liberties may be taken in writing, as if the graphic symbol were the norm"' (*OG* 325 n. 2, trans. mod.). Spivak's oversight in not supplying the italics for 'text' here tends to obscure the sharpness as well as the humour of Derrida's remark, in other words the bizarreness of this text that Saussure composes before our eyes: 'actually *wa* is written *oi*'.

– It is all about exploding the 'tranquil familiarity' (as Derrida calls it in the essay 'Différance') of our relationship to speech and writing, and unsettling 'our illusion that they are two' ('Différance' 5). The quotations from Rousseau and Saussure illustrate the troubling way in which writing seems to usurp speech: speech (which should be spontaneous, natural and *prior to* writing) is conceived as though it were based on writing, made in writing's image. Derrida is at once elucidating and analysing the quotations, and veering off somewhere else altogether. Everything gets inverted, perverted. The speculum and mirror are not 'in' Rousseau and Saussure but tilt into view in the extraordinary unfolding shadowshow of Derrida's remarks.

– You love this movement, this veering, this acceleration into the unknown. From the beginning of the book you have been trying to ponder the suggestion that 'the future can only be anticipated in the form of an absolute danger' (*OG* 5) and you sense this not only in what Derrida says but *how*, in the unforeseen, as if delirious shifts of his writing. As he notes in 'Force and Signification': writing is 'dangerous and anguishing', 'it does not know where it is going' (11). Such is the tone and the affect of this passage for you.

– You feel the strangeness of what is at once 'intolerable and fascinating'.

– It is erotic and disturbing at the same time, all this talk of mingling, intimacy, intertwining, promiscuity, complicity. Something is letting itself be seduced narcissistically. There is a sex scene going on, but where does it start? Or end? It is not about speech coming first and writing second, or the other way round. It is more to do with what Derrida calls that 'strange space [. . .] *between* speech and writing' ('Différance' 5). There is no longer any simple origin. It becomes elusive, enigmatic. You can't hold onto it. Bizarre, exorbitant, excessive, exaggerated: the passage veers magically in the direction of fiction or poetry. There are things like reflecting pools, and images, an infinite referral (*renvoi*: a dizzying word, that can also mean sending back, cross-reference, suspension, transfer . . .): where did these come from? What is this place? Where are we?

– This shadowshow, these spectacular sentences of delirious splitting and disorientation testify to the experience of what Derrida elsewhere refers to as the place 'where we believe ourselves to be' (*OG* 162), in other words *in the vertigo*.[1] In this vertigo of place, in which 'what is reflected is split *in itself*' and self-regard is intimately intertwined with otherness, some of the most insistent motifs of *Of Grammatology* are enfolded: representation, the supplement, the bizarre. It is a matter of what Derrida will later describe as the 'pre-originary intervention of the other in me' ('I Have a Taste for the Secret' 89).

– You have to break off, you know you do, but why don't you just add, by way of some brief illustration of the almost incredible logic of *renvoi* that seems, in turn, to be required for any properly attentive reading of Derrida, a few final indications of how this passage you love seems to send us back or away, as if for the first time, to other elsewheres in his work? Beyond the book called *Of Grammatology* and besides the numerous other analyses of the writings of Rousseau and Saussure, you might note, for example, the way the passage links with images and motifs of water, springs, sources, danger, fear of drowning, literature and doubles, duplicity without original, the uncanny (in 'Qual Quelle: Valéry's Sources', 'The Double Session', *Glas*, 'To Speculate – on "Freud"', 'Telepathy', etc.); with what he says about a deconstructive thinking of self and subject, the need for a new narcissism more open to the other ('Me – Psychoanalysis', 'Deconstruction and the Other', '"There is No *One* Narcissism"', 'Psyche, Invention of the Other', *Right of Inspection, Monolingualism of the Other*, 'Abraham, the Other', etc.); and with what his texts have to tell us about ghosts, not least as regards that spectral logic whereby 'one plus one makes at least three' (number is the ghost, as he suggests in *Spectres of Marx*, not to mention *yes*, what he says about yes, in 'Ulysses Gramophone' and 'A Number of Yes', and about 'etc.' (in 'Et Cetera'), etc., etc.).

– Us? Still harping on *us*? *Of Grammatology* is written in a quite philosophically traditional mode: there is, on occasion, an authorial 'I' as well as the perhaps more inclusive 'we' ('We must begin wherever we are' for example (*OG* 162)). Strikingly, it is not a book that addresses or engages with 'you'. Such dryness and formality as this might imply are in keeping with Derrida's avowed intention, from the outset, to 'respect classical norms' (*OG* lxxxix). Nevertheless you want to conclude by saying that you love this passage you have selected because it broaches, in however shadowy or subtle a fashion, an experience of delirious tone and *more than one voice*. In this sense you feel it is not after all so different from those numerous other, apparently more literary, poetic or dramatic texts by Derrida (some of which you have just named: 'Psyche, Invention of the Other', *Right of Inspection*, *Monolingualism of the Other*, 'Et Cetera') that take the form of dialogue. But it is never dialogue, you want to emphasize. It is always more than that: multiple voices, the call of the other, an irreducible polyphony. *One plus one makes at least three.*

DEREK ATTRIDGE, THE ARBITRARY (*OG* 44–7; *DG* 65–9)

The thesis of the *arbitrariness of the sign* (so grossly misnamed [*si mal nommée*], and not only for the reasons Saussure himself recognizes) must forbid a radical distinction between the linguistic and the graphic sign. No doubt this thesis concerns only the necessity of relationships between specific signifiers and signifieds *within* an allegedly natural relationship between the voice and sense in general, between the order of phonic signifiers and the content of the signifieds ('the only natural bond, the only true bond, the bond of sound'). Only these relationships between specific signifiers and signifieds would be regulated by arbitrariness. Within the 'natural' relationship between phonic signifiers and their signifieds *in general*, the relationship between each determined signifier and its determined signified would be 'arbitrary'. (*OG* 44; *DG* 65)

If, as Derrida says earlier in his reading of Saussure, 'the tone counts' (*OG* 34), we might begin by asking, 'Why should the thesis of the arbitrariness of the sign be "mal nommée"?' What has Derrida got against arbitrariness? Saussure's own discomfort arises because of possible misunderstanding: 'The term should not imply that the choice of the signifier is left entirely to the speaker [. . .]; I mean that it is unmotivated, i.e. arbitrary in that it actually has no natural connection with the signified' (*Course*, trans. Baskin 68–9). (Saussure goes on to dismiss two possible objections, pointing out that onomatopoeia and interjections, which might seem to be exceptions to the rule of arbitrariness, are 'never organic elements of a linguistic system' (*Course* 69) – an assertion to which Derrida devotes some acerbic comments in *Glas* (91b–94b)). Saussure's point is, of course, precisely the reverse of this misunderstanding: *because* the relation between signifier and signified is arbitrary and thus purely conventional, there can be no grounds for preferring a signifier different from the one sanctioned by the system; the operation of language would fail if speakers did not faithfully observe pre-existing paradigms.

It appears that for Derrida, however, this discomfort is not the only objection that can be raised against the term. He has observed earlier in the book that Saussure relies on the notion of arbitrariness to limit the kind of writing he discusses to phonetic, alphabetic writing, thus enabling the linguist to exclude it from the interiority of language – an exclusion which, Derrida argues, is not merely the result of a certain scientific exigency but one on which the possibility of scientificity itself depends (*OG* 32–3). And in a tone of mock surprise he has reminded us that it is 'the theoretician of the arbitrariness of the sign' himself who keeps returning to the notion of a 'natural' relationship – between concept and phonic signifier, and between speech and writing (*OG* 35). There are grounds, then, for being suspicious of the concept of arbitrariness, which is constantly in danger of being undermined. But we should note that in the passage quoted above the severity of Derrida's judgement is directed at the *naming* of the thesis, not at the thesis itself; his sentence implies that a worthwhile thesis has been given an inappropriate name – even though the note to this sentence cites 'an entire system of intralinguistic criticism [. . .] opposed to the thesis of "the arbitrariness of the sign"' (*OG* 326). The worth of the thesis, for Derrida, is immediately announced: it forbids 'a radical distinction between the linguistic sign and the graphic sign', a distinction which, as Derrida demonstrates, is a repeated theme in the *Course in General Linguistics*. (This is not, of course, how Saussure deploys the thesis of arbitrariness; but it's Derrida's point that the thesis can be used against itself.)

What makes a name inappropriate for that which it names? If words were wholly arbitrary in their relation to their meanings, there would be no room for a concept of appropriateness: any signifier would be as good as any other to refer to a particular signified. Saussure's explanation is well known:

> The idea of 'sister' is not linked by any inner relationship to the succession of sounds s-ö-r which serves as its signifier in French;

that it could be represented equally by just any other sequence is proved by differences among languages and by the very existence of other languages: the signified 'ox' has as its signifier *b-ö-f* on one side of the border and *o-k-s* [. . .] on the other. (*Course* 67–8)

(Notice that Saussure is already in trouble here, since 'ox' is a *sign*, not a signified, but let that pass. His claim here that the same signified is represented by different signifiers in France and in Germany is, of course, later complicated by his argument that the conceptual continuum is divided up by the particular language in a particular way, so there are no grounds for assuming a common signified on both sides of the border.) In invoking the possibility of misnaming, then, Derrida is already assuming that the operation of signs is not wholly governed by arbitrariness.

However, apparently accepting for the moment that the thesis of the arbitrariness of the sign is correct despite his unhappiness about the term (we might note the scare quotes round both 'arbitrary' *and* 'natural'), Derrida notes a tension in Saussure's thinking between, on the one hand, the 'arbitrary' relation between any given signifier (written or spoken) and its signified, and on the other the *general* relation between signifiers and signifieds, where one kind of signifier – phonic – bears a 'natural' relation to the signified while the other, by implication at least, is still arbitrary. (Oddly, the standard translation of the *Course* by Wade Baskin omits what, for Derrida, is the crucial adjective in Saussure's description of the phonic sign, cited many times in this chapter of the *Grammatology*: for Saussure's 'le lien naturel, le seul véritable' Baskin has 'the only true bond' (*Course* 25). Roy Harris, in his version of the *Course*, has 'the natural and only authentic connexion' (26).) Thus far in the argument, then, Derrida is pushing the claims of the arbitrary against a conception of natural relationship. (Much later he will comment on Paul de Man's reliance on the term 'arbitrariness', welcoming it as a name for the contingency and fortuitousness of the event but hesitating over its association in de Man's work with threat, cruelty, dismemberment and so on ('Typewriter Ribbon' 158).)

Now from the moment that one considers the totality of determined signs, spoken, and a fortiori written, as unmotivated institutions, one must exclude any relationship of natural subordination, any natural hierarchy among signifiers or orders of signifiers.

If 'writing' signifies inscription and especially the durable institution of a sign (and that is the only irreducible kernel of the concept of writing), writing in general covers the entire field of
linguistic signs. In that field a certain sort of instituted signifiers
may then appear, 'graphic' in the narrow and derivative sense of
the word, ordered by a certain relationship with other instituted –
hence 'written', even if they are 'phonic' – signifiers. The very idea
of institution – hence of the arbitrariness of the sign – is unthink-
able before the possibility of writing and outside of its horizon.
(*OG* 44)

If the relation of sound (or in Saussure's terms 'sound-image', though
Derrida doesn't make anything of this) to meaning is the 'natural
and only authentic' relation, it's clearly naturally superior to the
relation of writing to meaning; but if arbitrariness rules the field,
there must be no natural hierarchy. Once again, Derrida draws on
the maligned term to move the argument on. It leads to the classic
deconstructive account of the relation between speech and writing:
all linguistic signs are a kind of writing, because all involve inscription
of some sort. Derrida's act in retaining the term *writing* but changing
its meaning is exactly what Saussure has said the language-user
cannot do: this is the misunderstanding of 'arbitrariness' as 'open to
the choice of the speaker'. The violence involved here is indicated by
Derrida's use of scare quotes around several of his terms. When the
word 'written' appears in this extract in quotation marks, we register
that it does not have the meaning authorized by convention, but rather
Derrida's expanded notion; whereas 'writing', 'graphic' and 'phonic'
in this passage do have their conventional meanings, but require the
quotes to indicate that these conventional meanings are no longer
adequate.

Arbitrariness has now been both disparaged and misapplied –
though this hasn't prevented Derrida from making use of it – and
now it is put firmly in its place. Writing (which perhaps should
be 'writing'), we are told, is a precondition for arbitrariness, which
cannot be thought outside of its horizon. We cannot begin, as
Saussure wanted to do, from the principle of the arbitrariness of
the sign (Saussure's '*Principle I*'), because there is something more
fundamental, something that makes the principle of arbitrariness
thinkable in the first place. Here Derrida calls it *writing*; he will give
it other names in the pages that follow, including *trace*, *differance* and

supplementarity. He has also introduced the important notion of *institution*, which will help him take the issue of arbitrariness in a new direction.

> Let us now persist for a while in making use of this opposition of nature and institution, of *physis* and *nomos* [. . .] which a meditation on writing should disturb although it functions everywhere as self-evident, especially in the discourse of linguistics. We must then conclude that only the signs called *natural*, those that Hegel and Saussure call 'symbols', escape semiology as grammatology. But they fall a fortiori outside the field of linguistics as the region of general semiology. The thesis of the arbitrariness of the sign thus indirectly but irrevocably contests Saussure's declared proposition when he chases writing to the outer darkness of language. This thesis successfully accounts for a conventional relationship between the phoneme and the grapheme (in phonetic writing, between the phoneme, signifier-signified, and the grapheme, pure signifier), but by the same token it forbids that the latter be an 'image' of the former. Now it was indispensable to the exclusion of writing as 'external system', that it stamped [*vînt frapper*] an 'image', a 'representation', or a 'figuration', an exterior reflection of the reality of language. (*OG* 44–5, trans. mod.)

Derrida here acknowledges that he is, pro tem, making use of the discredited notion of arbitrariness to pursue the logic of his argument ('institution' is not identical to 'arbitrariness', but the opposition of institution and nature is clearly a version of the opposition between arbitrary and natural relations), even though writing, in his new sense, is prior to any opposition between arbitrariness or institution and nature, not only making them possible but at the same time limiting the absoluteness of their operation. The thesis of the arbitrariness of the linguistic sign allows us to exclude those signs that rely on a 'natural' or intrinsic relation between the properties of signifier and signified – what Peirce in his tripartite categorization calls *icons*. Concentrating for the present on these 'non-natural' signs, Derrida returns to the question of the relation between graphic and phonic signifiers. Since writing is, for Saussure, solely a representation of speech, it must be governed by the law of arbitrariness. How then, asks Derrida, can Saussure claim that writing gives us an image of speech? – this would be a non-arbitrary, motivated, natural connection. This may seem a little unfair to Saussure, who never extended the notion of arbitrariness to the relation between speech and writing; in this instance, he might have been reasonably happy with Derrida's refusal of both pure arbitrariness and pure natural-ness or motivation. But Derrida is intent on using Saussure's thesis against himself – there's an edge of sarcasm in his description of Saussure 'chas[ing] writing to the outer darkness [*les ténèbres extérieures*] of language' – and he insists that the inability to come down on the side either of convention or of motivation is a mark against Saussure. We may see this as characteristic of Derrida's readings of philosophers and linguists, a trait that has given rise to some misunderstandings: his barbed tone and evident delight in uncovering contradictions distract from the positive implications of his findings – here that Saussure, who 'saw without seeing, knew without being *able* to take into account' (*OG* 43), as Derrida put it earlier, reveals the inadequacy of both the conventionalist and the naturalist accounts of language. Putting Derrida's point more neut-rally, Saussure wants to assert both that writing is wholly exterior to speech, implying that the relation between them is arbitrary, and that writing is an image of speech, implying that the relation is motivated. A contradiction, yes, but one that Derrida is content to live with; if writing (in the limited sense) is the supplement of speech, as he will go on to argue, it is neither simply a conventional representation nor simply a motivated one, neither wholly outside nor wholly inside. Earlier Derrida had remarked that Plato's account of writing, speech and being or idea was fundamentally the same as Saussure's, but that the philosopher's tone was preferable, being 'more subtle, more critical, more troubled' (*OG* 33, trans. mod.)

In the paragraphs that follow, Derrida presses home his accusation, still leaning heavily on the notion of arbitrariness. 'What matters here is that in the synchronic structure and systematic principle of alphabetic writing – and phonetic writing in general – no relationship of "natural" representation, none of resemblance or participation [. . .] be implied' (*OG* 45). And again:

> One must therefore challenge, in the very name of the arbitrariness of the sign, the Saussurean definition of writing as 'image' – hence as natural symbol – of language. Not to mention the fact that the phoneme is *unimaginable* itself, and no visibility can *resemble* it, it suffices to take into account what Saussure says about the difference

between the symbol and the sign [. . .] in order to be completely baffled as to how he can at the same time say of writing that it is an 'image' or 'figuration' of language and define language and writing elsewhere as 'two distinct systems of signs'. (*OG* 45)

Gayatri Spivak must be held responsible for augmenting the tonal antagonism of Derrida's words – 'ne plus comprendre' becomes 'completely baffled' just as 'mal nommée' had earlier become 'grossly misnamed' – but the faux bemusement is there to a degree in the original. And one might ask, is it not possible for two distinct systems of signs to have a motivated relation to one another? A glance at the representations of the alphabet in one of the common sign languages will reveal a distinct system in which many of the shapes produced by the hands are imitative of the shapes of the letters. Poor Saussure is accused of something like Freud's 'kettle logic' ('a process exposed by Freud in *The Interpretation of Dreams*' (*OG* 45)) in advancing incompatible arguments in order to achieve his desired end: the discrediting of writing.

> Now we must think that writing is at the same time more exterior to speech, not being its 'image' or its 'symbol', and more interior to speech, which is already in itself a writing. Even before it is linked to incision, engraving, drawing, or the letter, to a signifier referring in general to a signifier signified by it, the concept of the *graphie* [unit of a possible graphic system] implies the framework [*instance*] of the *instituted trace*, as the possibility common to all systems of signification. [. . .] The instituted trace is 'unmotivated' but not capricious. Like the word 'arbitrary' according to Saussure, it 'should not imply that the choice of the signifier is left entirely to the speaker' [*Course* 68–69]. Simply, it has no 'natural attachment' to the signified within reality. For us, the rupture of that 'natural attachment' puts in question the idea of naturalness rather than that of attachment. That is why the word 'institution' should not be too quickly interpreted within the classical system of oppositions. (*OG* 46; *DG* 68)

Derrida is now ready to move to his own version of arbitrariness. Already the word 'unmotivated' ('immotivé') has begun to displace 'arbitrary', and 'unmotivatedness' ('immotivation') will soon displace 'arbitrariness', though it remains awkward in English (Spivak will put 'unmotivatedness' in scare quotes and then shift to 'immotivation' without quotes). Saussure's dividedness on the question of writing's relation to speech is now endorsed and amplified: writing is even more exterior and at the same time even more interior to speech than is allowed in Saussure's relatively timid account. And the notion of writing is generalized to the notion of the 'instituted trace', which underlies all sign systems and not just language. At first it seems as if Derrida is going to come down completely on the side of arbitrariness in his discussion of this generalized form of writing, echoing Saussure's cautionary remark about choice and asserting that the instituted trace has no 'natural attachment' to its signified content. (As always, Derrida's use of quotation marks is interesting: 'attache naturelle' looks like a quotation from Saussure that he has used earlier, but Saussure's phrase is 'lien naturel' so it must be an indication of the author's distance – quotation marks or 'guillemets' functioning as what Derrida, following Ponge, calls *pincettes* or tweezers (*Signéponge/Signsponge* 44–5).) But there is an immediate qualification: it is not that arbitrariness triumphs over naturalness, but that the concept of naturalness is not as simple as it seems. Hence the term 'institution' should not be taken to sit entirely comfortably on the side of, say, convention as opposed to nature, *nomos* as opposed to *physis*.

> The instituted trace cannot be thought without thinking the retention of difference within a structure of reference where difference appears *as such* and thus permits a certain liberty of variations among the full terms. The absence of *another* here-and-now, of another transcendental present, of *another* origin of the world appearing as such, presenting itself as irreducible absence within the presence of the trace, is not a metaphysical formula substituted for a scientific concept of writing. This formula, beside the fact that it is the questioning of metaphysics itself, describes the structure implied by the 'arbitrariness of the sign', from the moment that one thinks of its possibility *short of* the derived opposition between nature and convention, symbol and sign, etc. (*OG* 46–7)

Introducing the instituted trace – instituted rather than given, though this is no doubt another of those oppositions that must remain in question; trace rather than sign – allows Derrida to move on to his own version of Saussure's proposition, 'In language there are only differences *without positive terms'*. A few pages later, Derrida will remark,

> Henceforth, it is not to the thesis of the arbitrariness of the sign that I shall appeal directly, but to what Saussure associates with it as an indispensable correlative and which would seem to me rather to lay the foundations for it: the thesis of *difference* as the source of linguistic value. (*OG* 52)

The trace is offered as a way of conceptualizing difference that cuts across the oppositions with which Saussure continued to struggle, such as nature and convention, symbol (as motivated representation) and sign (as unmotivated representation), and, of course, presence and absence. And once more, the thesis of the 'arbitrariness of the sign' is pressed into service, albeit displaying still the tweezers of scare quotes: what is important is that we consider its operation before, or on this side of (*en deçà*) the oppositions Saussure clung to. Arbitrariness need not stay obediently on the side of convention and the sign but can denote a principle of differentiation that complicates, but also enables, all signifying processes. Another name, therefore, for the trace or – still to be discussed – supplementarity.

> I have chosen to demonstrate the necessity of this 'deconstruction' by privileging the Saussurean references, not only because Saussure still dominates contemporary linguistics and semiology; it is also because he seems to me to hold himself at the limit: at the same time within the metaphysics that must be deconstructed and beyond the concept of the sign (signifier/signified) which he still uses. But Saussure's scruples, his interminable hesitations, particularly in the matter of the difference between the two 'aspects' of the sign and in the matter of 'arbitrariness', are better realized through reading Robert Godel's *Les sources manuscrites du cours de linguistique générale*. (*OG* 329 n. 38 [note cited *OG* 73])

This is a note appended by Derrida at the very end of his discussion of Saussure. Up to now, the tone of Derrida's analysis or 'deconstruction' (he holds his own term in tweezers now!) has had the effect of presenting Saussure as a somewhat comically inadequate thinker. Plato was more subtle, critical and troubled than

Saussure (Spivak magnifies the latter's sins by translating 'plus inquiète' as 'less complacent') (*OG* 33), Saussure's 'irritation' drives him to 'pedestrian comparisons' (*OG* 38), he wants to set up a 'sort of intralinguistic leper colony' (*OG* 42), his statements are 'curious', he makes an 'apparently innocent and didactic analogy', and we 'have to oppose [him] to himself' (*OG* 52). But in this note Derrida lets him off the hook; his actual writings, as distinct from the book assembled from the lecture notes of his students, show him to be an exemplary thinker, pushing at the limits of conceptuality, anything but complacent, a forebear rather than an opponent. Derrida also refers from time to time to the *Anagrams*, where a Saussure who is much less sure of himself – and of the principle of the arbitrariness of the sign – emerges.

Derrida turns to the word 'arbitrary' in several other places in *Of Grammatology*: it appears in the reading of Lévi-Strauss, along with art, technology, law, institution, society and immotivation, as an example of the 'others' of *physis* (*OG* 103), as a characteristic of oppressive governments (*OG* 137), as a fault in Rameau's music (*OG* 210) and as a property of money, equated with phonetic writing (*OG* 301) (invoked these last three cases in the course of accounts of Rousseau's writing). In spite of the accusation of gross misnaming, it's obviously a very useful word in Derrida's thinking, but one that has to be handled with care – exploited but never wholly endorsed. He is willing to use the phrase 'the arbitrariness of the sign' without distancing quotation marks (*OG* 33, 35, 44, 45, 52), but he uses it just as often with them (*OG* 47, 48, 51, 57, 326). When we move from sign to trace, however, we find that he scrupulously avoids Saussure's term: as far as I know, he never refers to 'the arbitrary trace', preferring 'the unmotivated trace' or 'the instituted trace'. And with the trace, we shift to a new consideration: 'In fact, there is no unmotivated trace: the trace is indefinitely its own becoming-unmotivated' (*OG* 47). Saussure is eventually left behind, as the static notion of difference gives way to the movement of *différance*: 'In Saussurean language, what Saussure does not say would have to be said: there is neither symbol nor sign but a becoming-sign of symbol' (*OG* 47). Arbitrariness, it turns out, is not a foundation-stone, as Saussure would have it, but a temporary piece of scaffolding, to be set aside once its usefulness is over. And in stating that the thesis of 'the arbitrariness of the sign' is 'mal nommée' Derrida is not flagrantly exercising a power which according to that thesis he does not have, but marking a moment in his patient undoing of the oppositions on which the thesis relies, an undoing already implicit in Saussure's own 'scruples' and 'hesitations'.

SEAN GASTON, WRITING AND WORLD
(*OG* 47, 50, 65; *DG* 68, 73, 95)

How does Derrida treat the concept of world? In its classical forms, *kosmos* and *mundus*, it appears to be a profoundly metaphysical concept. One might expect that he would avoid the concept of the world or only use it in quotation marks. Encountering the inheritance of the suspension of the world in transcendental phenomenology and its intricate connection to *Dasein* in Heidegger's thought, Derrida can neither adhere to a clear denial nor to a persistent affirmation of world. Certainly, there are worlds that are cited from the works of Rousseau, Descartes, Jasper, Kafka and Lévi-Strauss, which often carry the heavy resonance of a quotation that should be placed in double quotation marks. For example, when Derrida quotes Lévi-Strauss's description of 'the lost world' (*le monde perdu*) of the Nambikwara, who are called a people 'without writing' (*OG* 107, 110; *DG* 157).

There are also passages where Derrida appears to use a concept of world in his own name. What kind of world is at stake when he writes of 'the ineluctable world of the future' in the Exergue (*OG* 5)? Though in this case, it is precisely a question of a 'future world' or 'monde à venir', a world to come, a world 'which breaks absolutely with constituted normality and can only be proclaimed, *presented*, as a sort of monstrosity' (*OG* 5; *DG* 14). But why evoke the world at all? Why retain a concept of world, even a world to come? If Derrida cannot entirely dispense with the concept of world, how are we to read his insistence that 'our entire world [*tout notre monde*] and language would collapse' without the exteriority of writing in general (*OG* 14; *DG* 26)? Does writing, as trace and *différance*, then *save* the world for us? Does it preserve that which it can also destroy?

Derrida refers on the first page of his work to a concept of writing that is 'in a world where the phoneticization of writing must dissimulate its own history as it is produced' (*OG* 3). What does it mean to have a concept of writing that is 'in a world' (*dans une monde*) (*OG* 11)? Must writing always be *in* a world? A few pages later,

Derrida gestures to one of the key problems in addressing the concept of the world:

> The system of 'hearing(understanding)-oneself-speak' ['s'entendre-parler'] through the phonic substance – which *presents itself* as the nonexterior, nonmundane, therefore nonempirical or noncontingent signifier – has necessarily dominated the history of the world during an entire epoch, and has even produced the idea of the world, the idea of world-origin, that arises from the difference between the worldly and the non-worldly, the outside and the inside, ideality and non-ideality, universal and nonuniversal, transcendental and empirical, etc. (*OG* 7–8; *DG* 17)

The phonocentric tradition casts language not *in* the world (the exterior, mundane, empirical and contingent) but as the origin *of* the world. Language is the transcendental possibility of the world. It is itself entirely free of the world: intelligible, necessary and universal. Without the ideality of the *phonē* and the *lógos*, there would be no 'idea of the world'.

For Derrida, despite the careful construction of a transcendental internal time consciousness, Husserl cannot avoid 'the time of the world' (*OG* 67). And despite his evocation of being-in-the-world, Heidegger succumbs to a notion of language 'which does not borrow from outside itself, in the world' (*OG* 20). We are left with what Derrida calls 'the *game of the world*' (*le* jeu du monde) (*OG* 50; *DG* 73). The challenge of 'the *game of the world*', Derrida argues, is to think of a writing 'which is neither *in* the world nor in "another world"', of a writing that marks 'the absence of another here-and-now, of another transcendent present, of *another* origin of the world' (*OG* 65, 47).

In 'Structure, Sign and Play' (1966), Derrida had associated *le jeu du monde* with Nietzsche's 'joyous affirmation of the play of the world and the innocence of becoming' (*Writing and Difference* 292). Derrida refers here to Nietzsche's description of the world as a '*game*' or 'play of forces', a continual becoming, passing away and destruction that Heraclitus had compared to the innocent play (*paidiá*) of a child (Nietzsche, *The Pre-Platonic Philosophers* 70–4; *Ecce Homo* 729; *Late Notebooks* 38; Heraclitus 102). Derrida was also inspired by the work of Eugen Fink (*OG* 326 n. 14). In *Nietzsche's Philosophy* (1960), Fink had written: 'The cosmos plays. [. . .] It plays joining and separating, weaving death and life into one beyond good and evil and beyond all value because any value only appears within the play' (172). From his reading of both Nietzsche and Husserl, Fink argued that one should not take the measure of the world through things or beings *in* the world but think *of* the world – from 'the *origin of the world*' ('Phenomenological Philosophy' 95–100).

For Derrida, the play of the world suggests that one can avoid thinking of world within the traditional Aristotelian structure of container and contained. As he remarks in a discussion from 1979: 'On the basis of thinking such as Nietzsche's (as interpreted by Fink), the concept of play, understood as the play of the world, is no longer play *in* the world. That is, it is no longer determined and contained by something, by the space that would comprehend it' (*The Ear of the Other* 69). Twenty years after *Of Grammatology*, Derrida described Heidegger's notion of 'the play of the world' in *Of Spirit* (1987) as a concentric 'becoming-world of world' that always tends towards 'collecting together' (*Versammlung*) (52). Derrida implies that Heidegger's use of world remained tied to the assumption of a 'clear difference between the open and the closed' (54). How does one open or close a world?

Language may relieve us of unrelenting reality, writing may evoke times long gone or even create wondrous fictional narratives, but it cannot engender another world, a clear escape or unbroken repose that is *always* elsewhere. If there is a world in Derrida's work, it is a world that provides neither ground nor pure possibility but is also a world that cannot be avoided or circumvented. We never stop passing through, finding ourselves in the midst of that which we are neither truly in nor truly above.

IAN MACLACHLAN, EMBARRASSING EXPERIENCE (*OG* 60; *DG* 89)

'Quant au concept d'expérience, il est ici fort embarrassant' (*DG* 89), Derrida notes in the course of an elaboration of the notion of 'arche-writing' as a generalized writing. Gayatri Spivak provides an idiomatic translation of the remark: 'As for the concept of experience, it is most unwieldy here' (*OG* 60). Experience is conceptually unwieldy, awkward, it is embarrassing in that it poses an obstacle which has to be crossed or crossed through, and it is far from alone in that: 'Like all the notions I am using here, it belongs to the history of metaphysics and we can only use it under erasure [*sous rature*]' (60). Its embarrassing but unavoidable baggage consists in its complicity with the metaphysical value of presence: ' "Experience" has always designated the relationship with a presence, whether that relationship had the form of consciousness or not' (60).

The local embarrassment posed by the concept of experience at this point of the chapter 'Linguistics and Grammatology' arises in relation to Copenhagen linguist Louis Hjelmslev's 'glossematics', proposed as the study of language as a formal system, that form being rigorously isolated from the material or immaterial substance of signifier or signified. Hjelmslev's exclusive focus on the fundamental linguistic unit of the 'glosseme' as form rather than substance seems to promise a grammatological corrective to the Saussurean phono-centrism that Derrida has just been examining. But, in so far as Derrida's 'arche-writing' designates the condition of possibility of a linguistic system, 'a field of transcendental experience' (*OG* 61), it would have been inadmissible to Hjelmslev's scrupulously demarcated 'immanent' linguistic system. Such an appeal to 'experience as arche-writing' is not made in order to take up a position firmly within the sphere of transcendental enquiry, but rather in order to avoid what Derrida detects as an unexamined metaphysics in Hjelmslev's immanent objectivism, the kind of surreptitious metaphysical baggage that he elsewhere describes as 'transcendental contraband' (*Glas* 244a). It is for this reason that a passage through a field of transcendental experience must, in this context, be hazarded:

> It is to escape falling back into this naive objectivism [of the Copenhagen School] that we refer here to a transcendentality that we elsewhere put into question. This is because there is, we believe, a short-of and a beyond of transcendental critique. To see to it that the beyond does not end up falling short is to recognize in this contortion the necessity of a pathway [*parcours*]. That pathway must leave a track in the text. (*OG* 61; *DG* 90, trans. mod.)

The recourse to experience, embarrassing though it may be, is under-taken precisely to avoid an unexamined recourse to experience in either of its purely empirical or transcendental guises. Indeed, 'experience as arche-writing' seems to name just that pathway or passage (*parcours*), a movement between or across versions of experience which might somehow maintain itself as that movement without falling back into one or other form of experience as 'relationship with a presence'.

Other paradigms for such a form of experience as passage or traversal that does not return to itself as presence are not signalled in these pages of *Grammatology*, but Derrida's 1967 essay on Georges Bataille does dwell on the latter's unsettling notion of 'interior' experience: 'That which *indicates itself* as interior experience is not an experience, because it is related to no presence, to no plenitude, but only to the "impossible" it "undergoes" in torture' ('From Restricted to General Economy' 272). Subsequently, it becomes something of a favoured term for Derrida, as for example in an interview of 1986 where, offered a range of words to describe his own itinerary, he declares a qualified preference: 'I rather like the word experience whose origin evokes traversal, but a traversal with the body, it evokes a space that is not given in advance but that opens as one advances. The word experience, once dusted off and reactivated a little, is perhaps the one I would choose' ('There is No *One* Narcissism' 207). This preference seems even more marked, from around that time onwards, in Derrida's frequent references to deconstruction as an experience of the impossible, or his explorations of the decision and the experience of undecidability. In relation to these, I would just like to observe that something of the hazardous, uncertain, tentative nature of the traversal evoked may be lost in the passage from *expérience* to 'experience', as translators as sensitive as Samuel Weber or Pascale-Anne Brault and Michael Naas take care to remind us in respect of the 'experience and experiment of the undecidable' (*Limited Inc* 116) or the 'experience and experiment of the impossible' (*The Other Heading* 44).

ANN SMOCK, THIS CONCEPT DESTROYS ITS NAME (*OG* 61; *DG* 90)

The concept in question here is that of the *arche-trace*. The statement that it destroys its name comes in a passage where Derrida acknowledges that certain terms (notably this one) are crucial to the development of a thinking that rules them out. They can't just be barred; they must make their necessity felt and *then* – or *thereby* – cross themselves out. It is precisely inasmuch as they have to be there that there is evidently no place for them. 'The concept of the arche-trace must do justice both to this necessity and to this erasure' (*OG* 61).

The trace of which Derrida writes is not a vestige of an origin that disappeared. What 'trace' means is that there never was an origin to disappear – that there never is any origin at all until belatedly, so to speak, via a deferral. Something non-original – a trace – constitutes it. Thus it must be said that the trace is the origin of the origin. Even though everything hinges on the trace's not being anything original at all, it is necessary to speak of an arche-trace because otherwise the concept of the trace would remain stuck in a classical schema where it means a lingering sign of something else which isn't a trace, but a presence. And the trace of which it's a matter here is not a trace of anything. It is not any such empirical mark. It must be wrested from the system which would consider it secondary – to something else, that is – by being given a position at the origin. And yet the meaning of this move is not that before the origin lies something more original, the arche-trace. Rather, the expression *arche-trace* means that there is no such primal position.

Derrida describes the necessary use of a name in order to bar it as a contortion in his text, and he says that in this contortion we should feel the necessity of a little circuit which leaves a trail in the text without which its stakes would not be clear. Derrida must manoeuvre vis-à-vis other philosophical discourses with which his can no more simply break than agree. For my part, though, I confess to a philosophically more naïve fascination, here and in other writing – Blanchot's for example – a fascination with words disqualified by what they designate. Or rather by words that name something in a way such that we dimly understand they aren't the name for it. Not that there are better, more appropriate names. The old ones are retained – not discarded or replaced – in order that they might convey their specific helplessness.

Innocent is an example in Blanchot. '. . . innocent, you alone have the right to say you are innocent. – If I have the right, [. . .] then I am not, innocence has no rights' (*The Step Not Beyond* 87; *Le Pas au-delà* 121).

In my understanding, no one can lay claim to innocence because it is the characteristic of an experience that does away with – or, in an odd way, leaves aside, or even spares – its subject. Suffering is innocent inasmuch as it is unbearable. It would like to become guilty in order to abate – it would like to have some rights and responsibilities. But the innocent are innocent of innocence, and if the word innocent had any bearing, it would be lost.

My attention is riveted by such words, ruled out by what, without being able to, they designate. Or by what their being unable to, designates. I think that writing, in Derrida's sense, might be defined as language subject to the demand to keep watch over and preserve the uselessness of such words; or writing might be described as the countless comings and goings, the exhausting circuits and trails required to help certain names convey their impropriety: show somehow, that is, that were there anything that could properly bear them, it certainly would not.

IAN MACLACHLAN, A HINGE (*OG* 65; *DG* 96)

What is a hinge? An answer to that question might hinge on whether or not one could say that it is the same thing as a *brisure*. It hangs or turns on the issue of how the links of a chain are articulated, how a reworked, perhaps somewhat unhinged, conception of writing might be required in order to think what it is that makes translation possible, or what more generally articulates sameness and difference, between languages but also within what is taken to be a language, as for example at the juncture between the graphic and the phonic: 'This articulation therefore permits a graphic ("visual" or "tactile", "spatial") chain. It is from the primary possibility of this articulation that one must begin. Difference is articulation' (*OG* 66).

The term *brisure*, evoking at once difference and articulation, a break or breach and a joint or link, is offered to Derrida by his friend Roger Laporte, and takes its place in *Of Grammatology* in a manner that itself forms something of a (dis)articulating hinge, in the internal border of an epigraph, the kind of textual juncture at which the names of Jacques Derrida and Roger Laporte crossed more than once. For example, Derrida invokes Laporte's recollection of an anecdote concerning posthumous Nietzsche publications in a post-scriptum to *Spurs: The Styles of Nietzsche* (139–40), and before writing on Laporte's work in more sustained fashion in the essay 'What Remains by Force of Music', Derrida's only published allusion to a writer whose work he had admired since Foucault had introduced him to Laporte's 1963 text *La Veille* (cf. Derrida and Bennington 330) had been in the margins of an essay largely devoted to textual marginality, in the prefatory 'Outwork' ('Hors livre') to *Dissemination*, in a parenthesis at the end of a footnote itself devoted to the status of the prefatory (and perhaps thereby acquiring a perverse centrality), where Laporte's *Fugue* (1970) is cited along-side Francis Ponge's *Fabrique du pré* as two exemplary 'treatises' on the *'pre written'* ('Outwork' 8 n. 11). In complementary fashion, Laporte's *Fugue* had already kept a special place for Derrida at its opening edge, bearing a dedication 'à Jacques et Marguerite Derrida' (*Fugue* 251).

The hinge with which Laporte provides *Of Grammatology* effects a link between sections of the book that also opens a breach in the book to its outside, to another signatory, for example. It opens, more-over, onto a correspondence, the kind of 'private' communication that is separate from the published work, but according to a mode of separation forming another undecidable *brisure* that may always take a public turn, as we are reminded in a different context when Derrida draws on a letter from Blanchot, a letter that 'does not belong to what we call literature' (*Demeure* 52), in a gesture of reading that exacerbates the ineluctable tension between fiction and testimony set up by Blanchot's third-person literary narrative *The Instant of My Death* (1994). The trace of Derrida's own correspondence in Laporte's writing is generously signalled in 'Bief' (the title denoting a kind of watery *brisure*, a channel that serves to connect or divide), Laporte's contribution to the issue of *L'Arc* devoted to Derrida in 1973. Here, Laporte identifies letters of 1965–66 from Derrida as key agents of a *brisure* between his previous work and *Fugue*, on which he began to work in 1967. In one sense, Laporte seems to mark a decisive break with his earlier work, going so far as to declare a wish to disown it, but the very terms in which he describes the impact of his friendship and correspondence with Derrida reveals that this *brisure* is also a conjunction: 'the *breakthrough* effected by Derrida reopened a path for me back to "myself", back to my "arche-project" as a writer' ('Bief' 68).

What is a hinge? It is the 'singular conjunction of *assembling* and *disassembling* – an indeterminable conjunction that is itself always in flight or movement – as one may discern in the word "disarticulation"', as Philippe Lacoue-Labarthe and Jean-Luc Nancy say of the contra-puntal texture of Laporte's writing in *Fugue* ('Entretiens sur Roger Laporte' 191). It is a point of disarticulation that is never located in the textual present, something which merely serves to connect or divide, providing a punctuation or scansion, but nothing in itself – or perhaps something a little more or less than nothing, perhaps not nothing. When the voracious textual machine of Laporte's *Fugue* seems to have consumed itself, 'what remains by force of music?', asks Derrida: 'Not nothing. But this *not nothing* never presents itself; it is not something that exists and appears. No ontology dominates it' ('What Remains by Force of Music' 89).

IAN MACLACHLAN, SOMETHING OTHER THAN FINITUDE (*OG* 68; *DG* 99)

Of all the challenges with which Derrida's early work presents us, one of the most persistently disorienting is whether we are to think of *différance* as infinite, as finite, or in some sense as neither or both. In fact, something of the intractability of the idea of *différance* seems to arise from the need to maintain apparently contradictory characterizations such as these in suspension, in an indecision that is required by the thinking of *différance*, but that is impossible, since the resulting aporia also demands to be resolved by a decision. Derrida suggests as much on numerous occasions, as for example in the eponymous paper first delivered in 1968, at a point where he is exploring the idea of *différance* as the 'detour' that at once facilitates the economic negotiation between pleasure and reality principles described by Freud in *Beyond the Pleasure Principle*, while at the same time effecting the ruination of a closed psychical economy in its dissipation of any possible return to presence:

> Here we are touching upon the point of greatest obscurity, on the very enigma of *différance*, on precisely that which divides its very concept by means of a strange cleavage. We must not hasten to decide. How are we to think *simultaneously*, on the one hand, *différance* as the economic detour which, in the element of the same, always aims at coming back to the pleasure or the presence that have been deferred by (conscious or unconscious) calculation, and, on the other hand, *différance* as the relation to an impossible presence, as expenditure without reserve, as the irreparable loss of presence, the irreversible usage of energy, that is, as the death instinct, and as the entirely other relationship that apparently interrupts every economy? It is evident – and this is the evident itself – that the economical and the noneconomical, the same and the entirely other, etc., cannot be thought *together*. ('Différance' 19)

But, as Derrida insists elsewhere, the thinking of *différance* entails precisely this impossibility, since it is at once the ground of economic relations of equivalence and difference, and the erosion of itself as economic ground in its unremitting transmutation of all stable values (e.g. 'Implications' 8–9). *Différance* is neither to be located once and for all within the finite systems that it enables nor elevated to an infinite dimension that would have definitively surpassed the finite. As an infinite differing and deferring, it is always drawn back into finite identities and differences; as the production of finite deferrals and differentiations, it always differs and defers once again, in-finitely.

So, for example, when Derrida famously declares in the final chapter of *Speech and Phenomena* that '*infinite* différance *is finite*' (102), it is in order to advance the argument that what he has just called, with respect to his account of Husserl's notion of ideality, 'the infinite *différance* of presence' (102, trans. mod.) can only appear as such on the condition of the mortal experience of finitude. But, as Derrida indicates there, finitude is viewed in this instance precisely as a *condition* of infinite *différance*, and not merely as a factical contingency, not just the re-grounding of a movement to the infinite in the empirical finitude of mortal existence. Geoffrey Bennington helpfully observes of Derrida's treatment of death in such contexts that it 'does not simply call the transcendental adventure back to the stern reality of human finitude, but shows up the metaphysical solidarity of that adventure *and* its recall' (*Interrupting Derrida* 187).

'Différance is also something other than finitude', (*OG* 68) Derrida declares, perhaps a little less famously, towards the end of the chapter on 'Linguistics and Grammatology'. In light of what we have just noted about the finitude of infinite *différance* as it is presented in *Speech and Phenomena*, the two remarks may not present us with as stark a contradiction as first appears, or if they do, perhaps they are, as Derrida says in another context, 'contradictorily coherent' ('Structure, Sign and Play', *Writing and Difference* 279). In relation to the argument he has just been pursuing, Derrida's point here is to insist that, notwithstanding the need to think the *logos* as never entirely separable from material inscription, this is emphatically not the gesture of an empiricist corrective that would merely be the mirror-image of a transcendental idealism: 'it would not mean a single step outside of metaphysics if nothing more than a new motif of "return to finitude", of "God's death", etc., were the result of this move' (*OG* 68).

The transition we have just been reading across these passages, from an infinite *différance* as finite to *différance* as something other than finitude, might itself be read in relation to *différance* as a differing-deferring sameness, always emerging otherwise, and not just according to 'different' contexts, but already in what we take to be the 'same' context, according to a ceaseless recontextualization that is also what gives us 'a context', and which Derrida elsewhere names iterability. So, it is doubtless the same thing that we read differently, or a difference inhabiting the same, when we turn to the same passage in the 1966 version in the journal *Critique* and read, after a reference to the need to 'destroy' rather than 'deconstruct' the metaphysical conceptuality that sets the finite and the infinite in clear opposition, that: '*Différance* is not finitude' ('De la grammatologie II' 36).

CHAPTER 3

OF GRAMMATOLOGY AS A POSITIVE SCIENCE

CHRISTOPHER JOHNSON, GRAMMATOLOGY AS A 'POSITIVE' SCIENCE (*OG* 81–3; *DG* 121–4)

Il faut sans doute entreprendre aujourd'hui une réflexion dans laquelle la découverte 'positive' et la 'déconstruction' de l'histoire de la métaphysique, en tous ses concepts, se contrôlent réciproquement, minutieusement, laborieusement. (*DG* 124; *OG* 83)

The paradox of grammatology is that it gestures towards a *science* of writing at a moment when '*the concept of science* or the scientificity of science' is recognized as a philosophical concept convergent with the history of logocentrism (*OG* 3). From this perspective, the title of the chapter 'Of Grammatology as a Positive Science' may seem perverse, even ironic, if one considers Derrida's consistently ambivalent formulation of this science. Despite this, the claim of grammatology to scientific interest is a serious one, a claim which again must be situated within the specific historical and intellectual context of structuralism. Lévi-Strauss's version of structuralism insisted on the scientific project of the human sciences, disciplines which were based on the empirical observation of facts and the theoretical processing of those facts in the form of general laws. In this respect, the human sciences were considered to have superseded traditional philosophical discourse, which could no longer justify its federating role as 'queen of the sciences'. Derrida's response to this attempted marginalization of philosophy is not the traditional humanist response, i.e., that the 'human' is not reducible to the terms of scientific analysis, but rather that the science of the human sciences remains too philosophical and is not sufficiently scientific. In the section entitled 'Science and the Name of Man', he asserts the independence of a future science of grammatology – based on contemporary research on the history of writing – from the discourse of the human sciences:

> Through all the recent work in this area, one glimpses the future extensions of a grammatology called upon to stop receiving its guiding concepts from other human sciences or, what nearly always amounts to the same thing, from traditional metaphysics [. . .].
>
> What seems to announce itself now is, on the one hand, that grammatology must not be one of the *sciences of man* [sciences humaines] and, on the other hand, that it must not be just one *regional science* among others.
>
> It ought not to be *one of the sciences of man* [sciences de l'homme] because it asks first, as its characteristic question, the question of the *name of man*. To achieve a unified conception of humanity is undoubtedly to renounce the old notion of peoples said to be 'without writing' and 'without history'. (*OG* 83; *DG* 124, trans. mod.)

The human sciences, in their haste to leave behind the history of metaphysics, have in the process failed sufficiently to take account of the deep determination of their 'science' by the discourse of metaphysics. As a result, many of their 'guiding concepts' are thoroughly philosophical, and therefore of little use to a critically reflexive grammatology. Grammatology will ask the question that the 'human' sciences do not, perhaps cannot, ask – that of the very name of humanity and the different criteria by which we judge or categorize different *kinds* of humanity. One of the guiding concepts of Lévi-Strauss's anthropology was indeed the notion of the cultural 'authenticity' of non-literate societies resistant to the 'dialectical' history of Western civilization. Significantly, at this point in his analysis Derrida refers to an alternative anthropology, that of the pre-historian André Leroi-Gourhan, to support his criticism of the ethnocentric distinction between literate and non-literate: 'the peoples said to be "without writing" lack only a certain type of writing' (*OG* 83). The reference to Leroi-Gourhan, and the commentary that follows, therefore gesture proleptically to the reading of Lévi-Strauss in the second part of *Of Grammatology*, providing a virtual indicator of what an authentically reflexive science of anthropology might look like. This, it could be said, is the basic function of the chapter 'Of Grammatology as a Positive Science' within the wider discursive economy of the book: to use the 'facts' provided by the extensive scientific literature on writing in order to support a critical rethinking of logocentrism from the point of view of grammatology. Even if the literature itself is not always theoretically adequate to the new information it presents (*OG* 81), grammatology must self-reflexively ground itself in this 'positive' knowledge if it is to avoid the spontaneous philosophy of the human sciences: 'a reflection must clearly be undertaken, within which the discovery of "positive" facts and the "deconstruction" of the history of metaphysics, in all its concepts, are subjected to a detailed and arduous process of mutual verification [*se contrôlent réciproquement, minutieusement, laborieuse-ment*] (*OG* 83; *DG* 124, trans. mod.).

PAUL DAVIES, WHY LEIBNIZ? (*OG* 76–81; *DG* 113–20)

Imagine a book collecting all the passages cited and quoted in *Of Grammatology*. They would appear or reappear without comment or correction, with all their ellipses, elisions, conflations and translations. Enough would be provided of their original contexts to show some-thing of the history and logic, the contingency and necessity, of their selection, and of the ingenuity and delighted opportunism of their selector. It would pronounce itself the book *Of Grammatology* relies upon, the book it reads and the book it would have us read or teach us to read. One of its signatories would of course be Jacques Derrida and two of the strangest entries would be taken from the *Monadol-ogy* and Leibniz's 1678 letter to Princess Elizabeth. In *Of Gramma-tology* they stand as perhaps the only time, when Derrida writes of being 'like Leibniz', perhaps the only time when Derrida writes his project and predicament with Leibniz's words.

In twenty years, Derrida will wonder about Heidegger's reluctance to read Spinoza, asking, conversationally, 'Why Leibniz rather than Spinoza?' Why is it always Leibniz to whom Heidegger turns when it is a question of reason, its grounds and principles? And why is it to Leibniz that Heidegger turns when he wants a figure who can be made to circumscribe and characterize the calculative-rationalist enterprise and epoch or, more accurately, a figure who can be made to circumscribe and characterize the rationalist enterprise and epoch *as* calculative? These are intriguing questions and they prompt thoughts about what in Spinoza might be seen to resist a Heideggerian interpretation, what it is that might tell against his being appropriated by and to Heidegger's history of being. But although 'Why Leibniz rather than Spinoza?' is no doubt a good question to ask about Spinoza and about Heidegger's reticence concerning Spinoza, it is not quite so obviously a good question to ask about Leibniz, as though there were not reason enough for Heidegger or anyone else to read and to re-read Leibniz. Nevertheless, it will surely be a useful question. It imagines Heidegger being forced to respond in one of two ways: either (i) what Spinoza says is essentially no different from what Leibniz says and so, with respect to the history of being or any of the versions in which Heidegger rehearses and re-describes the metaphysical tradition, Leibniz suffices; or (ii) what Spinoza says, however original, and it is startlingly original, has no relevance or purchase for the history of being et al. Derrida's question, two decades hence, will thus inquire into Spinoza's 'non-historicizable' originality and will consider what it might imply about Heidegger's notion of history and about his readings of the key moments in the history of philosophy. Everything is clear: 'Why Leibniz rather than Spinoza?' is simply another way of asking 'Why not Spinoza?' And yet, even in conversation, this is still a little unsatisfactory. It would be very odd for anyone, but perhaps especially for Derrida, to think that 'Why are you not reading Spinoza?' is a straightforwardly legitimate question to ask of someone reading Leibniz. Although Leibniz is not supposed to be the issue, the question must have some bearing on him. After all it is not being asked of someone reading Hegel, Husserl or Plato. When the question asks 'Why not Spinoza?' it is also necessarily asking 'Why Leibniz?' If the question and the subsequent project do then have a bearing on Leibniz there must be a hidden premise at work, one that does somehow make an issue of Leibniz. It would have to be a premise suggesting something in Leibniz's thought that both, on the one hand, renders it eminently qualified for a central role in Heidegger's critical and 'historicizing' engagement with metaphysics and, on the other hand, dulls the reader's sensitivity to the originality of Spinoza, to the originality of a philosopher deemed to be essentially other than Leibniz. A strange premise! At the very least it would itself depend on Derrida's having had a reason to distrust Leibniz or a reason to deny Leibniz the possibility of his own exceptionality. But what could such a reason be? And why Leibniz?

The matter of Leibniz's non-exceptionality is already raised at the very beginning of *Of Grammatology* where Derrida names the constituents of the ethnocentrism and logocentrism he wishes to read and from which he wishes to free reading. The second constituent is nothing less than 'the history of (the only) metaphysics, which has in spite of all differences not only from Plato to Hegel (even including Leibniz) but also beyond these apparent limits, from the pre-Socratics to Heidegger always assigned the origin of truth in general to the logos' (*OG* 3). No exception is to be made for Leibniz despite the fact that here is (i) a thinker who at the heart of phonocentrism envisages a symbolic non-phonetic writing (a universal Characteristic); (ii) a thinker who admits and notes the ways certain non-Western languages celebrate the possibilities of non-phoneticism; (iii) a thinker whose account of reason as calculative admits of infinite machinic operations where no 'present' can be secured logically and finally in its presence; and (iv) a thinker whose conception of modality seemingly binds even God to a principle that formalizes simple identity across infinite variety and possibility. But there has only ever been one metaphysics and it includes everything Heidegger would seek to describe as not yet and no longer metaphysical, that is the pre-Socratics and Heidegger himself. The epoch to be thought and named in *Of Grammatology* ('our epoch') will not count as post-metaphysical but will, as we know, find its clue in texts where 'writing' and the written 'mark' are not immediately subordinated to the ideal in speech and thought, where they remain in their materiality as the symptoms or traces of a struggle, a struggle that can be re-staged and re-read as though it were itself sufficient to characterize an 'age' or epoch, our own or Rousseau's. And it seems Leibniz can be and must be no help, for there is in Leibniz no equivalent struggle. The calculus of thought of which Leibniz dreams and which he begins to construct will always be subordinated to the higher and more profound dream of a perfect communication, the ideal calculation, a mechanically protected but still idealized present. If Leibniz looks to Egypt and China for hints as to how a language might be made to work against the subjectivity and complex content-dependency of meaning, sound and translation, the end is to have nothing in it of Egypt or China. It is to be the pure and perfect apprehension of truth, and although that apprehension is one more calculation, a further mechanical operation, and so is never able to claim for itself the qualitatively different status of a final end (a final truth), it imports into each of its 'ends' and calculations the values and features of the idealized end of logocentrism, the perfect absence of tension, tense, desire and imagination.[1]

What then is Leibniz doing in *Of Grammatology*, and why? There has been a temptation in some of the secondary literature to refer to

Leibniz's role as that of an awkward but useful mediator so that, for example, it is Leibniz whose references and appeals to the exoticism of Chinese non-phonetic writing are to count as evidence of an ethnocentrism, and it is by way of this implicit indictment of Leibniz and in explicit contrast to it that Derrida's own references and appeals to the very same writing can be excused or removed from controversy. If this does begin to offer a plausible defence of Derrida against a mean-spirited criticism or misunderstanding, it also forces Leibniz into a strange position. Those critics who think Derrida's descriptions of Chinese writing were themselves historically or ideologically problematic confuse Derrida with Leibniz. Leibniz, to the careful and to the mischievous reader, can sound a bit like Derrida. They might even share some interests and obsessions, but it is Leibniz who is problematic, ethnocentric, and as we know from the very beginning *even* he, whatever he says or writes, is to be included within logocentrism. Derrida's 'project' (both the project *Of Grammatology* is and the project it promises or imagines – that is the project it cannot be), by definition and in its description shares nothing with Leibniz's project of a universal characteristic.

In twenty years, Derrida will also look back at his own writing of epochs and epochality: 'And when I tried twenty years ago, to periodize and epochalize, I used these expressions, *présence* and the later Rousseauian-Cartesian *présence à soi*. And yet I was unhappy with these articulations, and I introduced so many quotation marks and ironic turns in order to avoid baldly stating that the concept of history (this is a tautology) implies this unfolding or refolding, this folding of presence as presence to oneself. I argued that if you give up these two values, then you give up history'.[2] *Of Grammatology* attempts to introduce and to *read* an epoch, the 'age' of Rousseau, and to do so in full awareness of having, as the preface tells us, to work against 'the categories of the history of ideas and the history of literature but also, and perhaps above all, the categories of the history of philosophy' (*OG* lxxxix). The first part of the book restates the need for such a new reading and develops some of the tools and terms that might sustain it. Rousseau and the 'age of Rousseau' will not simply function as examples because the new reading, freed from the categories that have determined all readings in and of history (and above all the history of philosophy), must concede that exemplarity is never simple but involves its own folds and repetitions. And so, twenty years later, is Derrida admitting a certain defeat? Any age or epoch, however conspicuous the quotation marks that protect or ironize its name, is complicit with the only history there can ever be, the history of presence and self-presence? In this context, the allusion to Spinoza and his absence in the work of the philosopher who, before *Of Grammatology*, envisages another history, a history of a withdrawal from all presencing, seems fortuitous. Spinoza, uniquely according to Derrida in 1987, will not think of history, of presence or self-presence. But it cannot now, as it was twenty years ago, be a matter of writing and reading an 'age' of Spinoza or an 'age of Spinoza'.[3] The uniqueness must be marked or mentioned differently, here as a challenge and a check to Heidegger. Even Heidegger's history of being can permit no room for this name and for this thinker. Heidegger's *Der Satz vom Grund* develops a subtle double reading of both Leibniz and Heidegger's own earlier interpretation of Leibniz. It is a reading in which the same Leibnizian dictum ('Nothing is without reason') can be referred first to the history of metaphysics construed as ontotheology and secondly to the interrupted and interrupting history of being. In this telling ambiguity, Heidegger detects Leibniz's unwitting capacity to think and to name the essence of an epoch. For the Derrida who signs *Of Grammatology* and who wishes to think an 'age' resistant to the categories even of Heidegger's histories, Leibniz is permitted no ambiguity and no originality. Whatever he says and thinks, even unwittingly at Heidegger's hands, he belongs unequivocally to the metaphysics of presence. Leibniz is a philosopher to whom Derrida might be expected to feel a certain proximity. To negotiate this proximity and this philosopher by writing that opening 'even including Leibniz' requires a background reading in which Leibniz's place has already been established. And whose reading can that be if not Heidegger's? The distance Derrida keeps from Heidegger, the distance *Of Grammatology* announces, can perhaps only be sustained by accepting the Heideggerian judgement of Leibniz. Do we have here the bones of an answer to our question 'Why Leibniz?' Might it not be that in the background to *Of Grammatology* and to its denial of Leibniz's exceptionality is Heidegger's reading, and especially the reading developed in *Der Satz vom Grund*? If so then Leibniz's uniqueness and ambiguity are in some sense successfully captured in Heidegger's reading and when they are mentioned or recontextualized in *Of Grammatology* they appear without ambiguity and without uniqueness, returned along with Heidegger's reading to logocentrism. When Derrida, twenty years on, asks 'Why not Spinoza?' it is asked necessarily only of Heidegger and so also necessarily only of Heidegger's Leibniz, and it is this Leibniz and this reading that Derrida is accepting and relying on both for the project of *Of Grammatology* and for the very different intervention of 1987. Whether employed as a symptom of ethnocentrism in his unique enthusiasm for the non-phonetic or conceded a certain ambiguity (the ambiguity at the heart of calculative rationality) in his Heideggerian retrieval, there is a sense in which for Derrida there is no reason to re-read Leibniz. Strictly speaking, there will be no Derridean reading of Leibniz.[4] Perhaps it has always been a matter of maintaining these distances: from the standpoint of 1987, Spinoza is essentially other than Leibniz, and from the standpoint of 1967, the 'project' is essentially other than the project of the universal characteristic. Curiously we seem to be left with Leibniz as exceptionally unexceptional, a philosopher and a work that will not need to be read otherwise, with an eye and an ear for *its* uniqueness.

All of which is offered as preparation and context and for a brief look at how at one moment in *Of Grammatology*, Leibniz's own writing is cited and summarized. Among all of Derrida's many instructions to the reader as to what else it would be necessary to do time and space permitting, among all the nods to alternative texts, sources and itineraries, and among all the suggestions about implications and applications, there are surely few that sound quite as peculiar or that unfold in such a peculiar manner as those found in a footnote to 'Of Grammatology as a Positive Science'. It begins:

> Cf., for example, among many other texts, *Monadology* 1 to 3 and 52. It is beside the point both of our project and of the possibilities of our demonstrating from internal evidence the link between the characteristic and Leibniz's infinitist theology. For that it would be necessary to go through and exhaust the entire content of the project. (*OG* 331 n. 14)

The footnote falls in the middle of the five or so pages Derrida devotes to Leibniz and between the second and third sentences of the following passage:

> In spite of all the differences that separate the projects of a universal language or writing at this time [. . .] the concept of the simple absolute is always necessarily and indispensably involved. It would be easy to show that it already leads to an infinitist theology

and to the logos or the infinite understanding of God. [Here we find the number to the relevant footnote] That is why appearances to the contrary and in spite of all the seduction that it can legitimately exercise on our epoch, the Leibnizian project of a universal characteristic that is not essentially phonetic does not interrupt logocentrism in any way. (*OG* 78)

Imagine a reader following or trying to follow Derrida's instructions to the letter, a reader who sits with both the *Grammatology* and the *Monadology* to hand and who wonders what the former is saying about the latter. Imagine as well that this reader wonders how Derrida might deal with Leibniz's commitments to non-phonetic universality, to the mark that will permit reason to calculate, to work as though reasoning were calculating. It may be that this reader is interested in the Leibnizian project and in its (analytical) descendants in the Fregean and neo-Fregean traditions. The appeal to a metaphysical simple, indispensable to the project of a universal non-phonetic language, is always dependent on a theological infinity, on an infinite being. It would, we are told, be easy to show this. And because this is so, because the Leibnizian project is irreducibly theological and because it can be so easily demonstrated, there is no way that Leibniz can be said to interrupt logocentrism and no need for Leibniz to take up too much of our attention. We might find ourselves 'seduced' into thinking that Leibniz offers a challenge to the essential linking of phonocentrism and logocentrism, and such a seduction is under-standable, indeed 'legitimate', but it is easily avoided or survived. Nothing can come from it and 'our epoch' need spend no time regret-ting any dalliance. The footnote presumably provides the requisite demonstration for those pedantic enough to demand it. Except that it doesn't. The footnote begins by suggesting that so many texts could be called upon here but if we must have one, the reader might look to four propositions from the *Monadology*. The first defines the monad as a simple, that is as something without parts. The second states that there must be such simples given the fact that there are compounds. The third argues that as all physical atoms or simples are not literally so, the monad must count as the true (metaphysical) simple, as the ultimate element of things. And the fourth, or 52nd, reminds us that as no true simple can effect or impinge upon another, the organizing and relating of monads is dependent upon God who, in accordance with rational principles, actualizes and arranges every separate and individual thing. In short, the four propositions we are invited to read bind the monad and God to the principle of sufficient reason. Again here we have the kernel of the Leibnizian system that Heidegger reads, as it were, for Derrida. But Derrida's emphasis here is not quite on the principle of sufficient reason, it is on Leibniz's theism, more precisely it is on the implicit theism of rationalist universalism. Elsewhere in this section of *Of Grammatology*, Derrida will discuss Descartes, conflating Descartes's and Leibniz's thoughts of the possibility of a perfect language and will leave to one side the fact that Descartes and Leibniz will disagree on the whole question as to whether logic – reason and its principles and methods – belongs to the nature of God or whether God himself can or could be essentially other than the reason whose principles and methods we deduce and describe. Given Derrida's emphasis, the selections from the *Monadology*, rather than demonstrating the ties between the characteristic and theism, merely reassert them. The footnote admits as much: 'It is beside the point both of our project and of the possibilities of our demonstrating from internal evidence the link between the characteristic and Leibniz's infinitist theology. For that it would be necessary to go through and exhaust the entire content of the project'. Our literal-minded reader tries to retrace their steps. The footnote is appended to a sentence that insists on the ease with which a link can be shown. It seems reasonable to expect the footnote to show the link. However what the footnote does is first restate the link in Leibniz's own words and then declare that the demonstration is redundant, 'beside the point' of both the project of the *Grammatology* and the attempt to marshal internal evidence from Leibniz's own writings, beside the point we might say of both the *Grammatology* and the *Monadology*. How and why could it be beside the point of a reading of Leibniz to demonstrate the link in Leibniz between the search for a universal language and the existence of God? The answer seems to be that it would take too long and that such a reading and demonstration could only properly take place when we have been through and exhausted 'the whole project'. Far from demonstrating the ease with which Leibniz's projected characteristic entails and is entailed by his theological infinitism, the footnote announces that such a demonstration requires the completion of 'the whole project'. But which project, the *Grammatology*, the project it writes and promises, or the *Monadology* and Leibniz's universal characteristic? The footnote seems to say that in order to provide the easy demonstration championed by the main text we would need either (i) to read and complete that text and the project it outlines or (ii) to read the whole of the Leibnizian text and the project it outlines or (iii) to do both. But neither the project of the *Grammatology* nor Leibniz's project of a universal characteristic is or can be completed. Each of the authors admits as much. It seems that no demonstration even of this 'easily shown' link between the characteristic and theism is or can be forthcoming.

Here, finally, is the footnote in full:

> Cf., for example, among many other texts, *Monadology* 1 to 3 and 52. It is beside the point both of our project and of the possibilities of our demonstrating from internal evidence the link between the characteristic and Leibniz's infinitist theology. For that it would be necessary to go through and exhaust the entire content of the project. I refer on this point to works already cited. Like Leibniz when he wishes to recall in a letter the link between the existence of God and the possibility of a universal script, I shall say here that 'it is a proposition that [we] cannot demonstrate properly without explaining the foundation of the characteristic at length . . . But at present suffice it to remark that my characteristic is also the demonstration for the existence of God for simple thoughts are the elements of the characteristic and simple forms are the source of things. Now I maintain that all simple forms are compatible among themselves. It is a proposition that I cannot demonstrate properly without explaining the foundation of the characteristic at length. But if it is granted, then it follows that the nature of God which holds absolutely all simple forms, is possible. Now we have proved above, that God is, provided He is possible. Therefore He exists. Which had to be demonstrated'. (Letter to the Princess Elizabeth, 1678) There is an essential connection between the possibility of the ontological argument and that of the Characteristic.

Leaving aside the awkwardness of the reference to 'works already cited', the footnote continues with an extract from Leibniz's famous letter to Princess Elizabeth, the letter in which he goes to some lengths to distinguish his ontological argument from those of Descartes. And this extract again simply repeats the claim that there is a link between the characteristic and the existence of God. When the extract concludes, Derrida offers his own conclusion: 'There is an essential connection between the possibility of the ontological argument and that of the Characteristic'. Our reader might be tempted to gloss the whole passage, main text and footnote, in four stages:

(i) Derrida (main text): There is an essential connection between Leibniz's theological metaphysics and the universal characteristic, and this can be easily shown;

(ii) Leibniz (footnote, *Monadology*): There is an essential connection between the existence of God and the existence of the monad.

(iii) Leibniz (footnote, letter to Elizabeth): There is an essential connection between the possibility of the ontological argument and that of the Characteristic.

(iv) Derrida (footnote): There is an essential connection between the possibility of the ontological argument and that of the Characteristic.

And our reader is not obviously wrong, but so read it must stand as one of the least helpful or clarificatory footnotes ever provided. Notice however that Derrida offers the similarity between his gesture and Leibniz's as an analogy and as an alibi. Leibniz, in the letter, cannot provide the complete demonstration, for that one would need a full and exhaustive account of the foundation of the characteristic but if the reader (Elizabeth) would accept that, given such an account, there would be such a demonstration, she can appreciate the superiority of Leibniz's reasoning over that of Descartes. Derrida cannot provide the full demonstration, for that one would need such a science as the dreamed-of 'grammatology' but if the reader would only countenance such a science as a possibility then she or he can begin to appreciate if not the superiority of Derrida's project over Leibniz's then certainly its irreducibility to Leibniz's. The analogy might support such an interpretation. But is Derrida here not explicitly 'like Leibniz?' Is he here not letting Leibniz's words describe his own predicament and the predicament with 'grammatology as a positive science?' It would take the whole of grammatology as such a science, the whole project of grammatology and the project of the *Grammatology* to comprehend the whole of Leibniz and the whole of the project of the characteristic. It would take all of this to justify the easily read and incorporated 'even including Leibniz' that would rob Leibniz's thought of any (legitimate) seductive power, anything that would confer on it the power and the appeal of an exception. Finally, it would take all of this to demonstrate finally Leibniz's complicity with logocentrism. But if the reader would just accept it just this once and with just this one philosopher, we and grammatology and *Of Grammatology* could advance . . .

CHRISTOPHER JOHNSON, WRITING IN EVOLUTION, EVOLUTION AS 'WRITING' (OG 83–7; DG 124–31)

A. Leroi-Gourhan ne décrit plus ainsi l'unité de l'homme et de l'aventure humaine par la simple possibilité de la graphie en général: plutôt comme une étape ou une articulation dans l'histoire de la vie – de ce que nous appelons ici la différance – comme histoire du gramme. (*DG* 125; *OG* 84)

Derrida's reading of Leroi-Gourhan in 'Of Grammatology as a Positive Science' is qualitatively different to his treatment of other sources in the chapter. This is because, beyond his critique of ethnocentrism, Leroi-Gourhan can be said to offer a scientific account of the evolution of living forms that is convergent with the grammatological understanding of arche-writing, *différance* and the trace. The following points can be extracted from Derrida's reading of *Gesture and Speech*:

1. *The transcendence of the program.* In his landmark text *Gesture and Speech* (1964–65), Leroi-Gourhan emphasizes the *mechanical* continuities of structure and function which determine the evolution of living forms. In doing this, his analysis short circuits the sequence of concepts normally used to distinguish the human from other living forms (instinct, intelligence, speech, society, etc.), and indeed the living from the non-living. As Derrida notes, the operative concept here is that of the *program*, in the cybernetic sense of the term, which itself is generalizable under the category of the trace or gramme (*OG* 84). The program is transcendent in the sense that it is the condition of possibility of all structured form and all ordered (sequential) function, from DNA to primitive nervous systems to the human brain to what Leroi-Gourhan terms the 'externalization' (*extériorisation*) of the brain in the electronic memories, calculators and logical machines described in cybernetics. Within this generalized operation of the pro-gram, both *before* and *after* the human, the human itself is simply 'a stage or an articulation in the history of life', while 'intentional consciousness', so-called 'conscious subjectivity', are merely 'emergent' features (*OG* 84).

2. *Hand and face, gesture and speech.* For Leroi-Gourhan, gesture and speech are co-emergent features of the becoming-human of the

human. The relationship between the hand and face in humans is a continuation of the structural and functional evolution of the *champ antérieur* ('anterior field'), the forward-facing organs – fin, paw, hand, mouth, etc. – which ensure locomotion, orientation and the capture and processing of food in all bilaterally symmetrical vertebrate species. With the advent of bipedalism in humans, there is a 'liberation' of the hand for technical activity and of the face for the operations of articulated speech. The articulations of human speech have the same neurological basis as manual articulation, hence the circular or cybernetic (retroactive, feedback) relationship between hand and face, gesture and speech. Leroi-Gourhan's analysis therefore provides a natural scientific grounding for one of the central arguments of Derrida's grammatology: the structural continuity of writing and speech. At the same time, Derrida notes the care or caution that is needed in our transactions with the language of this 'positive' science: 'In all these descriptions, it is difficult to avoid a mechanistic, technicist, and teleological language at the very moment when it is precisely a question of retrieving the origin and the possibility of movement, of the machine, of the *technè*, of orientation in general' (*OG* 84–5; *DG* 126, trans. mod.). What is required, then, is a vigilant and reflexive manner of inhabiting the language of science, one that allows us to think for example the structural unity of gesture and speech without confusing them (*OG* 85).

3. *The future(s) of the human.* Leroi-Gourhan's narrative of human evolution in *Gesture and Speech* describes a species, *homo sapiens*, which biologically has ceased to evolve but which continues to do so via its technological 'externalizations'. However, the exponential development of technology in the contemporary world threatens to destabilize the 'precarious equilibrium' of the form of manual-visual coordination which has so far ensured the evolutionary success of *homo sapiens*. The continued externalization of human functions, speculates Leroi-Gourhan, may in the long term lead to an anatomical counter-adaptation involving the loss of the hand, the recession of the teeth and the suspension of bipedal locomotion (*OG* 85). Derrida does not pursue the implications of this projected (monstrous) mutation of the human form – Leroi-Gourhan's anxiety concerning the 'fate' of the hand is in fact symptomatic of the kind of 'humanism of the hand' (*humainisme*) that Derrida will later come to question and criticize (*On Touching* 152–3). Instead, he focuses on another possible future of the human articulated in Leroi-Gourhan's text, one involving

a cognitive, rather than an anatomical, transformation of the species. Again, it is the contemporary state of technological development, the new electronic and computing technologies characteristic of the age of cybernetics, which open the way to this rethinking of the human, through their revelation of the limits of the linear model of cognition imposed by alphabetic (phonetic) writing. What these new technologies permit, argues Leroi-Gourhan, is a more disseminated, 'multi-dimensional' mode of thinking closer to that of the symbolic systems (pictographic, ideographic) which preceded linear script. While the latter was historically – and quite literally – *instrumental* in the establishment of Western science, this science and its technology are now, dialectically, describing the end or the limits of linearization. The night of logocentrism begins to clear 'at the moment when linearity – which is not the loss or absence but the repression of pluri-dimensional symbolic thought – relaxes its oppression because it is beginning to sterilize the technical and scientific economy that it has long favored' (*OG* 86; *DG* 128, trans. mod.). The future of humanity to which Derrida gestures in 'Of Grammatology as a Positive Science', via Leroi-Gourhan, is therefore a kind of future anterior in which the multidimensionality of human cognition is restored, liberated from its colonization by a particular (Western) mode of writing.

PEGGY KAMUF, GRAMMATOLOGY AS GENERAL SCIENCE (*OG* 84; *DG* 124–5)

Of Grammatology frequently signals a certain respect for Rousseau's insights as a thinker, even if these insights more often than not are forced to give way to the impossible and inexorable logic of the auto-affective desire for presence, which is the same logic that has to condemn, in Rousseau's economy, 'l'habitation des femmes' (*OG* 155; *DG* 223–4). Given this condemnation and this denial, it is all the more paradoxical perhaps that one of Rousseau's most far-reaching intuitions will have been, in Derrida's estimation, his sense of the inscribed, scriptural nature of social space, indeed of every kind of space. Nothing less than 'a transcendental question about space' in all its difficulty is outlined in terms that neither Kant nor Husserl took into account. What Rousseau's differential account of language origins lets one envision is how a 'transcendental question about space concerns the prehistoric and precultural layer of spatio-temporal experience that provides a unitary and universal ground for every subjectivity, every culture, on this side of the empirical diversity, the proper orientations of their space and their time. If one lets oneself be guided by inscription as habitation in general' (*OG* 290; *DG* 410, trans. mod.).

I will continue this quotation and restore its fuller context later (see Part II, 221–3), but already one may venture a provisional consequence of this conditional proposition: if one thinks inscription as habitation in general, then this mode of thought and inquiry, if not this science, deserves perhaps to be called as well *ecography,* or better yet *habitography*. As best I can tell, the latter not very elegant term has the advantage of being entirely up for grabs, whereas 'ecography' has so far been put to some minimal use in the biological and ecological sciences, although needless to say without incorporating any reflection on the 'strange graphic of differance' as the spatiotemporal inscription of life. Ecography also refers one to the *oikos* of economy, ecology and so forth, and thus to the laws or logic of conservation and even capitalization (conserving and enhancing the 'riches of nature') that preserve, with the very desirability of their aims and goals, a double-entry accounting of good vs. bad life, and even life as opposed to death. As an alternate name of grammatology, however, (eco)habitography would reaffirm the *program* that Derrida announces early on under that title and would underscore what has too frequently been overlooked there: namely, as neither 'one of the *human sciences*' nor 'just one *regional science* among others', the pertinence of thinking 'inscription as habitation in general' extends across the whole 'ecosystem' of life, from minimal organisms to the most advanced 'human' technologies, which would include technologies of death: not only weapons of all sorts, but in general every technology that can go awry, through some virus or mutation of its 'genetic' program, and produce destruction instead of useful tools or functions – which is to say any technology.

> Instead of resorting to concepts that habitually serve to distinguish the human from other living beings [. . .] one calls upon the notion of *program*. This term must be heard, to be sure, in the cybernetic sense, but this is itself intelligible only on the basis of the history of the possibilities of the trace as unity of the double movement of protention and retention. This movement largely exceeds the possibilities of 'intentional consciousness'. The emergence of the latter causes the gramme to appear *as such* (that is according to a new structure of non-presence) and makes possible

no doubt the rise of systems of writing in the narrow sense. From 'genetic inscription' to 'short programmatic sequences' regulating the behaviour of the amoeba or the annelid up to passage beyond alphabetic writing to the orders of logos and of a certain *homo sapiens*, the possibility of the gramme structures the movement of its history according to rigorously original levels, types, and rhythms. But one cannot think them without the most general concept of gramme. The latter is irreducible and impregnable. (*OG* 84; *DG* 124–5, trans. mod.)

FORBES MORLOCK, DIFFERANCE –
A LITTLE NOTE (*OG* 84; *DG* 125)

Of Grammatology is full of calling. One of the novelties of the book, especially Part I, is its vocabulary – and the powerful sense it gives that new thinking requires a new language. Even as it rewrites existing words, including 'writing', it is calling. 'What we will call (logocentrism)', 'what we call (erasure)', 'what we have called (the metaphysics of the proper)', 'one could call (play)', 'one can call (arche-writing)', 'one should not call (its ambiguity)', 'one calls (sign)', 'could be called (writing)', 'is called (writing)' (*OG* 3, 61, 26, 50, 92, 71, 62, 93, 4, trans. mod.). These are the grammatical constructions of inhabiting language like a garden. We are very near, if not at, the beginning.

So much of *Of Grammatology* is concerned with articulating the impossible necessity of the beginning, the origin. *Arche-écriture, trace, espacement, différance*. And what of their own origins, 'arche-écriture', 'trace', 'espacement' and 'différance's' beginnings? One could tell a story of the birth of *différance* – more briefly and less beautifully than Rousseau's pages on the birth of society.

'An exceptional moment'. A still-astonished Derrida remembers the summer of 1965 with the wonder – and pride – of a first-time father (Derrida and Dick, *Derrida*, Special Features/Derrida Interviews/Eureka). 'Différance' appears very late in the second of the two parts of the essay 'De la grammatologie' that will arrive into print around the end of that year. The new word – with its inaudible difference – occurs twice in the last lines of the article's last paragraph, where it is already one in a list of names (the book later hedging those 'names' as 'strategic nicknames') (*OG* 93; *DG* 142; 'De la grammatologie II' 53). It occurs just once before that in 'De la grammatologie'. Otherwise all 'a's' in Part I of *Of Grammatology* were 'e's' on their first publication (if there is a corresponding passage). Every other 'différance' was mere difference.

The first occurrence of 'differance' in *Critique* then has the performative quality of an event, as if the writing called its word, and its concept, and its name, into the world. 'One can speak of a "liberation of memory", of an exteriorization of the trace, which [. . .] enlarges difference (we will say *differance*) [*la différence* (*nous dirons la* différance)]' ('De la grammatologie II' 46; cf. *OG* 84; *DG* 125). Nous dirons 'la différance'. We will say 'differance'. We are already saying 'differance'. We – with Derrida – have been saying 'differance with an *a*' ever since.

SARAH WOOD, THE CONSTITUTION OF GOOD AND BAD OBJECTS (*OG* 88; *DG* 132–4)

Here Derrida insists on the necessity of the mysterious 'investments of writing'. On page 18 a widely credited notion of 'good writing' is revealed as promoting bad writing. By 'bad writing' I have in mind an idea of writing that doesn't like writing, unnecessary, predictable and unaware of the something other than language that moves us and leaves us guessing, thinking and reading on. Derrida suggests we might think differently about good and bad, by his use of Melanie Klein's psychoanalytic notion of 'good' and 'bad' objects. These are constituted subjectively, that is by and for the psychic investments of particular finite individuals. Klein's work recognizes that before writing signifies there is a general possibility of fantasmatic attachments to the written mark: for example, letters and pairs of letters. No philosophical or theoretical account of the ideal constitution of the written object can fathom, or do without the force of these investments. Marks are invested by someone who believes, invents, listens and composes. They are marks *for* someone. It's going to be idiosyncratic. The isle is full of noises. Full of letters and surprises.

Listen while Elie listens to Melanie Klein. (Elie is Derrida's other name, a sort of private writing-name. He tells its story in 'Circumfessions' and comments: 'I don't know if it's true, spontaneous, or if I reinvented it little by little, if I made it up, if I told myself a story in this regard, and in fact rather late, only in the last ten or fifteen years' (Derrida, 'A "Madness" Must Watch Over Thinking' 344). So *Of Grammatology* belongs to the time before the acknowledgement of this name that 'is not inscribed in the civil record'. I use it here because I've noticed its letters $e - l - i - e$, which of course recur in various formations of the verb $l - i - r - e$, and are therefore in French the letters of reading, sometimes come up a lot when Derrida writes about writing in this period. For example in the two essays on Jabès in *L'écriture et la différence*. And they feature here – as *i*, *e* and *l* – in the long quotation from Klein that Derrida appends to page 88.) Klein recounts the way Fritz, a boy who suffers from 'an inhibition in respect of writing and reading', talks about writing. For Derrida beginning to write about the intimate life of letters, it's a find. Fritz imagines the letters *i* and *e* riding together on a motorbike and speaks of the love that exists between these *motocyclettres*: 'they love one another', according to the boy, 'with a tenderness quite unknown in the real world' (*OG* 333 n. 37). It's the inhibition, a malfunctioning in respect of the movement between signifier and signified that makes us poets, lovers, true readers, capable of experiencing, obscurely, non-conceptually, what *Of Grammatology* calls 'the force without which an objectivity in general would not be possible' (*OG* 88).

Why read, why write, if not in search of something quite unknown in the real world? What would be mad in everyday life can happen here. There is a fearlessness attached to what happens in Derrida's writing. He says in an out-take from *Derrida: the Movie* that when he writes there is a feeling of necessity, a force stronger than himself. It concerns the truth. He says elsewhere 'when something appears to me to be "true" (but I am now giving this word an altogether different meaning that I cannot explain here), no power in the world, no torture could keep me from saying so. It's not about courage or defiance, it is an irresistible impulse' ('From the Word to Life' 9). Perhaps he had no fear because he had no anticipation: anticipation requires a kind of continuity that writing can dispense with. And one cannot anticipate the truth. On page 5 of *Of Grammatology* it says that the future (*avenir*) 'can only be anticipated in the form of an absolute danger', or cannot be anticipated except in that form. When he wrote, he said more than once, he tried to make it so he didn't know where he was going. Afterwards, he found ways to stand by his gesture. And he said that the reader should not anticipate. He names the 'fearful reader' in 'Envois' (4). 'It is bad, and I know no other definition of the bad, it is bad to predestine one's reading, it is always bad to foretell'. The fearful reader 'wishes to expect what has happened'. So-called 'good writing' and 'the idea of the book' allow readers to think of writing as what has happened (*OG* 18, again).

JEAN-LUC NANCY, L'OUVERTURE BLANCHE (*DG* 142)

Nous sommes à la fin de la première partie, c'est-à-dire de l'exposition de ce que doit être cette 'grammatologie' dont on entreprend d'inaugurer la toute nouvelle discipline. Ce qu'elle se devra d'être. Ce qu'elle est donc sans doute déjà en quelque façon puisqu'elle se montre ici capable d'anticiper son devoir-être. Au moins sur un mode formel.

Cette formalité se donne à travers quelques termes: 'pointer au-delà', 'hors de', 'index indéterminé d'une époque à venir', 'ce que nous savons déjà n'avoir pas encore commencé à faire'. Il y a donc un *déjà* par lequel est anticipé cet *à venir* dont nous ne pouvons rien savoir puisqu'il est tout entier dans cet 'à' qui le désigne autant comme attente, désir, expectative, suspens – tout à la fois – que comme venue, approche, arrivée. Le *venir* est tout entier dans son *à*. Mais si ce dernier porte éloignement et proximité, c'est qu'il fait sentir l'approche. Comment opère cette sensation ou ce sentiment, ce pressentiment?

C'est lui qui nous fait *savoir déjà* ce qui pourtant n'a pas *encore commencé*. Un tel savoir ne peut être celui d'une 'science', terme que la première phrase a rangé avec le terme 'philosophie' du côté de l''époque passée' qu'englobent deux termes du texte: l'*épistémè* dont le nom rassemble en silence ceux de Foucault et de Platon, et la *logique* au sens qu'il faut donner à 'logie' suffixe ou désinence de 'grammatologie': logique ou savoir, raison suffisante. Le suffixe se détache, par l'italique du *gramma* dont il ne saurait donc rendre raison. Heidegger est encore présent ici, caché dans ce déplacement d'accent entre le suffixe et son substantif, déplacement pareil à celui que Heidegger propose entre 'onto' et 'logie' dans les *Beiträge* (Derrida ne pouvait les connaître à l'époque: la rencontre est d'autant plus frappante).

Dans le nom de la discipline dont ce livre construit le concept et décrit le champ, le suffixe tiré du *logos* doit être affecté d'un indice d'incertitude et de fragilité. De lui, quelque chose est déjà passé, tandis que son autre s'approche. Cet autre n'est dit '*pensée*' que par économie et stratégie – pour s'appuyer à Heidegger tout en évitant de déplier les implications de l'écart qu'on signale envers lui. Mais on nous donne un indice: Heidegger veut *transgresser*. C'est ce que ne veut pas le penseur ici au travail. Transgresser suppose le seuil d'un interdit et la possibilité – illégale – de le franchir. Cela suppose

JEAN-LUC NANCY, BLANK OPENING (*OG* 93)

We are at the end of the first part, that is, of the exposition of what this 'grammatology' is to be, this entirely new discipline whose inauguration is being undertaken. What it will owe itself to be. What it therefore doubtless already is in some fashion, since it here shows itself capable of anticipating its having-to-be. It does so formally, at least.

This formal mode is proffered by way of a number of terms: 'point beyond', 'outside of', 'indeterminate index of an epoch to come', 'what we already know we have not yet begun to do'. There is therefore an *already* which anticipates the *to come* about which we can know nothing since it is entirely within this 'to' which marks it out as much, on the one hand, as awaiting, desire, expectancy, suspense – all at once – as, on the other, coming, approach, arrival. It *comes* entirely within its *to*. But while the latter may convey distancing and proximity, that's because it has us sense an approach. How does it take effect, this sensation or sentiment, this presentiment?

This presentiment is what allows us to *already know* that which has nonetheless *not yet begun*. Such a knowledge cannot be that of a 'science', as this is a term that, along with that of 'philosophy', the first sentence ranks under the heading of a 'past epoch' encompassed by two other terms in the text: *epistémè* whose name silently summons up those of Foucault and Plato, and *logic* in the sense that is to be attributed to the 'logy' that appears as suffix or inflexion of 'grammatology': logic or knowledge, sufficient reason. The suffix gets detached by virtue of the italicized *gramma* for which it cannot therefore give any reason. Heidegger is still present here, hidden in this shift of emphasis between the suffix and its substantive, a shift which is similar to the one Heidegger proposes between 'onto' and 'logy' in the *Beiträge* [Heidegger, *Contributions to Philosophy*] (which could not have been known to Derrida at the time, making the convergence all the more striking).

In the name of the discipline whose concept this book constructs and whose field it describes, the suffix derived from the *logos* has to bear an indication of uncertainty and fragility. Something of this suffix has already passed, while its other is still approaching. It is only for economic and strategic reasons that this other is called '*thought*' – to take support from Heidegger at the same time as avoiding unfolding all the implications of the divergence from him that is being signalled. But we are given a clue: Heidegger is intent on *transgressing*. That is what the thinker at work here does not want to do. Transgressing presupposes the threshold of an interdiction and the

donc la loi et la distinction des registres (permis/défendu, profane/ sacré).

Sans doute, la transgression à laquelle Heidegger procède est 'analogue' – et par conséquent ici aussi il s'agit d'une transgression; mais elle n'est pas 'identique' – et par conséquent ou bien elle ne transgresse pas le même seuil, le même interdit, ou bien elle ne transgresse pas de la même manière. La seconde hypothèse semble la mieux autorisée puisqu'il s'agit de part et d'autre de transgresser 'tout philosophème'.

Qu'est-ce qu'un philosophème? Et comment pouvons-nous ou bien devons-nous imaginer la différence entre les deux modes de sa transgression? Il n'est pas certain qu'il nous soit possible d'aller jusqu'au bout de la distinction ni de savoir pour finir jusqu'où et comment elle écarte l'une de l'autre, en les contrastant mais sans les opposer, les deux démarches qu'une stratégie rend complices sans pour autant permettre de les conjoindre.

Un philosophème est un énoncé à teneur philosophique. Pourquoi désigner la philosophie par le biais de ce terme quelque peu barbare? Peut-être pour ne pas la nommer 'philosophie' et ainsi réserver la possibilité qu'elle ne se confonde pas sans reste avec l'ensemble des philosophèmes. Ces derniers doivent répondre à certains requisits: ils doivent porter des significations dont ils assurent de pouvoir, en dernière instance, rendre raison. Cela se nomme, dans l'acception la plus ample, *logique*. Non seulement conformité à un ensemble de conditions formelles, mais proposition d'une justification, d'une fondation ou d'une vérification dans une instance ultime de sens. Ce qu'on cherche à nous faire entendre est que la philosophie, elle-même, n'est pas limitée à cette logique. C'est-à-dire que la transgression pourrait ne pas la transgresser, ou bien que la philosophie pourrait détenir en elle la force transgressive.

Quel est l'enjeu de cette différence? Il est de suggérer qu'en définitive il n'y a pas proprement transgression, même s'il y a outrepassement, excédence ou débordement. Là où Heidegger entend se séparer de la philosophie et passer ailleurs – nommément, dans la 'pensée' – Derrida veut pratiquer en elle une *ouverture*. Ouvrir n'est pas transgresser.

Nous ne sommes pas sur le seuil d'un temple et nul état d'exception (produit par un sacrifice, une consécration, ou bien par un défi impie et violent) ne se peut décider au-delà de la loi. Il ne s'agit pas de loi ni de seuil. Il s'agit d'une *ouverture*. Ce n'est pas un seuil, une frontière

(illegal) possibility of crossing it. It therefore presupposes the law and a distinction of registers (permitted/forbidden, profane/sacred).

No doubt the transgression on which Heidegger embarks is 'analogous' – and consequently, here too it is a question of transgression; but it is not 'identical' – and consequently, either it does not transgress the same threshold, the same interdiction, or else it does not transgress in the same manner. The latter hypothesis seems to be the one most clearly sanctioned, since in either case it is a question of transgressing 'all philosophemes'.

What is a philosopheme? And how can we or even must we imagine the difference between the two ways in which it may be transgressed? It is not certain that it will be possible for us to reach the end of the distinction, or finally to know to what extent or in what way the distinction, establishing a contrast but not an opposition between them, holds apart these two procedures that are made complicit by a certain strategy without, nonetheless, allowing their conjunction.

A philosopheme is an utterance of a philosophical tenor. Why designate philosophy by means of this somewhat barbarous term? Perhaps so as not to name it 'philosophy', thereby preserving the possibility that it might not be unreservedly equated with the set of philosophemes. The latter must meet certain prerequisites: they must be the bearers of significations which they must ultimately guarantee to be able to justify. In the widest sense of the term, that is called *logic*: not just as conformity with a set of formal conditions, but as the postulation of a justification, a foundation, or a verification in relation to a final authority of meaning. What we are being led to understand is that philosophy, itself, is not limited to such a logic. In other words, that transgression might not transgress it, or else that philosophy might harbour a transgressive force within itself.

What are the stakes of this difference? They come down to the suggestion that, ultimately, there is no transgression properly speaking, even if there is surpassing, exceeding or overflowing. Whereas Heidegger intends to break with philosophy and move elsewhere – precisely, into 'thought' – Derrida wants to effect an *opening* in philosophy. Opening is not transgressing.

We are not at the threshold of a temple and no state of exception (produced by a sacrifice, a consecration or even by a violent, impious act of defiance) can be determined beyond the law. It is not a matter of a law or a threshold. It is a matter of an *opening*. This is not a threshold, a frontier, or a demarcation. It relates to an *inside* and an *out*.

ni une démarcation. Cela relève d'un *dedans* et d'un *hors*. Alors qu'un seuil est défini par des déterminations préalables de domaines et de dominations, une ouverture se produit de façon mal déterminée, par accident, rupture, ou bien par pression ou par enfoncement. Elle peut aussi être ménagée à l'avance. Tout cela peut même aller ensemble, peut-être. Mais cela ne définit pas une disjonction ni une discrépance de lois. C'est une continuité qui est mise en jeu, un passage, non un franchissement. Un écoulement, non une écluse, une expansion, non une conquête. C'est une contagion et un partage.

Le texte désigne ce partage à l'aide du verbe *s'entamer*. Un seuil, en effet, ne peut relever de l'entame – à moins de ne considérer en lui que le 'dedans' du seuil, celui 'sur' lequel on se tient et qui garde au seuil, aussi longtemps qu'on s'y tient, une façon et une valeur d'ouverture. L'entame ouvre un dehors dans le dedans. Elle introduit un dehors dedans, elle explore, exploite et expose le dedans comme tel.

La *pensée* dont parle le texte n'est pas le régime autre d'un dépassement de la science et de la philosophie. Elle *s'entame*, c'est-à-dire qu'elle s'amorce et qu'elle se fend ou se fissure. Elle s'inaugure, elle s'écarte, elle s'amorce. C'est à la fois la déhiscence d'une substance et l'écartement d'une articulation. Et c'est, sous quelque forme qu'on puisse l'envisager, une action exercée sur soi-même: ça *s'*entame signifie que l'entame lui vient de soi. Lui vient à soi comme du dehors. Lui vient en soi d'un dehors qui s'y trouvait donc déjà et qui déjà s'y ouvre. C'est, pour tout dire d'un mot que Derrida aurait tenu à distance, un phénomène vivant. (Peut-être la vie est-elle par excellence ce qui s'entame – mais ce n'est pas le lieu de s'y arrêter.)

'Mesuré à la *taille* de l'écriture' cela ne fait que *s'entamer*. Car l'entame est aussi petite, mince, seulement initiale et inchoative. La taille de l'écriture n'est pourtant pas 'grande', ni 'large', ni 'terminale'. Elle ne se 'mesure' que selon le double sens de 'taille': la grandeur et la coupe. L'écriture coupe et divise – quoi ? simplement le sens (autre 'gros mot' – selon ses propres mots – qu'il aurait refusé). L'écriture, le gramme, le graphe – le glyphe ajouteraient certains Américains – ne désigne pas autre chose que l'entaille et l'entame du *logos* compris comme sens, ou comme sens et savoir (sens du savoir et savoir du sens: science du sens ou la philosophie).

Ce qu'entreprend *De la grammatologie*, ce livre au titre si soigneusement savant, n'est rien de moins que l'exploration 'nécessaire

Whereas a threshold is defined by the prior determining of domains and dominations, an opening comes about in an ill-defined way, by accident or rupture or else by pressure or by breaking through. It may also be prepared in advance. All of these possibilities may perhaps co-exist. But none of this defines a disjunction or a discrepancy in relation to laws. What is brought into play is a continuity – a movement of passage, not of crossing: a flowing motion, not one dammed in by a lock; an expansion, not a conquest. This is a contagion and a sharing out.

The text marks this sharing out with the help of the expression *is broached*, or *broaches itself*. A threshold cannot in fact be a matter of broaching – unless all that is considered of the threshold is its 'inside', the one 'on' which one stands and which, as long as one stands there, allows the threshold to retain a form and a value of opening. Broaching opens up an outside within the inside. It introduces an outside within, it explores, exploits and exposes the inside as such.

The *thought* of which the text speaks is not the surpassing of science and of philosophy in some other mode. It *is broached* or *broaches itself*, that is to say, it launches itself and it splits or cracks itself open. It inaugurates itself, pushes itself off, launches itself. It is both the bursting open of a substance and the opening of a gap in an articulation. And, in whatever form it may be envisaged, it is an action that something carries out on itself: something broaching *itself* means that the broaching comes to it from itself. Comes to it from itself as if from outside. Comes to it in itself from an outside that was already within and was already opening itself up there. It is, to sum it up in a phrase that Derrida would have kept at a distance, a living phenomenon. (Perhaps life is above all that which broaches itself – but we can't dwell on that notion here.)

'Measured by the *tally* of writing', all it does is *broach itself*, as this broaching is also slight, slender, merely initial and inchoative. However, the tally of writing is not 'great' or 'wide' or 'terminal'. It may only be 'measured' according to the double sense of a 'tally': size and cutting. Writing cuts and divides – what? Simply, sense (another 'crude word' – in his own words – that he would have rejected). Writing, the gram, the graph – the glyph, as some Americans might add – names nothing other than the notching and broaching of the *logos* understood as sense, or as sense and knowledge (the sense of knowledge and the knowledge of sense: the science of sense, or philosophy).

The undertaking proposed by *Of Grammatology*, this book with such a deliberately learned title, is nothing less than the 'necessary

et difficile' de ce dont l''écriture' en son concept séculaire de simple exécution des signes graphiques, deux fois éloignés du sens en son émission présente, actuelle et vive forme la *trace* qui oblige à être lue non seulement comme le dépôt second et mort mais en même temps comme le passage – ni passé ni futur, mais en venue, venant, de ce dont l'essence même – l'inessentielle essence – est de ne point accomplir un *logos*.

Ce n'est pourtant pas autre chose que *logos* même si c'est tout autre chose que -*logie*. Et c'est en quoi il n'y a pas la transgression heideggerienne – si du moins elle est bien telle, ce qu'on pourrait discuter longuement. Mais la grammatologie n'a pas à discuter: il lui faut entamer, s'entamer ; c'est urgent, à ce temps-là, et Derrida est le savoir de cette urgence et de ce temps, de ce *kairos*.

Oui, il est ce savoir. Il ne l'a pas, il l'est, c'est-à-dire qu'en lui ou dans son écriture ce savoir s'ouvre et s'entame. Lui, il n'ignore pas qu'il faut encore – en ce temps-là – rouvrir les clôtures du 'champ de l'*épistémè*'. Mais il ne croit pas, à la différence de Heidegger, qu'ouvrir soit transgresser et dépasser. Il sait qu'ouvrir se fait dans l'attention et la sensibilité à l'entame. En fait, il sait que Heidegger, quoi qu'il prétende, est déjà lui-même dans cette attention et plus encore qu'il en provient. Car il s'agit moins de 'Heidegger' que de l'époque, du temps, de la suspension qui ouvre les temps l'un après l'autre. Deux fois 'époque' scande cet alinéa, et une fois 'aujourd'hui'. L'aujourd'hui est celui du partage et du clivage entre une pensée qui se pense savoir ce qu'elle présente au-delà 'de tout philosophème' et une pensée qui sait qu'elle doit dire, ici et maintenant, que son nom de 'pensée' '*ne veut rien dire*'.

Que veut dire en effet 'vouloir dire'? Que veut dire la subordination du 'dire' à un 'vouloir'? Cela veut dire le vouloir-dire, précisément. Cela veut reconnaître en sa naissance même, en sa levée, en son désir, l'intention de modeler le dire selon la visée d'un sens, si ce n'est même du sens, absolument. Cela veut dire vouloir le dire comme lui-même un vouloir – non pas un désir mais bien la capacité d''être par ses représentations cause de la réalité de ces mêmes représentations' (Kant). Mais si le dire était précisément tout sauf une 'cause' et moins encore une 'cause de réalité', c'est-à-dire une production dans l'empirie? Si le 'dire' était un 'écrire', à savoir un frayage ne 'produisant' rien mais ouvrant dans le réel la trace de sa réalité même?

and difficult' exploration of what is *traced* by 'writing' in its secular conception as the mere execution of graphic signs, the latter being doubly removed from sense as a present, current and live utterance: a *trace* which demands to be read not just as a secondary, dead deposit, but at the same time as the passage – neither past nor future, but on its way, coming – of that which has as its essence (its inessential essence) not to complete a *logos*.

This is, however, nothing other than *logos* even if it is something entirely other than *-logy*. And that is why there is no Heideggerian transgression – if there even is such a thing, which one could debate at length. But grammatology does not have to debate. What it must do is broach, broach itself; at this time, it's urgent, and Derrida is the knowledge of this urgency and of this time, this *kairos*.

Yes, he is this knowledge. He doesn't have it, he is it, in other words, in him or in his writing this knowledge opens and broaches itself. It's not that he is unaware that one must still, in this time, open up again the closures of the 'field of the *epistémè*'. But, unlike Heidegger, he doesn't believe that opening is transgressing and surpassing. He knows that opening comes about in attention and sensitivity to broaching. As a matter of fact, he knows that Heidegger, whatever the latter may claim, is himself already in this attention and even more that he comes from it. Because it's less a question of 'Heidegger' than of the epoch, the time, the suspension that opens times, one after the other. The word 'epoch' twice punctuates this paragraph, and 'today' does so once. This today is one of a sharing out and a cleaving between a thought which thinks of itself that it knows what it presents beyond 'all philosophemes', and a thought which knows that it must say, here and now, that its name of 'thought' *'means or wishes to say nothing'*.

What in fact does 'meaning or wishing to say' mean to say? What is the meaning of this subordination of 'saying' to a 'wish'? It means, precisely, wishing to say. It wishes to acknowledge in its very birth, in its rising, in its desire, an intention to model saying in terms of aiming at a sense, perhaps even at sense itself, absolutely. This means wishing a saying that would itself be a wish – not a desire but that very ability to 'be through its representations the cause of the reality of those same representations' (Kant). But what if saying were precisely anything but a 'cause', much less a 'cause of reality', that is, the production of something empirical? What if 'saying' were a 'writing', namely a breaching 'producing' nothing, but opening up in the real the trace of its very reality?

Sa réalité n'est que son effectivité de chose au monde, de chose et de monde, de monde de choses. La trace de la réalité en tant que telle inscrit – fugitive, précaire – la contingence du monde. Sa non-nécessité et la nécessité de cette non-nécessité. L'écriture, celle qu'il nomme 'archi-écriture', n'est pas la notation graphique d'un dire plein de sens. Elle est ceci: que l'archie *est* écriture, à savoir aventure insensée du 'sens'.

Cet *être*, à bien l'entendre (et c'est ce que Heidegger a su entendre), n'est jamais substantif mais verbe. L'écriture est verbe, c'est-à-dire ouverture. Ouverture du sens là où le sens s'ouvre, s'entame, s'aventure. Ouverture donc *blanche* – 'un blanc textuel' – et par conséquent ne dévoilant rien comme un autre pays ou un autre régime. Ne dévoilant rien, mais ouvrant le rien lui-même.

'La pensée' ne veut rien dire: imaginez la ressource qu'il cache et qu'il déclare dans ces mots. D'une part, le mot 'pensée' ne veut rien dire: on ne lui présuppose aucun sens et surtout pas le sens d'une transgression aboutie. D'autre part, la pensée – la chose – ne veut pas dire. La pensée n'intentionne pas. Est au-delà de l'intention. Est tension sans direction, sans objectif, sans fin. Et cela même est 'pensée': s'ouvrir de l'entame de 'rien', s'ouvrir à l'entame de 'rien'. Tenir seulement à l'ouverture, non comme à une générosité, une curiosité, une réceptivité – mais comme à l'*à* lui-même. À cet *à* non intentionnel mais tendu. Tendu vers ce qui s'ouvre ou bien tendu comme l'est l'ouverture elle-même.

Pour savoir que nous ne pensons pas 'encore' (comme Heidegger le disait) il faut déjà penser. La philosophie a toujours déjà-pensé. S'il n'y a pas une transgression identique à celle de Heidegger ou bien s'il n'y a pas vraiment de transgression, c'est qu'il s'agit pluôt de laisser s'ouvrir ce dont l'ouverture s'est toujours déjà entamée. Mais il ne s'agit pas non plus de regagner un passé plus originaire, pas plus que de franchir la ligne et le suspens d'une époque. On se tient dans l'ouverture, sur le bord de la science et de la philosophie, mais non pas dehors. En même temps, on témoigne de l'ouverture grâce à laquelle on est sur le bord.

L'ouverture est blanche, elle est faite d'un 'blanc textuel'. Ce dernier, sans doute, n'est pas un blanc au sens d'un silence ou d'une absence de signification. S'il est 'textuel' c'est qu'il assume en tant que *blanc* la vérité textuelle. Qui n'est pas celle de la *logie* mais celle, précisément, de l'ouverture. On appelle 'texte' ce qui ouvre au dehors, ce qui s'entame au lieu de se fonder. Le *blanc* de l'ouverture ou bien

Its reality is just its effectiveness as a thing in the world, as thing and as world, as a world of things. The trace of reality as such inscribes – fleetingly, precariously – the contingency of the world: its non-necessity and the necessity of this non-necessity. Writing, the writing he names 'arche-writing', is not the graphic notation of a saying full of sense. It is this: that the arche *is* writing, in other words, the senseless adventure of 'sense'.

The being of this *is*, if it is well understood (and this is what Heidegger was able to understand), is never a substantive but always a verb. Writing is a verb, that is, an opening. An opening of sense at the point where sense opens itself, broaches itself, ventures itself. An opening that is therefore *blank* – 'a textual blank' – and consequently unveiling nothing like another land or another regime. Unveiling nothing, but opening that nothing itself.

'Thought' means or wishes to say nothing: just imagine the resources he is concealing and declaring in these words. On the one hand, the word 'thought' means to say nothing: in it, there is no presupposition of a sense, and certainly not the sense of a successfully completed transgression. On the other hand, thought – the thing – does not mean to say. Thought does not intend. Is beyond intention. Is a tension with neither direction, nor objective, nor end. And that's just what 'thought' is: opening itself with the broaching of 'nothing', opening itself to broaching by 'nothing'. Just holding fast to the opening, not as if to a generosity, a curiosity or a receptivity – but as if to the *to* itself. To this *to* that is not intentional but tensed or stretched. Stretched towards what is opening itself, or else stretched as the opening itself is.

In order to know that we are not 'yet' thinking (as Heidegger used to say), one must already think. Philosophy has always already-thought. If there is no transgression identical to that of Heidegger, or if there really is no transgression at all, this is because it's rather a question of allowing to open itself that by which the opening has always already broached itself. But neither is it a matter of getting back to a more originary past, any more than it is of crossing over the line or the hiatus of an epoch. One stands in the opening, on the brink of science and philosophy, but not outside. At the same time, one testifies to the opening thanks to which one stands on the brink.

The opening is blank, it is formed by a 'textual blank'. Doubtless, the latter is not a blank in the sense of a silence or an absence of signification. If it is 'textual', this is because, as a *blank*, it takes on textual truth. Which is not that of the *logy* but precisely that of the

son caractère *neutre* indiquent simplement ceci, que c'est ouvert et que nous ne sommes pas 'muré[s] dans la présence'.

Nous ne sommes pas murés parce que la présence s'entame et s'ouvre. C'est-à-dire aussi bien se présente. N'est pas le présent donné, posé d'une identité, mais la venue en quoi consiste cette différance qui porte manifestement ici l'enjeu – donc l'ouverture elle-même. Elle n'annonce pas une perpétuelle remise à plus tard: elle indique qu'aucune différence ne se résorbe, pas plus qu'elle ne se maintient. Mais toute différence va et vient, joignant et disjoignant ses termes qui ne sont tels que selon leur rapport incessant. De cette manière est toujours promis un surcroît sur chaque position et de toute position – ou présence. Rien n'est achevé ni achevable. Rien n'est muré ni emmuré.

Pas même 'l'écriture' ni le gramme ou le graphe délié de toute *logie*. Rien n'est fermé. Le projet grammatologique à peine entamé s'entame déjà lui-même et 'pointe au-delà'. Il pointe vers nous, qui le lisons aujourd'hui selon de nouvelles entames, non moins blanches et non moins ouvertes. Nous lisons, nous écrivons. Ni science ni philosophie de l'écriture. Aucune assurance mais un élan, une pulsion et un désir que nous ne pouvons méconnaître: la vie même du 'ne rien vouloir dire', la vie au-delà de toutes ses significations et de toutes ses insignifiances. Pensée pointée au-delà: ici même. Pensée pointue qui ne veut rien dire, mais qui pique et qui perce – qui entame et qui ouvre.

opening. What is called a 'text' is that which opens to the outside, that which broaches itself rather than founding itself. The *blank* of the opening or its neutral character simply indicate this, that it is open and that we are not 'walled in within presence'.

We are not walled in because presence broaches and opens itself. Which is also to say, presents itself. Not the given, established present of an identity, but a coming, that is what is constituted by this differ*a*nce on which the stakes – and therefore the opening itself – obviously rest here. It does not announce a perpetual postponement: it indicates that no difference ever seals itself up again, any more than it maintains itself. But rather, every difference comes and goes, connecting and disconnecting its terms which are only what they are by virtue of their incessant relation. So it is that there is always the promise of an excess over each position and of each position – or presence. Nothing is or may be completed. Nothing is walled in or up.

Not even 'writing', nor the gram or graph detached from any *logy*. Nothing is closed. No sooner broached, the grammatological project already broaches itself and 'points beyond'. It points towards us, who read it today according to new broachings, no less blank and no less open. We read, we write. Neither a science nor a philosophy of writing. No assurance, but a surge, a drive and a desire that we cannot fail to recognize: the very life of 'meaning or wishing to say nothing', life beyond all its significations and insignificances. A thought pointed beyond: right here. A pointed thought meaning to say nothing, but which pricks and pierces – which broaches and opens.

Translated by Ian Maclachlan

PART 2

NATURE, CULTURE, WRITING

THE VIOLENCE OF THE LETTER: FROM LÉVI-STRAUSS TO ROUSSEAU

MICHAEL NAAS, *LEURRE*, LURE, DELUSION, ILLUSION (*OG* 139–40, 20, 39; *DG* 201–2, 34, 58, 59)

The French word *leurre* is one of just a handful of terms – along with *brisure* and *bricole* – that Derrida himself not only comments on but gives the origins of in *Of Grammatology* (*OG* 65; *DG* 96). Like the *bricole*, says Derrida, the *leurre* designates first a hunter's stratagem. A term of falconry, a *leurre* is 'a piece of red leather', Derrida writes citing *Littré*, 'in the form of a bird, which serves to recall the bird of prey when it does not return straight to the fist' (*OG* 139; *DG* 201). The *leurre* is thus a decoy, snare, distraction or enticement, an artefact that presents itself as something natural and alive – perhaps even more alive than what is actually living. The *leurre* thus becomes a *leurre* of life by making itself as transparent as possible, that is, by effacing by means of a supplement everything that would suggest artifice and deception in order to give the impression of life and naturalness. The *leurre* is thus a kind of 'illusion' – one of the ways *leurre* has been translated into English in *Of Grammatology* since it appears in a couple of passages to be more or less synonymous with the French *illusion* (*OG* 12, 75, 82, 120, 130, 154, 163, 188, 272).

In the following passage from an early section of *Of Grammatology* Derrida uses both the terms *leurre* and *illusion* to speak of the way in which the voice *seems* to present meaning itself, that is, the way the phonic signifier *appears* to efface itself or make itself transparent in order to give immediate and direct access to the signified.

> This experience of the effacement of the signifier in the voice is not merely one illusion [*illusion*] among many. [. . .] This illusion

[*leurre*] is the history of truth and it cannot be dissipated so quickly. Within the closure of this experience, the word [*mot*] is lived as the elementary and undecomposable unity of the signified and the voice, of the concept and a transparent substance of expression. (*OG* 20; *DG* 34)

Though the phonic signifier *is* indeed a signifier, the product of difference and absence, it has a way of *appearing* to efface itself *as* a signifier in order to give immediate access to the signified. Writing, on the contrary, does not so easily lend itself to this illusion or this lure; it wears its artificial status on its face, so to speak. It does not give the impression of transparency and is not experienced as an 'undecomposable unity'.

The *leurre* is thus always an illusion within experience of presence, integrity and life. It is not only what characterizes but what sustains one side of a whole series of so-called *binary oppositions* co-extensive with a logocentric metaphysics. It is the *experience* of a voice that seems to efface itself and to give rise – or seems to do so, for that is the illusion – to the immediate apprehension of meaning. This explains why, as Derrida demonstrates throughout *Of Grammatology*, logocentrism is so often related to phonocentrism, to a hierarchy of speech over writing, and why both are often in complicity with a thinking of the unity and integrity of the *word*. In the logocentric and phonocentric tradition that Derrida is reading throughout *Of Grammatology*, the *leurre* is given in experience though it is not, of course, presented to experience *as a leurre*. The *leurre* presents itself – for that is the *leurre* – of being something other than itself; it claims to be, for example, a speech uncontaminated by writing, a signifier united with its signified, a life protected from death. In the following passage where Derrida is speaking of Saussure's seemingly unjustified exclusion of writing from his general linguistics, one will notice the emphasis Derrida places on the *declaration* that speech is exterior to writing, on the *self-proclaimed* reduction of language properly speaking to living speech and so on.

A particular system which has precisely for its *principle* or at least for its *declared* project to be exterior to the spoken language. Declaration of principle, pious wish and historical violence of a speech dreaming its full self-presence, living itself as its own resumption;

self-proclaimed language, auto-production of a speech declared alive, capable, Socrates said, of helping itself, a logos which believes itself to be its own father, being lifted thus above written discourse. [. . .] Self-proclaimed language but actually speech, deluded [*leurrée*] into believing itself completely alive, and violent, for it is not 'capable of protect[ing] or defend[ing] [itself]' [. . .] except through expelling the other, and especially *its own* other, throwing it *outside* and *below*, under the name of writing. (*OG* 39; *DG* 58–9)

The *leurre* whose power or effectiveness takes root in experience is thus sustained by speech's self-proclamation of its own exteriority to writing and its self-attribution of life.

But there is perhaps more. In speaking here of a 'dream' or a 'pious wish', Derrida's notion of the *leurre* seems to bear something of a family resemblance to what Freud in *The Future of an Illusion* calls illusion (*Illusion*) or to what in his reading of Gradiva in *Delusion and Dream* he calls delusion (*Wahn*). What these works make clear is that the lure or delusion is always a self-delusion (see *OG* 298). Speech would proclaim itself to be co-extensive with language, exterior to all writing and so protected from it, not because that it is the way things are but because that's the way we *want them to be*. Writing would thus be not only subjugated to speech but *repressed* by it.

Though Derrida is very clear in 'Freud and the Scene of Writing' (1966) and elsewhere that deconstruction cannot be confused with a psychoanalysis of the text, the work of deconstruction nonetheless seems to aim for something analogous to psychoanalysis: a recovery of what has been 'repressed', a making manifest of what is 'latent' – it being understood, of course, that what is recovered or made manifest will never have the quality of a presence. Deconstruction would thus aim for a 'respect' for a 'condition of origin' that the metaphysical tradition has not respected, a respect for *writing*, for example – for spacing and *différance* – as the condition of speech. It is only through this respect for what has hitherto not been respected that the *leurre* or delusion begins to lose some of its power. For even if experience might continue to live off that delusion, our theoretical discourse will not or will not in the same way once it begins to take the *leurre* explicitly into account.

Let us return, then, to the passage cited at the outset, the one in which Derrida refers to the origins of the word *leurre*. Here is how Derrida introduces that passage:

> The ethic of the living word would be perfectly respectable, completely utopian and a-topic [*utopique et atopique*] as it is (unconnected to *spacing* and to différance as writing), it would be as respectable as respect itself if it did not live on a delusion [*leurre*] and a nonrespect for its own condition of origin, if it did not dream in speech of a presence denied to writing, denied by writing. The ethics of speech is the *delusion* [leurre] of presence mastered. (*OG* 139–40; *DG* 201–2)

The *leurre*, delusion or illusion, of speech is related to a non-respect, an ignoring or a repression, of the writing, the spacing and the difference, that makes it possible. Though it comes second, therefore, it always presents itself through a sort of 'retrospective illusion' as coming first (*OG* 102). It thus leads to an ethics that privileges speech over writing as virtue over vice – a perfectly respectable privileging were it not based on a *leurre*, as Derrida writes and underscores. (The fact, moreover, that this ethics of speech is the *leurre* of 'presence mastered' licenses us to see in this term an avatar of what Derrida will call in many later texts, from *Glas* right up through *Rogues*, the 'phantasm' in general and the 'phantasm' of sovereignty in particular.)

After using the word *leurre* twice in two sentences and then giving us the definition of the word ('it is a term of falconry . . .'), Derrida goes on to describe what would appear to be the task or work of deconstruction: a making explicit of the conditions that make the *leurre* possible, a certain *recognition* of the *leurre as a leurre*.

> To recognize writing in speech, that is to say différance and the absence of speech, is to begin to think the lure [*leurre*]. There is no ethics without the presence *of the other* but also, and consequently, without absence, dissimulation, detour, differance, writing. [. . .] In the texts that we must now read, Rousseau is suspicious also of the illusion [*illusion*] of full and present speech, of the illusion of presence within a speech believed to be transparent and innocent. (*OG* 139–40; *DG* 201–2)

Whereas Derrida referred earlier to a certain Rousseau who seems to privilege an 'ethic of the living word', an 'ethics of speech' – that is, an ethics of self-presence – we now see him referring to a Rousseau who, like Derrida himself, will be 'suspicious of the illusion of full and present speech', suspicious of the supposed transparency and innocence of speech. By playing one Rousseau off the other, Derrida makes the *leurre* apparent *as a leurre*, demonstrating that 'there is no ethics [. . .] without absence, detour, différance, writing'. The ethics of deconstruction, if such a phrase is permissible, would thus entail the deconstruction of all the *leurres* of ethics, and, first among these, the 'ethics of speech'.

FORBES MORLOCK, THE SUBJECT OF READING-1
(*OG* 117; *DG* 172)

' "I see yellow" ' (*OG* 117).

By this point the use of the first-person singular is not unexpected. The pronoun 'I' has appeared many times in *Of Grammatology*. Always – as here – in quotation marks. Except that these quotation marks don't mark a quotation. Or, rather, 'I see yellow' may be a quotation, but it is not one for which *Of Grammatology* gives an author or a source.

The reference in the text is clear enough. Descartes's *Regulae ad directionem ingenii* discusses the experience of someone who thinks everything is coloured yellow (47). In Descartes's text, though, this sufferer from jaundice does not speak. He does not speak in his own voice, in Descartes's voice, in the work's voice. The *Regulae* certainly resorts to the first-person singular, but not in this case.

So, who is the 'I' in *Of Grammatology* who declares that he or she sees yellow? Philosophers may object to his or her (or its) being called the 'philosophical "I"'. They might prefer the 'logical "I"' or the 'propositional "I"'. We can proffer the 'universal "I"' and the 'impersonal "I"', but any of these designations risks giving a name to or deciding the context of what is hardly conscious, voluntary or intentional – a textual tic. The question of the 'I' is as much one of fidelity as philosophy. The introduction to Part II has suggested that we approach a reading of Rousseau through the texts of Lévi-Strauss because of the place there of 'the theory of writing and the theme of fidelity to Rousseau' (*OG* 100). The 'I' is to be read.

'Let us paraphrase this text' (*OG* 133). Faithfully? Let us dramatize this text. Faithfully. Derrida's account of the argument of Descartes's *Regulae* is admirably economic – and not unfaithful. The 'I' seeing yellow is very nearly the *Regulae*'s, almost Descartes's, but it is not quite one or the other. At the same time, the quotation marks hint that the jaundiced eye is not Derrida's or his text's own either.

Mettre le je en jeu. In the name of the subject of reading, let us put this 'I' – the seventeen instances of this 'I' – into play.

CHAPTER 2

'. . . THAT DANGEROUS SUPPLEMENT . . .'

MICHAEL NAAS, *ENTAMER*, *ENTAMÉ*, TO INITIATE OR OPEN UP, TO BREACH OR BROACH (*OG* 20–1, 163, 182; *DG* 34, 233, 259 AND *PASSIM*)

Next to terms such as the trace, deconstruction or *différance*, the verb *entamer* (along with its past participle – which is also used as an adjective – *entamé*) would appear scarcely worthy of serious consideration. Indeed the term can easily go unnoticed since it is variously translated throughout *Of Grammatology* – and always for good reason – as 'broach', 'breach', 'interfere', 'infiltrate', 'cut into', 'break into', 'usher in' and so on. But as we will see, this term is almost as important and useful to Derrida as the term *différance* or *différer* and Derrida's multiple and varied uses of it can do much to help illuminate what is at stake in these other, better-known terms.

In fact, just like the verb *différer*, there are two different though related meanings of *entamer* – one related to time and one to space. The verb first means simply to begin, to initiate, to enter into or open up. Derrida thus speaks in an early passage of how the question of the meaning of being initiates or 'broaches [*entame*] philosophy (for example, in the *Sophist*) and lets itself be taken over by philosophy' (*OG* 20–1; *DG* 34). The verb *entamer* here suggests the opening up or beginning of a new movement or historical epoch. Derrida writes much later, commenting on or parsing Rousseau, 'the invasion of the northern barbarians ushered in [*entame*] a new cycle of historical degeneration' (*OG* 202; *DG* 288–9). Or again, 'If [imagination] is able to corrupt us, it is first because it opens the possibility of progress. It *broaches* [entame] history' (OG 182; *DG* 259, Derrida's emphasis). Though Derrida would surely caution against thinking deconstruction itself as a movement that is simply opened up in time or as an epoch that begins at some particular moment in time, the verb *entamer* is sometimes used to signal this opening as well. Derrida thus speaks of 'broaching [*entamer*] the de-construction of *the greatest totality* – the concept of the *epistémè* and logocentric metaphysics' (*OG* 46; *DG* 68; see *OG* 162; *DG* 231).

If Derrida opposes throughout *Of Grammatology* the *end* of metaphysics to its *closure*, one might see here the makings of an opposition between *beginning* or *initiating* deconstruction and its being *broached*. For if, as Derrida shows, what appears to have been initiated or begun at a certain moment in time *will have already* begun before its supposed beginning, then the transitive verb *entamer* or the reflexive *s'entamer* would be a better way to describe the way in which some historical movement is *opened up* in a time that cannot be merely linear. Derrida thus concludes an analysis of Rousseau: 'If culture is thus broached [*s'entame*] within its point of origin, then it is not possible to recognize any linear order, whether logical or chronological' (*OG* 267; *DG* 377). The notion of an originary 'broaching' is thus not unlike an original 'deferral', where the '*birth of society*', for example, would be 'not a passage' but 'a point, a pure, fictive and unstable, ungraspable limit. One crosses it in attaining it. In it society is broached and is deferred from itself [*s'entame et se diffère*]' (*OG* 267; *DG* 377).

Like the verb *se différer*, then, to which it is explicitly connected in the preceding lines, the verb *s'entamer* has a very distinct *temporal* meaning that Derrida wishes at once to exploit and inflect: what begins will have already begun, but not in a past that can ever be identified as a past present. But just like the verb *différer* or that infamous Derridean neologism *différance*, the verb *entamer* has a *spatial* meaning as well, as if its meaning too already differs from and defers itself, as if its meaning could never be univocal but already multiple, disseminated, in a word, *broached*. The second meaning of the verb *entamer* in *Of Grammatology* is thus to undermine or unsettle, or, better, to break into, cut or eat into, or again, to breach or broach. Early in the work, for example, Derrida speaks of the way writing has been characterized throughout the tradition as infiltrating, breaching or contaminating speech and its relation to the soul and the living breath. Writing, he argues, is the 'eruption of the *outside* within the *inside*, breaching [*entamant*] into the interiority of the soul, the living self-presence of the soul within the true logos' (*OG* 34; *DG* 52). Later Derrida demonstrates how writing will have '*breached* [entamait] living speech from within and from the very beginning' (Derrida's emphasis), before adding, 'as we shall begin to see, difference cannot be thought without the *trace*' (*OG* 56–7; *DG* 83). Hence the verb *entamer* is brought into proximity not only to a thought of *differing* and *deferral*, that is, to *différance*, but, as we see here, to a thinking of the *trace*. There is no coincidence in this.

What is breached is always some supposedly pure inside by the outside, living speech, for example, by writing, a singular presence by repetition and absence, the putative origin by the supplement: 'the indefinite process of supplementarity has always already *infiltrated* [entamé] presence, always already inscribed there the space of repetition and the splitting of the self' (*OG* 163; *DG* 233, Derrida's emphasis). What is breached, cut into, compromised or contaminated, is thus, according to a certain tradition of which Rousseau would be exemplary, life and the energy of life: 'What Rousseau in fact describes is that the lack, adding itself as a plus to a plus, cuts into [*entame*] an energy which *must* (*should*) *have* been and remain intact. And indeed it breaks in [*entame*] as a dangerous supplement, as a *substitute* that *enfeebles, enslaves, effaces, separates,* and *falsifies*' (*OG* 215; *DG* 308). The supplement is thus, writes Derrida elsewhere, what 'breaches [*entame*] both our pleasure and our virginity', that is, it is what opens or initiates our pleasure and, in so doing, compromises our virginity (*OG* 154; *DG* 222).

At the core of these various uses is the notion that a putatively intact realm is from the very beginning *entamé*, that is, that a supposedly pure moment has been contaminated from the outset. In each case, it is a putatively unbroached or uncompromised purity, a supposedly 'intact purity [*une pureté inentamée*]' (*OG* 246; *DG* 349), 'pure enough to have remained unblemished [*inentamée*] by the work of difference' (*OG* 249; *DG* 353), that shows itself to have been compromised from the very beginning. In each case, it is a supposedly originary presence or natural plenitude, a certain 'integrity', that is breached (*OG* 112; *DG* 166), the 'exemplary model of a pure breath (*pneuma*) and an intact life [*une vie inentamée*], [. . .] of speech without spacing' (*OG* 249; *DG* 353; for *inentamé* see *OG* 282; *DG* 400). Echoing the argument he makes in *Voice and Phenomena* (1967) and elsewhere about the way in which the ear is always contaminated or compromised by the eye, Derrida writes: 'Visibility [. . .] is always that which, separating it from itself, breaches [*entame*] the living voice' (*OG* 306; *DG* 432).

What *seems* intact and uncompromised has thus *always already* been breached. What Rousseau would have thus said without saying it is that 'substitution has always already begun; that imitation, principle of art, has always already interrupted natural plenitude; that, having to be a *discourse*, it has always already broached [*entamé*] presence in différance' (*OG* 215; *DG* 308). The notion of a life untouched by death, of an originary presence uncompromised by absence and supplementarity, would thus be but a *phantasm* or what Derrida calls in *Of Grammatology* a *leurre*, a delusion. 'A life that has not yet broached [*entamé*] the play of supplementarity and which at the same time has not yet let itself be violated [*entamer*] by it: a life without différance and without articulation' (*OG* 242: *DG* 344) – this thus would be, for Derrida, *no life at all* since it would be devoid of all desire and all time. Any life, nature, origin, plenitude or presence that would claim to precede the play of supplementarity would thus be but an illusion or phantasm made possible by the supplement. Derrida writes: 'the unity of nature or the identity of origin is shaped and undermined by a strange difference which constitutes it by breaching [*entamant*] it' (*OG* 198; *DG* 283). Difference at once breaches this supposed unity of nature or this identity of origin *and* constitutes it, constitutes it *by* breaching it. This suggests that there *is* no pure presence, no intact nature, which would *then* or *subsequently* be opened up, compromised or contaminated. The purity of the inside is *from the origin* opened up and compromised, and it is only through this *original breach* that the origin is then constituted *après coup*, that is, retrospectively or after the fact.

For Derrida as a reader of a tradition that would *feign* or *claim* to grant access to a nature without the supplement of culture, to an origin uncontaminated by repetition, the task would be to read this tradition and to demonstrate how this nature and this origin are broached or breached from the very outset – always already *entamé*. More than thirty years after *Of Grammatology*, Derrida would write in one of the concluding sentences of 'Faith and Knowledge' (1996): 'Emblem of a still life [*une nature morte*]: an opened pomegranate [*la grenade entamée*], one Passover evening, on a tray' (66; 100). It is a memory, it seems, from Derrida's childhood, the image of a pomegranate that is not intact but already opened up, already cut, its 613 seeds on display, already in dissemination, shattering the illusion of a phantasm of purity or integrity, of an origin before

language, of a nature before culture, of a life before violence, absence
and difference.

FORBES MORLOCK, THE SUBJECT OF READING-2
(OG 142; DG 205)

'If I were present, one would never know what I was worth' (*OG* 142).
Jacques Derrida quotes Jean Starobinski quoting Jean-Jacques
Rousseau (*Les Confessions* 116). Before and after *Of Grammatology*
quotes (the Starobinski quoting) the Rousseau a second time, it would
tease out the economy of this sentence. It paraphrases. And, in paraphrasing, it dramatizes, specifically that it is getting closer to (the text
of) Rousseau than Starobinski does. It is reading, more closely.

At the same time, for the first time in *Of Grammatology*, an 'I'
appears outside quotation marks. 'To the *I am* or to the *I am present*
thus sacrificed, a *what* I am or a *what I am worth* is *preferred*'. Three
times – and Spivak follows scrupulously the aberrancy of the fourth –
a phrase is underlined, emphasized, italicized. An 'I' is underlined,
emphasized, italicized, but not quoted. The 'I' is almost Rousseau. It
is a possible Rousseau, which is also a possible Derrida. As Rousseau
assesses relations between 'I's' here in the *Confessions*, *Of Grammatology* is assessing its own relation to that 'I', those 'I's'. It is assessing
the relation between its 'I' and Rousseau's. (Jean-)Jacques?

There are no more than seven passages (in the French of *De la
grammatologie*) where a 'je' appears that is not the 'I' of another
author, signature or proper name. And all seven, if that is the
number, appear in the part on Rousseau.

Part II of *Of Grammatology* reads Rousseau, it reads *Rousseau's
text [le texte de Rousseau]* (*OG* lxxxix, 41, 153, 160, 161, 163, 188,
199, 218, 246, 265, 294, 301, 307, 309). Part II reads the text and not
the book (*OG* 18), the document (*OG* 149), the thought (*OG* 329 n. 38)
or even, by implication, the corpus or oeuvre: it reads Rousseau's
texts (*OG* 145, 183), a certain number but not all of them (*OG* 162).

The object of reading? The text: 'the system of a writing and of a
reading' (*OG* 164). A text somewhere between writing and reading, a
text like *Of Grammatology*, a text like the *Confessions* it would read
here ('Rousseau', according to the conventions which Starobinski
follows, reading 'Jean-Jacques'). The object of reading in this case is
also somehow its subject. (Jean-)Jacques.

Where are we in Part II of *Of Grammatology*? 'We are *in* Rousseau's text' (*OG* 160, trans. mod.). And we are in Derrida's text. 'I renounce my present life'. I, writer/reader, Rousseau/Derrida – we can figure (but only figure?) the problem in terms of the French reflexive verb or the Greek middle voice. The less than two. Either way, we lose count after one. The 'I' is plural and yet not 'we'. It cannot say 'I'. It is a text, but it can never be the author, voice or subject of a text. 'There is not, strictly speaking, a text whose author or subject is Jean-Jacques Rousseau' (*OG* 246). A text whose author or subject is Jacques Derrida.

Where are we here in Derrida's reading of Rousseau? The 'I' in this paraphrase measures, marks or establishes a distance – and an identity. In 'Rousseau', in reading, in *Of Grammatology*. The distance and identity of identification. 'The battle by which I wish to raise myself above my life even while retaining it, in order to enjoy recognition, is in this case within myself [*la guerre est ici en moi*], and writing is indeed the phenomenon of this battle' (*OG* 142; *DG* 205, trans. mod.).

Writing, the writing of the *Confessions*, the writing of *Jean-Jacques Rousseau. La transparence et l'obstacle*, the writing of *Of Grammatology* – the battle is here in the 'I'. In this apparently egoistic economy, these writings are indeed the phenomena of the question of reading.

FORBES MORLOCK, THE SUBJECT OF READING-3 (*OG* 156; *DG* 224–5)

On hundreds of occasions throughout the book, others speak in the first-person singular. Rousseau, Peirce, Saussure, Laporte, Descartes, Leibniz, Février, Leroi-Gourhan, Klein, Lévi-Strauss, Bataille, Duclos, Lanson, Masson, Warburton, Homer, Kafka, the author of the article 'Métaphore' in the *Encyclopédie*, Condillac – all are able to speak as themselves, to say 'I' in *Of Grammatology*. Of course, it may be their characters or their arguments that articulate these 'je's', but in each case something speaks for itself. Someone speaks in his or her own voice. Derrida, it seems, does not.

There are perhaps seven passages (at least in the French) where a 'je' appears that is not the 'I' of another author. These 'je's' are not quite the 'I's' of *Of Grammatology*'s author, not wholly the 'I's' of Jacques Derrida. They are the 'I's' of a reading subject. I, the subject of reading – and reading *Of Grammatology*.

It is not hard to find the grammatical 'I' of an author, something that might pass for the 'I' of Derrida, in the other books of 1967, *Speech and Phenomena* and *Writing and Difference*. *Of Grammatology*, though, alters even what we might take as their most minimal authorial interpolations: its unstyled or editorial 'emphasis added' or 'my emphasis'. '*Je souligne* [I underline]' acknowledges the writer's slightest intervention in what he or she quotes and reads – the line, the underline. It acknowledges the least mark or trace of reading. But I do not underline in *De la grammatologie*. *Nous soulignons*.

A matter as unsigned as editorial practice, as unauthored as house style (all three books are published by different publishers), is also the question of reading – of the subject of reading. The question: Who underlines? is also: Who or what reads? Who or what speaks, writes, inscribes, performs, registers or declares a reading? The oft-derided notion that a text articulates or governs the logic of its own reading – that it reads itself (*se lit*) – is not wholly a conceit.

Certainly, the autonomous, autarkic, proper 'I' does not read. Entirely itself, it is too much itself to read.

Reading is, rather, an auto-affective disorder. As all orders, including consciousness, the imagination and the universal structure of experience, are auto-affective disorders (*OG* 98, 186–7, 165–6). I touch, I am what is touched, I touch me, I am what is touched by me. '*Auto*-affection constitutes the same (*auto*) as it divides the same. Privation of presence is the condition of experience, that is to say, of presence. In as much as it *puts into play* the presence of the present and the life of the living, the movement of language does not, one suspects, have only an analogical relationship with "sexual" auto-affection. It is entirely indistinguishable from it' (166–7). Just in case you suspected that all this – or all Derrida – was so much wanking.

'As I thus harm only myself, this perversion is not truly condemnable'. I, Rousseau, masturbating; I, Derrida, introducing the less-than-proper topic of masturbation into philosophy. I, the reader, reading books that 'can only be read with one hand' (*OG* 340 n. 8; *Les Confessions* 40); I, the writer, finding it 'difficult to separate writing from onanism. [. . .] In both cases, the possibility of auto-affection manifests itself as such: it leaves a trace of itself in the world' (*OG* 165). The last assumption about writing may be Rousseau's, Derrida's, or simply male, but it cannot detract from the universally auto-affective nature of reading.

Of Grammatology's polemic against commentary is justly celebrated. '[I]f reading must not be content with doubling the text, it cannot legitimately transgress the text toward something beyond it' (*OG* 158). Neither the image nor the other of the text.

Reading is close, very close, to absolute proximity.

PEGGY KAMUF, *L'HABITATION DES FEMMES* (*OG* 155; *DG* 223–4)

Perhaps a major reason the thinking of in-habitation rarely advances to the front line of Derrida's lexical armoury is simply that it is given so little play in Rousseau's own text, which is here standing in for the metaphysical text in general at a certain epoch of its history, the 'epoch of Rousseau', precisely. Certainly its range of possibilities – lexical, semantic, syntactic, rhetorical – are far more limited and limiting than the range of supplementarity, and not only in Rousseau's text. But there is at least one very significant occurrence of *habitation*, which Derrida does not fail to place and to underscore early in his reading of Rousseau. Its significance is such, I venture to say by way of hypothesis, as to cause it to radiate throughout the text as Derrida reads it, and from there to cross through the thin membrane between the text read and the text reading. I will venture further to say that, once again unlike what happens with the vocabulary of supplementarity, this crossing happens almost silently or without remark, although I'll stop short of surmising that it is uncalculated or inadvertent, still less 'unconscious'. Instead of according to such figures of intentionality, this crossing or transfer or exchange of fluid language occurs, I am proposing, through the very medium or milieu that is named by Rousseau 'l'habitation' in the particular sense it can be given in the French idiom by the phrase 'l'habitation des femmes'.

This phrase is picked out early in the reading of Rousseau, when Derrida has just begun to track the 'dangerous supplement'. He sets up the context of the phrase in these terms:

> It is from a certain determined representation of 'l'habitation des femmes' that Rousseau had to resort throughout his life to that type of dangerous supplement that is called masturbation and that cannot be dissociated from his activity as a writer. Up until the end. (*OG* 155; *DG* 223–4, trans. mod.)

The phrase Derrida remarks is then cited in context in the next long quotation from *The Confessions*, one of a series that has been strung on the thread of this reading of the 'dangerous supplement' – which in the same work Rousseau also refers to as his 'pernicious habit [*funeste habitude*]'. In this passage, Rousseau is explaining the initial plan to abandon Thérèse, his long-time companion as the phrase goes, as he takes flight from Paris after the public banning of *Émile* and its author. He piles on the excuses for having wanted to put distance between himself and Thérèse, and then finally he adds: 'Besides, I had observed that intercourse with women [*l'habitation des femmes*] distinctly aggravated my ill-health' (*The Confessions* 581; *Les Confessions* 595, trans. mod.).

Translations of *The Confessions* usually render the phrase either, as here, 'intercourse with women', or perhaps 'cohabitation with women', which are both no more than adequate given that Rousseau's language pointedly dispenses with the 'with'. According to the *Dictionnaire Littré* and as Rousseau's Pléiade editors also point out, the more customary or habitual form of the expression to indicate 'le commerce charnel' is 'habitation avec des femmes'. By contrast, Rousseau's curious expression can be compared, at least syntactically, to the sense of inhabiting some surrounding space – a dwelling, a city, a country, a continent: *l'habitation d'une maison, l'habitation de Londres, l'habitation du Canada*, etc. One effect of this inhabitual turn of phrase is to project a habitation that is not a living- or a being-with, not even a having-sex-with although the phrase in question would isolate a complaint about precisely that experience. Oddly, it would be a (co)habitation (with) women without women and thus perhaps a variation on what Derrida underscores, using Rousseau's own language, of that 'state almost inconceivable to reason'. The elision of the word and thus the idea of 'avec' inscribes, in other terms, the economy of auto-affection that Derrida finds written large and small across Rousseau's text – indeed, *as* Rousseau's text, whether it is describing certain sexual habits that supplement the writer's unhealthful 'habitation des femmes' or the self-awakening power of imagination, which 'receives nothing that is alien or anterior to itself. It is not affected by the "real". It is pure auto-affection'.

By bearing down on Rousseau's somewhat aberrant usage, I've sought to shore up a little my hypothesis that Derrida would have perhaps seen there a reason to take on the condition, state or experience called 'habitation' so as to in-habit it otherwise, in a certain way. By inhabiting Rousseau's text in another way, in a way that will in effect restore the elided spacing of the *avec*, the reading he produces yields another thinking of habitation-with which the same inhabited text – but can we still call it the same text? – seeks to conjure away in a flight from every worldly habitation, of women *and* of men, as it works towards a final chapter titled *Reveries of a Solitary Walker*.

CHAPTER 3

GENESIS AND STRUCTURE OF THE 'ESSAY ON THE ORIGIN OF LANGUAGES'

3.1 THE PLACE OF THE 'ESSAY'

SEAN GASTON, PITY, VIRTUALITY AND POWER
(*OG* 171–92; *DG* 243–72)

Derrida argues at the start of his reading of Rousseau that, contrary to the view of Jean Starobinski, the 'Essay on the Origin of Languages' was not written before the *Second Discourse* (1754–55). The Essay can be dated to 1754–61 (*OG* 170–2, 192–4). Starobinski had suggested that the Essay must precede the *Second Discourse* because it offers such a different account of natural pity. In a note from 1995, he both acknowledges his error and criticizes Derrida's 'selective' (*ponctuelles*) remarks on Rousseau's theory of pity ('Note sur l'établissement du texte', cci–cciii). In the *Second Discourse*, *la pitié* is a natural sentiment that arises from the immediate repugnance of seeing others like oneself suffer or die. In the Essay, on the other hand, pity is mediated by the imagination. In the *Second Discourse*, Rousseau had insisted that natural man has neither imagination nor foresight (143, 155). In the Essay, he argues that it is only through the imagination that I can go out of myself and enter into the feelings of others.

For Derrida, as 'the first *diversion*' of natural self-love, pity is '*almost* primitive' and already placed somewhere between nature and culture (*OG* 174). Natural pity also protects us from the corruption of the amorous passions and socially constructed sexual desire (*OG* 175). To do this, pity must be supplemented by the imagination to produce a restrictive 'moral love' that can redirect the energy of 'physical love' and desire (*OG* 177–9). As Derrida observes: 'pity never stops being a natural sentiment or an inner virtue that only the imagination has the power to awaken or reveal' (*OG* 184). As a proposed structure of 'absolute identity', pity cannot avoid relying on a re-presentation and 'a certain non-presence within presence' (*OG* 173, 189–91). Derrida writes: 'Without imagination, this pity does not awaken to itself in humanity, is not accessible to passion, language, and representation, does not produce identification with the other as with another me. Imagination is the becoming-human of pity' (*OG* 185; *DG* 262, trans. mod.).

For Derrida, this supplementary relation between pity and imagination gives rise to an Aristotelian structure of potentiality and actuality in which the 'real presence' of the natural is held back and takes on the form of a virtuality:

> This appeal to activation and to actualization by the imagination is so little in contradiction with other texts that one can follow everywhere in Rousseau's work a theory of innateness as virtuality or naturality as sleeping potentiality. Not a very original theory to be sure, but one whose organizing role is indispensable. It asks us to think of nature not as a given, as a real presence, but as a *reserve*. (*OG* 185)

This Aristotelian gesture raises the problem of rethinking the inheritance of potentiality and power. This notion of a reserve, Derrida writes, 'is itself confusing [*déroutant*]: one may determine it as a hidden actuality, dissimulated deposit, but also as a reserve of indeterminate power' (*OG* 187; *DG* 263). Perhaps less confusing than disconcerting (*déroutant*), which suggests a resistance or holding back, a reserve offers two possible interpretations: one determined (*actualité*) and one indeterminate (*puissance*). But the reserve *itself* is also disconcerting: it can be determined as a hidden actuality, an actuality waiting to take place and, *at the same time*, as an indeterminate power that may be more or less than an assured resource for actuality.

Derrida suggests that Rousseau's need for the imagination to supplement pity disorders the proper relation between potentiality and actuality: 'It awakens the potential faculty but just as quickly transgresses it. It brings forth [*met au jour*] the power which was held back [*se réservait*] but, by showing that power what lies beyond it, by "superseding" it [*la "devançant"*], imagination signifies for it its powerlessness [*impuissance*]. It animates the faculty of enjoyment but inscribes a difference between desire and power' (*OG* 185; *DG* 263). In this context, imagination disconcerts potentiality as a power, but it does not fall back on powerlessness as an untouchable pure possibility. It exceeds both potentiality and actuality (as the proper expression of the potential). It exceeds power and powerlessness by inscribing a difference. Having started with Starobinski's dating of the Essay, and characterized its relationship to the *Second Discourse* through the imagination supplementing natural pity and reconfiguring the natural as a kind of virtuality, Derrida concludes his analysis of 'the economy of pity' by outmanoeuvring the Aristotelian ordering of *dūnamis* and *entelēkheia*. He writes:

> Thought within its concealed relation to the logic of the supplement, the concept of virtuality (like the entire problematic of power and act) undoubtedly has for its function, for Rousseau in particular and within metaphysics in general, the systematic predetermining of becoming as production and development, evolution or history, through the substitution of the accomplishment of a *dynamis* for the substitution of a trace, of pure history for pure play [. . . .] Now the movement of supplementarity seems to escape this alternative and to permit us to think it. (*OG* 187; *DG* 265–6, trans. mod.)

CLARE CONNORS, PREFERENCE AND FORCE
(*OG* 178; *DG* 253)

'Telle est l'histoire de l'amour' (such is the history of love) (*DG* 253; *OG* 178), writes Derrida, at the start of a paragraph summing up the bit of Rousseau's *Second Discourse* which describes the advent of human love, and its birth as a diversion and orientation of natural desire. This sentence might be flagged with a 'mark of irony' (*point d'ironie*) (*OG* 227; *DG* 324). We can certainly hear in it the accent that marks a diversion from what one seems to be declaring, the tension of a tone that holds things off, denies ownership of an utterance, puts into question the universal acknowledgement of a truth by marking one's own preference and prejudice. *Rousseau's* history of love is, roughly, an account of the cultural and feminine prejudice that a single man in fortunate possession of a wealth of desire must be in want of a wife. This generally held prejudice is not a truth he acknowledges himself. *He* cleaves, in the name of nature, to a less domesticated vigour – to the vim and virility of the forces of desire. But Derrida's opening irony – if such it is – here holds at a distance Rousseau's disdainful and rather distasteful history of love. On the other hand, his words communicate telepathically with Rousseau's. We've seen '*tel*(*le*) *est*' crop up twice just a few pages before, in a quotation from a slightly earlier bit of the *Discours*: 'tel est le pur mouvement de la Nature' (such is the pure movement of nature), 'telle est la force de la pitié naturelle' (such is the force of natural compassion) (*DG* 246; *OG* 173; Rousseau, *Discours sur l'inégalité* 155). Such is the movement and force of writing and reading, télé-reading, remarking what has gone before in different accents, affectionately and with an altogether novel kind of love.

'Telle est' . . . 'tel é . . .' frame the paragraph I want to read here. I chose this paragraph because I love it; because its aphoristic energy inscribed it in my memory, detached – until I re-read it – from its context. It's a grand and awkward paragraph. It moves quickly, gathering, abstracting, synthesizing, translating and supplementing on the way, from the history of love, as told by Rousseau in his second *Discours*, to history *tout court* in its emergence and divergence from nature, to the supplement and its relationship to force, to the role of preference vis-à-vis force, to the *étonnement* – the astonishment – that marks the genesis of, and structures, Rousseau's thought.

The language of force comes in through Rousseau's mention of the spontaneous and indifferently oriented 'énergie' of physical desire, which in human society is hijacked by the cultural and 'moral' codes of love that bind it to an 'objet préféré'. Derrida's unfolding of this history in terms of force explicates once more the logic of the supplement, the late-coming addition that is also a necessary condition. Force in Rousseau's account is natural and undifferentiated, a spontaneous and unchecked overflow of powerful feeling, that disports itself no matter where. It only subsequently becomes channelled and bound, undergoes the agony of choice and decision. And what channels it cannot be thought about as being itself forceful, insofar as it is a mere representation, displacing force by parasiting it. Rousseau's account, though, is a wishful thinking, is itself a forcing. It has the kettle-logic coherence in contradiction, the wildly comic or utterly infuriating pig-headed persistence in having it all ways at once, that expresses the force of a desire. Force cannot be indifferent, ever, for it only gets its edge by its resistance to what it is not.

It might seem, then, that in the propositional content of this paragraph Derrida describes and dispatches the economy of forces with a lofty dispassion. But that's not quite how he writes it:

On ne pourra jamais expliquer à partir de la nature et de la force naturelle que quelque chose comme la différence d'une *préférence* puisse, sans force propre, forcer la force (One can never explain, in terms of nature and natural force, the fact that something like the difference of a *preference* might, without any force of its own, force force). (*DG* 253; *OG* 178)

This is the sentence I really love, in spite, or perhaps because, of its odd neutrality. It is not certain to whom or to what this necessary preference belongs. *It* is not bound to a single theme, subject, object or genre, but rather comes first, preferred, borne before, before there is anyone there to do the preferring. And so the sentence seems to get carried away a bit, borne onwards by its echoing resonance (différence / *préférence*) and consonance (all those p's and f's!), till we get to 'forcer la force', the little accent that is what tips and orients force, and gets it going.

But if this preference, the bias force comes in on, cannot be owned, it can nevertheless give rise to a body of work, by skewing and styling it. It is his astonishment by and at the barely-there force of this preference, and his explicatory *impuissance* before it, that gives both force and form, genesis and structure, to Rousseau's thinking: 'Un tel étonnement donne tout son élan et toute sa forme à la pensée de Rousseau' (Such an astonishment gives all its oomph and all its form to Rousseau's thought) (*DG* 253; *OG* 178, trans. mod.). 'One [*on*]' can never explain, but then this 'on' itself can only ever come in on a bias, a bit eccentrically, accented and inflected minutely differently – viz 'an' and 'en'. 'On' can never explain, but preference is always signed, *en avant*: *différence, préférence, étonnement, pensée, élan* – the accents of **Jean,** remarked by Jacques, in the thinking of Rousseau.

PEGGY KAMUF, BEING-IN-NATURE (*OG* 186; *DG* 264–5)

Unlike the key lexicon of supplementarity, out of which Derrida draws both the main axes of his reading of Rousseau's text and, through a far-reaching generalization of this example, the displacement of the metaphysical, historical obliteration of *differance*, the lexicon of habitation is never given, by that name, a leading role in the analyses. This is despite its playing a part that is perhaps somewhat analogous to the important role Rousseau and, in turn, Derrida assign to the imagination, namely, as the virtual faculty that awakens all the others by first awakening itself. Here, for example, is Derrida commenting on a passage from *Émile* in which Rousseau evokes the self-starting capacity of imagination to awaken itself and thereupon the other sleeping faculties, most important of which is pity, the opening to 'the suffering of the other as other':

> One will have noticed [. . .] that the imagination that excites the other virtual faculties is none the less itself a virtual faculty: 'the most active of all'. And that therefore this power to transgress nature is itself in nature. It is part of the natural fund of resources. Better: we will see that it holds the reserve in reserve. This being-in-nature thus has the strange mode of being of the supplement; it designates both the excess and the lack of nature *in* nature. It is upon the meaning of *being-in* that we locate here, as upon one example among others, the trembling of a classical logic. (*OG* 186; *DG* 264–5, trans. mod.)

The 'trembling of a classical logic', which is shaken in that distinction of inside from outside on which all its other conceptual distinctions depend, takes place on the site of the meaning of being-in. Rousseau situates imagination 'in' nature – it is, he insists, a natural faculty, although he does not extend it to the nature of other living beings – but it is 'in' in 'the strange mode of being of the supplement' to what is lacking 'in' nature. The meaning of being-in trembles with this awakening of imagination to itself as to its outside. In a parallel manner, we saw Derrida evoke in-habitation (with a hyphen now to mark this spacing of difference within) as what can awaken to itself as a certain way of in-habiting that shakes up the very structures housing it (see *OG* 24).

CLARE CONNORS, *DYNAMIS* AND *ENERGEIA* (*OG* 187; *DG* 265–6)

There's a theory of latency lurking in Rousseau which remains latent in all the scholarship about him, insofar as it is 'misrecognized' (*méconnu*) by it. Scholars have, indeed, *remarked* it. Derrida mentions Durkheim and Derathé. But the work it does has been misread or underestimated. Derathé – in the passage to which Derrida points us in his footnote (*OG* 342 n. 20) – suggests, for example, that it is the theory of a 'faculté virtuelle' which allows Rousseau to 'rester d'accord avec lui-même', to remain in agreement or accord with himself (Derathé 148). That lovely phrase notwithstanding, virtuality here is triumphantly named as the idea that keeps the succession between nature and society in place, and Rousseau consistent in his theories, against the apparent evidence. Nature is imagined as a reserve, a pent-up *puissance, potentially* social, else it could never *become* social, but not *actually* social, else it wouldn't be natural. Nature is lured beyond itself and made social by imagination. This is the 'accomplishment of a *dynamis*' that Derrida names. But – so his commentary goes – imagination is itself in Rousseau a natural and virtual property, and so the question – whence originates the social? – risks simply being displaced.

At issue here is philosophy's powerlessness in the face of possibility, potential and *dynamis*. From Aristotle to Rousseau and beyond, *dynamis* and *energeia*, power and act, potentiality or possibility and actuality, force and its effects, lead inexorably from one to the other. *Of Grammatology* holds the pair apart for a long while – from page 187 to 311, or page 266 to 439 in the French. This protension – *dynamis* . . . wait for it . . . *energeia* – mimes what the terms name, *dynamis*'s orientation towards a telos at which it will eventually arrive, effacing itself as it comes into being, making itself present. The orientation and thinking of *dynamis* 'undoubtedly has for its function, for Rousseau in particular and within metaphysics in general, the systematic predetermining of becoming as production and development, evolution or history' (*OG* 187). Any attempt to know or to theorize potential abrogates it a priori, insofar as, by establishing what it is, it renders it actual and thus rends its potential.

In a sense, then, *dynamis* can only be *méconnu*, badly known, mis-recognized and missed. And yet we can still imagine it. Imagination, for Rousseau, as Derrida conjures him in these pages, has an extraordinary property (another translation of *dynamis*). It is the only power capable of bringing itself into the world, of imagining *itself* into being, making itself up as it goes along. This is, of course, impossible, a romantic dream, 'pure auto-affection' par excellence, or, to gloss a bit Byronically, a frigging of the imagination. But it's a dream that the experience of reading, and of reading *Of Grammatology*, allows us to bear and to bear with, an entertaining of the impossible. For John Keats, 'the imagination may be compared to Adam's dream – he awoke and found it truth' (*Letters* 37). For Jean-Jacques Rousseau, quoted by Jacques Derrida, right at the end of *Of Grammatology*, imagination and what it dreams up are less certain to make this passage to actuality. Doing what others fail to do, he gives his dreams as dreams, and leaves 'the reader to discover whether there is anything in them which may prove useful to those who are awake' (*OG* 316). Like the 'philosophical *dynamis*' which, in his interview with Derek Attridge in *Acts of Literature*, Derrida describes as a property of 'literature and poetry' rather than of philosophy, this is a *dynamis* which can 'be developed only in response' ('This Strange Institution' 45–6).

3.2 IMITATION

ANN SMOCK, *ESTAMPE* (OG 208–9; DG 296–7)

Estampe means print, stamp or engraving – very often a copy of an original artwork. Also a tool for imprinting (a stamp). Rousseau is so confident that signs are effective not on their own but strictly via what they express (that which they imitate or convey) – he is so sure we are moved by the thing, or better, the passion that is exposed, and not at all affected by the outward exposition – that he says what touches us in a painting is what would touch us just as much in a print (*une estampe*) (*OG* 208–9; *DG* 296–7). It follows that an engraving of a painting is at least as good as the original and that indeed the very essence of painting is really nothing but what lends itself to being reproduced. The copy, then, is art's model; the possibility of the print is the origin of art, which means that art's death and art as death are mixed up in the birth of the work and entangled with the principle of life. This is one of Derrida's swiftest and most telling demonstrations of the justice Rousseau's text does to exactly what he does not wish to say.

The stamp has an interesting development in Derrida's work. I think it belongs among the multiple puns and other plays on words that spread across his *oeuvre* not only helping to locate writing where it isn't traditionally supposed to be (as in the passage from *Grammatology* just cited), but also attributing to it (to the letter, the mark, the imprint) a musical ring and indeed to the vital depletion that launches and sustains the living word a specifically vocal resonance.

For example, the stamp reappears as *timbre* in *La Carte postale*: postage stamp, and also label or seal, official mark on an authenticated document – such as an invoice – and the instrument used to print the mark, and then too a little drum or bell, and also a resounding voice (*voix timbrée*) – if not a slightly crazy one (*voix timbrée*). Quite regularly in *La Carte postale timbre* designates the particular character or quality of a vocal sound (apart from its pitch or intensity). 'And often I cease paying attention to what you say [on the phone] so that the timbre might resonate all by itself, as in a language all the closer for being foreign and incomprehensible to me' ('Envois' 19; 24, trans. mod.). 'So it's this timbre you address to me, with no message, none other that counts' ('Envois' 15; 11, trans. mod.).

Philately has to do with *atéléia*, we read: acquittal of a charge. Whence the stamp (*timbre*): an official indication payment has been made. Unless the stamp exempts from paying. For to stamp, to frank – *affranchir* – is to free from a charge, dissolve an obligation. A stamp, in other words, is never just one; philately is stamp *collection*. And it is love (*philos*, friend) – it is love of the stamp with or without it. Love of the bond that also unbinds and by dismissing engages. It is love with or without love – stamped and validated conjugal love ('l'amour timbré'), or 'l'amour timbré', crazy love.

What is all this – this love, 'our' love, with or without? Nothing that is (*est*); instead it remains (*reste*). Or would – having the virtue of music. 'What would remain of us [*ce qui resterait de nous*] has the force of music' ('Envois' 32; 37, trans. mod.). And, 'there remains but the song [*ne reste que le chant*], it is reborn every time, nothing can do anything against it and I love only the song, in the song' ('Envois' 43; 49, trans. mod.).

GEOFFREY BENNINGTON, FRACTAL GEOGRAPHY
(*OG* 216–18; *DG* 309–12)

Deconstruction is fractal. As in a Julia set, for example, an arbitrarily small segment of the curve is sufficient to generate the whole. The deconstructive equivalent of this is that according to the general 'logic' or *graphic* of the trace, and its more special instantiation in the graphic of the supplement, every trace is the trace of a trace, and

every supplement is the supplement of a supplement. A further speci-
fication of this graphic would have supplements always generating
representations or stories about themselves (like the smaller, always
slightly displaced versions of itself contained in the so-called Mandelbrot set), about what and how they supplement, even if those stories
or representations take the form of denial, repression or some other
less acute version of avoidance. Such stories are part of the 'what of
the signifier *gives itself out as* a [. . .] signified', (*OG* 160; *DG* 229,
trans. mod.) often part of the 'intended meaning' of the text, what it
declares if not always what it *describes* (to use the *Grammatology*'s
most common pair of terms for this), what it claims if not always what
it does, *how it reads itself,* if not always how it can most interestingly
be read. So, for example, towards the very end of the *Grammatology*,
and itself readable as an unmarked supplement to the more famous
'Exorbitant: Question of Method' section, in presenting Rousseau's
account of the festival, the *fête,* which he is opposing to the theatre,
Derrida says that Rousseau interprets the *fête* in terms of an absence
of *play* if not an absence of *games*:

> There are indeed *games* [jeux] in the public festival, but no *play*
> [jeu], if one understands under that singular the substitution of
> contents, the exchange of presences and absences, chance and
> absolute risk. [. . .] At any rate, play is so much absent from the
> festival that dance is admitted into it as initiation into marriage
> and contained within the closure of the ball. Such at least is the
> interpretation to which Rousseau, in order to fix it prudently,
> subjects the meaning of his text on the festival. One could make
> it say something very different. (*OG* 307; *DG* 433, trans. mod.)

We could have it or make it say something very different: how? Well,
by taking into account the general structures of trace and supplement
that are what allow us to *read* rather than merely *decipher* (or even
interpret). So now the general, 'theoretical' justification of the possibility, in reading, of having a text also saying something other than
what it says:

> And Rousseau's text must ceaselessly be considered as a complex,
> layered structure: in it, certain propositions can be read as inter-
> pretations of other propositions that we are, up to a certain point and
> with certain precautions, free to read otherwise. Rousseau says A,

then for reasons that we must determine, interprets A as B. A, which was already an interpretation, is reinterpreted as B. After taking note of that fact we can, without leaving Rousseau's text, isolate A from its interpretation as B and discover in it possibilities and resources in it that indeed belong to Rousseau's text, but have not been produced or exploited by him, which, for reasons that are also legible, he *preferred to cut short* by a gesture that is neither conscious nor unconscious. (*OG* 307; *DG* 433–4, trans. mod.)

Rousseau's version of the *fête* is also a story, not necessarily just a bad story, about the management of textuality itself, of how to deal with the possible proliferation of, for example, the 'substitution of contents'. And it turns out that Rousseau's work is full of such stories, is really nothing but itself a proliferation of stories about how to handle or manage proliferation, substitution and supplementation, in other words, how to manage or handle textuality 'itself', the writing that is most obviously a 'supplement of the supplement' (*OG* 281, 295, 298) and the treatment of which motivates the focus the *Grammatology* as a whole places on the 'age of Rousseau' as an age where a certain Cartesian-type self-presence needs to be shored up against the threat of writing (*OG* 98–9). Whatever Rousseau's ostensible subject, it turns out that he is always trying to read the text he has written in spite of himself, the textuality into which he has fallen in one or other of his very many 'fatal instants', of which the emblematic one would be the moment of falling into writing itself on the road to Vincennes (see the beginning of Book VIII of the *Confessions*), constantly trying to catch up with that textuality and close it back off into a consistent totality no longer available for further reading, or for any reading other than the reading it provides of itself (for any interpretation of A other than B), with the dramatic turn that once the fall into textuality has happened, even silence makes more text and lends itself to reading (see the preface to the *Lettre à d'Alembert*). Our 'freedom to read otherwise', limited though it may be by what Derrida often calls 'prudence', is what drove Rousseau (rather literally) mad.

A peculiar instance of this structure (which is, then, absolutely generalizable, and not just in Rousseau) shows up in the 'Essay on the Origin of Languages' and its fantastic, phantasmatic geography. Rousseau, according to the most commonly used description in the *Grammatology*, 'declares' one thing (that language has *one* absolute origin point in passion, and therefore in the South), but 'describes' another (that languages are always differentially structured by a structure with *two* poles of attraction: passion and need, South and North). Here is the passage:

> We are thus brought back to discourse as supplement. And to the structure of the Essay (origin of language, origin and degeneracy of music, degeneracy of language) which reflects the structure of language not only in its becoming but also in its space, in its disposition, in what may literally be called its *geography.*
>
> Language is a structure – a system of oppositions of places and values – and an *oriented* structure. Let us rather say, only half in jest, that *its orientation* is *a disorientation.* We can call it a *polarization.* Orientation gives direction to the movement by relating it to its origin as to its orient. And it is on the basis of the light of the origin that one thinks of the West, the end and the fall, cadence or deadline, death or night. Now according to Rousseau, who appropriates here a very banal opposition in the [eighteenth] century, language *turns,* so to speak, as the earth turns. Here neither the orient nor the occident is privileged. The references are to the extremities of the axis around which the earth *turns* (*polos, polein*) and which is called the *rational* axis: the North Pole and the South Pole.
>
> There will be neither a historical line nor an immobile picture of languages. There will be a *turn* of language. And this movement of culture will be both ordered and rhythmed according to what is most natural in nature: the earth and the season. Languages are *sown.* And they themselves pass from one season to another. The division between languages, the sharing out, in the formation of languages, between the systems turned toward the North and the systems turned toward the South – that interior limit already leaves its furrow in language in general and each language in particular. Such at least is our interpretation. Rousseau *would like* the opposition between southern and northern to place a *natural* frontier between several types of languages. However, what he *describes* forbids us from thinking it. That description allows us to recognize that the opposition north/south – being rational and not natural, structural and not factual, relational and not substantial – traces an axis of reference *inside* each language. No language is from the south or the north; no real element of the language has

an absolute situation, only a differential one. That is why the polar opposition does not divide up a set of already existing languages; it is described, though not declared, by Rousseau to be the origin of languages. We must measure this gap between the description and the declaration.

What I shall loosely call the polarization of languages repeats within each linguistic system the opposition that allowed emergence of language from nonlanguage to be thought: the opposition of passion and need and the entire series of connotative significations. Whether from north or south, every language in general springs forth when passionate desire exceeds physical need, when imagination is *awakened,* which awakens pity and gives movement to the supplementary chain. But once languages are constituted, the polarity need/passion, and the entire supplementary structure, remain operative within each linguistic system: languages are more or less close to pure passion, that is to say more or less distant from pure need, more or less close to pure language or pure nonlanguage. And the measure of that proximity furnishes the structural principle of a classification of languages. Thus the languages of the north are *rather* languages of need, the languages of the south, to which Rousseau devotes ten times the space in his description, are *rather* languages of passion. But this *description* does not prevent Rousseau from *declaring* that the one group is born of passion, the other of need: the one group expresses *primarily* passion, the other expresses *primarily* need. In southern lands, the first discourses were songs of love, in northern countries 'the first word . . . was not *love me* [aimez-moi] but *help me* [aidez-moi]'. If one took these declarations literally, one would have to judge them to be contradictory both with the descriptions and with other declarations: notably with the one that excludes the possibility of a language arising out of pure need. But although they are not merely apparent, these contradictions are regulated by the desire to consider the functional or polar origin as the real and natural origin. Not being able simply to accept the fact that the concept of origin has merely a relative function within a system situating in itself a multitude of origins, each origin capable of being the effect or the offshoot of another origin, the north capable of becoming the south for a more northern site, etc., Rousseau would like the absolute origin to be an absolute south. It is on the basis of this schema that the question of fact and principle, of real and ideal origin, of genesis and structure in Rousseau's discourse must be asked anew. This schema is undoubtedly more complex than is generally thought.

One must here take into account the following necessities: the south is the place of origin or the cradle of languages. Given this, the southern languages are closer to childhood, nonlanguage, and nature. But at the same time, being closer to the origin, they are purer, more alive, more animated. On the other hand, the northern languages are distant from the origin, less pure, less alive, less warm. In them one can follow the progress of death and chill. But here again, what is unrepresentable is the fact that this distancing brings closer to the origin. The northern languages lead back to that need, to that physics, to that nature to which the southern languages, which had just left it, were in the closest possible proximity. Again the impossible design, the unbelievable line of the supplementary structure. Although the difference between south and north, passion and need, explains the origin of languages, it persists in the constituted languages, and at the limit, the north comes back to the south of the south, which puts the south to the north of the north. Passion animates need more or less and from the inside. Need constrains passion more or less, and from the inside. This polar difference should rigorously prevent the distinction of two series simply exterior to one another. But we know now why Rousseau is determined to maintain that impossible exteriority. His text moves, then, between what we have called *description* and *declaration,* which are themselves structural poles rather than natural and fixed points of reference. (*OG* 216–18; *DG* 309–12, trans. mod.)

In the familiar terms of declaration and description, then, Rousseau declares one thing (the origin of language takes place in an absolute south), and describes something a little different (all languages are struck by a 'polar' tension between north and south, and their associated values), or describes the 'A' of a polar tension but interprets it as the 'B' of an absolute origin.

Before returning to the claim (the declaration) at the end of the passage that the relation between declaration and description is *itself* quasi-geographical, a polar structure of attraction rather than a simple oppositional classificatory pair, let's take a moment to wonder about (and indeed at) the bizarre outcome of Rousseau's *description* (as it undermines or deconstructs his *declaration*), and more especially about what in it merits Derrida's characterization of it as 'unrepresentable' (see too *OG* 211, 271). At the origin of language, humans emerge from an animality defined as pure need into a humanity defined as the possibility of passion. The pure passionate origin of language (which is more song than talk) is thus absolutely close to the other (mere animal need) from which it will most vigorously be distinguished. As language moves north, it gets further away from that origin (passionate song) and takes on characteristics that are not fully spelled out in the passage, but which are described at length elsewhere in the reading, all of which tend towards the pole of need (harshness, consonants, articulation, writing). But by the same token, as it were, that distancing from the origin also, simultaneously and 'unrepresentably' brings language back towards that origin (or that origin's origin or pre-origin), in that pure need is just what immediately precedes the pure passion that is the origin of language. Perhaps with Heidegger's *Entfernung* in mind, Derrida reads Rousseau describing (against his declarations, then), though not representing (it is 'unrepresentable'), a contradictory possibility of nearing and distancing at the same time. The further north we go, the further from the south, the closer we get to the south from which we are taking our distance. This unrepresentable, contradictory character would be definitive of supplementarity, indeed its very non-linear 'graphic'.

This extra turn in the description of supplementarity seems to go a little farther than Rousseau's explicit 'description' as opposed to his 'declaration'. If Rousseau interprets A as B, Derrida does not simply restate A, but interprets it as C. For Rousseau nowhere explicitly describes a geography in which the south is to the north of the north and the north to the south of the south. This, then, seems to be Derrida *reading* Rousseau (he still calls it 'interpretation' in the passage, but my suggestion is that there is good reason to link this with what at the beginning of Chapter VII of *Speech and Phenomena* is said to be 'neither commentary nor interpretation', a reading *through* (à travers) the text (88; 98)). And this supplementary turn in the exposition of the logic of supplementarity seems to go further (or to be 'more powerful', as Derrida often says, a little mysteriously) than a mere 'polar' structure, and thus more powerful too, methodologically speaking, than the much-used pair of declaration and description itself, which is, strikingly, described at the end of the passage as being *itself* a polar structure.

It looks as though the reason for this possibility is still legible in Rousseau's text. For although Derrida is clearly correct in saying that what matters in Rousseau's description is not the classical passage from East to West, but a non-oppositional relation of north and south, it seems as though Rousseau's 'geography' is not in fact exactly polar either. The clearest way to put this is probably to point out that Rousseau's 'absolute South' is not, after all, the South pole, but somewhere more in the middle, more literally *Mediterranean.* On the terrestrial globe, there is an awful lot of south to the south of that 'absolute south'. Rousseau's geography, in fact much more quadratic than hemispheric, maps the globe from somewhere towards the middle towards one of the poles, from an origin towards a north: but one might imagine that if Rousseau (or world-history as available to him) had explored south of the equator, then moving south from the south would have looked somewhat similar to going north from the south in the description he actually gives. This hypothesis gives more immediate plausibility to the paradoxical structure whereby the north can be said to be south of the south, and the south north of the north, in that now the 'polar' relation of north and south has become a relation between an equator (what Rousseau calls 'south') and *either* pole. In Rousseau's geography, moving away from the origin means moving polewards, and therefore towards the cold.

This strange structure might, of course, simply be a result of spherical geometry, which itself presents a number of peculiarities that might be summed up by the proper name 'Reimann'. In a certain sense (though most obviously at the poles, precisely) it is always only possible to move in one direction from any point on a sphere: if you are standing at the North Pole, every direction is south, and if you are standing at the South Pole, every direction is north. Rousseau's description has in fact displaced the 'polar' structure by arbitrarily assigning a pseudo-pole (what in French he calls the 'midi') from which all directions are called 'north'. According to a logic that years ago intrigued me in Flann O'Brien (but that I did not then know was derived – a little fancifully, it is true – from actual mathematical propositions advanced by Theodor Kaluza in 1919 postulating the existence of a fourth (cylindrical) dimension of space, laying some distant foundations for string theory), this thought can be extended to the globe in general, so that on this view there is only one direction it is ever possible to take, and that one direction always returns one to the point of departure. Whatever the merits of this logic (which leads Flann O'Brien's character to conclude that the earth is not spherical at all, but 'sausage-shaped'), it does give a sense of the havoc that may be wrought by structures of supplementarity on common-sense understanding.

One might imagine that this 'unrepresentable' situation (though the so-called 'horn torus' might be an interesting approximation here) would have some impact on any future non-physical geography that counted on the simple sphericity of the globe, or even its straight-forward polarization. All of Derrida's more recent interest in *mondialisation* and his resistance to the Anglo-American term 'globalization' could be re-read from this point, as could his repeated references to the role played in Kant's cosmopolitanism of the spherical form of the earth's surface. More immediately, this very resource in the 'description' part of the description/declaration distinction must also complicate Derrida's characterization of *that* structure as 'polar'. Supplementarity, like *différance*, always in fact means something more and a little other than a field of tension organized around two poles of attraction: what Rousseau's impossible geography suggests is rather that the absolute south of declaration (the supposedly perfect coincidence of what I mean and what I say) is compromised by a 'description' that is not even a pole, but a movement (what I have been calling 'reading') that moves away from and back towards that 'origin' (which is merely 'somewhere where we are, in a text already') in a process of approximation that simultaneously gets closer to and further from what the text declares.

ANN SMOCK, ACCENTS (*OG* 212–16, 223–9; *DG* 303–9, 318–26)

'Accents' are the voice's changeable tones, its varying pitches and intensities. These modulations can cause us to say of a voice that it's altered (by fear, by joy, by grief . . .). Pascal Quignard, for example, speaks of the loveliest *altérations* into which emotion can pitch a voice, and likens these inflections to a sort of *age* tuning and changing the voice the way puberty changes a boy's (he calls the lowering of a young boy's register *l'affection* of his voice (*La Leçon de musique* 18)).

Accents, as Derrida demonstrates, are the part of melody that Rousseau, for his part, values, as opposed to harmony, because, precisely, accents express the passions and faithfully imitate nature (*OG* 212–16). 'Harmony' on the other hand (scales and calculated intervals) doesn't express or imitate anything. Harmony for Rousseau is analogous to colour in painting – colour considered as a graduated scale of tints, a chromatic sequence – whereas the contours of the shapes in the painting (the drawn part of it) correspond to melody: they are expressive and move us because they imitate the forms in Nature. Moreover the gamut of colours – that series of intervals – degrades the art of drawing, and just so do the accents of emotion that animate melody get deadened by harmony. Likewise 'articulations' threaten the tunefulness of speech – the intonations of the speaking voice that keep language in contact with song, its origin. The more articulation comes to characterize a tongue the more it lends itself to writing, giving up its music and departing its origin.

Derrida brings this system of corresponding relations into sharp focus: vocal accents are encroached upon by harmony in Rousseau just as drawing is by colour, the expressive voice by articulation and songlike speech by writing. But furthermore Derrida traces the twisty logic Rousseau must adopt to keep these symmetrical oppositions in place – the awkward manoeuvres he is obliged to introduce in order to avoid spoiling his design or better, as Derrida puts it, in order to avoid declaring the contraband his writing carries. For all the while he duly declares one thing, for example that articulation (the tendency in speech to give in to writing) *survient à l'origine* – falls upon our original tongue at some point from outside – in fact he describes how this becoming-writing *survient à l'origine*: happens right *at* the origin (*OG* 229; *DG* 325–6). Or again, while he declares that grammar with its cold, abstract rules impedes the heartfelt melody in speech, he nevertheless describes grammar's presence in melody *making possible* the tune which never could have warmed up without this chill. Thus the origin, whose live presence and plenitude Rousseau aims to affirm without fail, proves in his very words divided and deferred, while the process of decline – the general worse-ward drift he laments – turns out to be not just a loss but also a gain in vitality, a movement in two directions, not one. Rousseau's discursive intention appears to have smuggled in with it everything it takes to annul the thought of an unequivocal end as well as of an unambiguous beginning – teleology along with archeology.

But what of accents in Derrida? What of inflection, modulation – *altération, affection* – when language is understood to *arise* from an encroachment upon it and simply to *be* its becoming-writing?

It could be that this understanding of language is all about voice. Jean-Luc Nancy, in a footnote to a discussion of rhapsody, indicates that everything Derrida calls writing concerns what in his pages is called voice (*Le Partage des voix* 64). And a short piece that Derrida devoted to Roger Laporte's *Fugue* and its successor *Supplément* – 'Ce qui reste à force de musique' – suggests that his thought about writing cannot do without a musical vocabulary, to which, however (not that he employs it with gratifying assurance) he gives an unheard-of inflection ('What Remains by Force of Music').

Laporte's *Fugue* bears as an epigraph a dictionary definition of *fugue* which cites Rousseau: a fugue is a kind of counterpoint, we read, whose theme and its successive imitations seem ' "to flee and pursue one another" ' (*Fugue* 253). Indeed, as Derrida demonstrates from every angle, Laporte's writing is a pursuit of writing – which it keeps outstripping. Writing flees ahead and lags behind itself both, which is to say it has no 'itself', and is not properly anything, at least not anything the verb *to be* can capture, so that in it a question blinks: is there anything? Has anything happened? Struck by this uninterrupted alteration of nothing that ever has been, '*Fugue* is not nothing', Derrida states. He suggests it *remains* ('reste sans être'), and asks – asks, that's all – what relation this inexhaustible remainder without being bears to *affection*: to that which injects or infects itself and us with music ('s'affecte et nous affecte de musique') ('What Remains by Force of Music' 89; 104).

FORBES MORLOCK, THE COPYIST (*OG* 227–8; *DG* 323–5)

Rousseau's text.

To what extent is Part II of *Of Grammatology* a reading, and a reading of the 'Essai sur l'origine des langues'? Derrida's text never states that the 'Essai' – or Rousseau – is its text, but its weaving together of Rousseau's words and works suggests a textile construction. Its own practice, as it unpicks the heterogeneous threads of different texts, supplements both etymology and its understanding of Rousseau's practice: 'On each occasion one would notice: 1) That Rousseau weaves his text with heterogeneous threads' (*OG* 200; see also 14, 150, 159, 204, 221).

Of Grammatology tears Rousseau's text apart – into pieces and by disrupting the order of its argument. And at the same time it claims that that text was never anything but a (re)configuration of torn parts. 'As usual, Rousseau brings the borrowed pieces into play in a perfectly original organization. He cites and recites [*cite et récite*] of course here and there [. . .] [And] even when he does not cite, he draws from passages [*puise dans des passages*]' (*OG* 228; *DG* 324–5, trans. mod.). Rousseau's drawings, his method, would be his reader's own.

Certainly Derrida does not read the 'Essai sur l'origine des langues' in order: Chapter XX, its end, appears near the end of 'The Violence of the Letter', where Chapter V brings 'The Theory of Writing' (and the book) to a close. As a reader, Derrida performs enormous violence on the work (if not its letter). He takes great liberties with Rousseau's text – in the name of that text – and all the while continues faithfully to read.

The extent of Derrida's quotations from the 'Essai' suggests his making Rousseau's text his own. His reading of it involves writing out very nearly half of it. Only two of its twenty chapters escape the scribe's attention. Nor does the occasion (apparently – in 1967 – the most recent edition of the 'Essai' had been published by Belin in 1817) obscure the method (*OG* 338–9 n. 2). Derrida reads (and teaches himself and us to read) by writing, by writing out, by copying out in his own hand.

Hence his fascination with Rousseau's fascination with the figure of the copyist. As fidelity: 'The good copyist must resist the temptation of the supplementary sign'. To be set against the figure of the good copyist, though, is the fact that copyists as such are bad: 'Accents are, like punctuation, an evil of writing: not only an invention of *copyists* but of copyists who are *strangers* to the language which they transcribe' (*OG* 227). *Nous soulignons* – we underline, even faithful Derrida accents.

The combination of accent and economy, violence and fidelity, is *Of Grammatology*'s extraordinary challenge. In reading Rousseau's 'Essai', Derrida *rewrites* it in the senses of both copying it out and changing it. Rewriting, he repeats the text and, in this repetition, alters it: 'Writing, which would seem to fix language, is precisely what alters it; it changes not the words but the spirit' (*OG* 314; quoting

'Essai' 388, trans. mod.). The logic – like the words – is the 'Essai''s own. Derrida works through Rousseau.

CLARE CONNORS, ARTICULATION, ACCENT AND RHYME (*OG* 226–7; *DG* 321–3)

Derrida devotes these and surrounding pages to an unfolding and refolding of Rousseau's geographical account of the origin of languages; to the differences between the languages of the north and of the south; and the corresponding affiliations between these poles and the polarities of need and passion, articulation and accent, speech and song, speech and writing. I'd prefer not to reconstitute that elaboration as such.

But there's a remarkable moment in Derrida's reading when his writing goes wild. It comes when he's summing up the 'thèse centrale' of the 'Essai' about the generation of writing out of the articulation of a language. Starting with that articulating conjunction 'or' (now) which marks a break and the suturing of a new element – 'Or l'écriture est au nord' (Now, writing is at the North) (*DG* 321; *OG* 226, trans. mod.) – the writing begins to roil and mate with itself, in a frenzy of auto-affection or disaffection, generating itself out of itself – from 'or', to 'nord', 'force' and 's'efforcer' to 'mort' – and then that minute turn (a 'demi-tour' or u-turn, its accent almost inaudible to an English ear, though the writing helps us see it) that gives us 'tour'. The writing rings with rhymes and half-rhymes, eye-rhymes and ear-rhymes, assonances and consonances – 'mangée [. . .] rongés par les consonnes' (eaten [. . .] gnawed through by consonants) (*DG* 322; *OG* 226) – and some of them make themselves felt in English too – vigour, rigour (*OG* 226). These chimes are easy enough to hear, see and mark. But what are we to do with them?

Obeying the sleekly utilitarian dictates of close reading, we might want to put them to work, by exploring the work that they do, looking at how the sounds serve the sense. Work – the labour necessitated by the hard northern climes – does not lessen but represses and displaces passion, supplements it, staves off death through its own deathliness, defers it. Like the reality principle, it aims to give us pleasure, in time and given time, and also to return us as nearly as possible to quiescence, to a state where love rather than need prevails. The labour of close-reading has similar ends and aspirations, producing the unity of a reading from the diremption of the elements it explicates. And of course we don't have a choice about working, however much we might prefer not to. Work, we must know, if we have read *Of Grammatology*, is already at work, insofar as need operates within passion itself. There is no shirking work.

A 'close reading' then: One can see very quickly how the rhymes here, *as* rhymes, are generated out of the articulations which joint language, its divisions and sutures, its sameness and its differences. In this way Derrida's rhymes mime the articulations they describe, dramatizing them for us a little. As the writing unfolds out of itself, so it performs the upping of the ante – the 'plus . . . plus . . . plus . . . plus' – discussed. The more language is articulated, the more it lends itself to writing, and the more it therefore summons writing too – 'plus elle se prête à l'écriture, plus elle l'appelle. Telle . . .' (the more it yields to writing, the more it calls writing forth. This . . .) (*DG* 321; *OG* 226). In its flighted, self-delighting, articulate energy, *this* writing – *elle-même* – is true not so much to what Rousseau declares, the deathliness of writing, as to what he describes without wanting to – writing's own force and passion, its 'énergie passionn**elle**' (*DG* 340; *OG* 340).

This reading isn't untrue, exactly. But to *stop* there, as though that were the end and the truth of it, the pay-off from our labours – well that would itself be deathly, a headlong precipitation towards the signified, and effacement once more of the writing. The 'or' that resounds through Derrida's French is not (although it allows us to hear it) the English 'or' of logical alternatives: form or content, signifier or signified, passivity or activity, pleasure or meaning, accent or articulation, Derrida or Rousseau. It's a 'now' – not as temporal marker of a presence, but as a conjunction that involves us by summoning us, coming early to surprise us, in at the ear before there's any choice in the matter. And, if we listen, it's listen too – 'now, listen' – exigent because it button-holes us, but pleasurable because it holds us for a moment. Like a story-teller's now – 'now, once upon a time' – it marks a re-beginning, a let's begin-again, a break and a start, a let's read again. It names and appeals to (*appelle*) an intimacy and relation that it instantiates. This little nugget of golden 'or' isn't the profit from the work of reading, or the wages of hand-maidenly service. There's nothing to capitalize on here. But it's nevertheless something that we can pirate away as contraband, and treasure as the reminder of a consonance before clarity.

3.3 ARTICULATION

MICHAEL NAAS, BUTADES, THE INVENTION OF DRAWING AND THE 'IMMEDIATE SIGN' (*OG* 233–5; *DG* 333–4)

In a later section of *Of Grammatology* that revolves around a close reading of Rousseau's 'Essay on the Origin of Languages', Derrida evokes Rousseau's notion, his dream, as we will see, of an *'immediate sign'*. The term is used in a paraphrasing of Rousseau's conception of gesture as what would precede even speech. For if *Of Grammatology* traces the hierarchy and supposed priority of speech over writing in the Western philosophical tradition (including in Rousseau), there is also in Rousseau a desire to return to a moment before even speech, that is, to a 'language of gesture'. This would be the place for Rousseau of what might be thought of as an 'immediate sign'. But in his reading of Rousseau's 'Essay' Derrida questions the dream of such immediacy and the very possibility and meaning of an *immediate* sign. Notice in the following lines where Derrida is preparing us to read this passage on gesture from Rousseau the way in which this language of gesture is characterized in Rousseau's terms as a realm of liberty, immediacy, presence, selfsameness and muteness, the place of a 'sign without speech', as opposed to a realm of slavery, mediation, the infinite circulation of signs, articulation and difference.

> The mute sign is a sign of liberty when it expresses within immediacy; then, what it expresses and he who expresses himself through it are *properly* present. There is neither detour nor anonymity. The mute sign signifies slavery when re-presentative mediacy has invaded the entire system of signification: then, through infinite circulation and references, [. . .] the selfsameness [*propre*] of presence has no longer a place: no one is there for anyone, not even for himself. [. . .] As it is speech that has opened this endless movement [*l'abîme*] of signification – thus constantly risking the loss of signification – it is tempting to return to an archaeological moment, a first moment of sign without speech, when passion, beyond need but short of articulation and difference, expresses itself in an unheard of way [*voie inouïe*]: an *immediate sign*. (*OG* 233–5; *DG* 333–4)

Gesture would thus be, for Rousseau, a 'sign without speech', a 'mute sign', a gesture of the hand without any sound from the mouth.

But could such a sign really be as immediate and without difference as it pretends? Derrida's scepticism is conveyed simply by his characterization of gesture as what expresses itself in a *voie inouïe*, that is, literally, in a way that does without *ouïe*, without hearing, without sound, but *also* in a way that is unprecedented, incredible, unbelievable [*inouïe*]. A sign without difference or mediation would thus be this unprecedented, truly incredible thing: an *immediate sign* – a paradoxical, oxymoronic notion that Derrida draws attention to here by underscoring it. Derrida goes on to cite Rousseau from the 'Essay on the Origin of Languages' where this language of gesture is described and where we see Rousseau yielding to what Derrida called the 'temptation' to return to an 'archaeological moment':

> Although the language of gesture and spoken language are equally natural, still the first is easier and depends less upon conventions. For more things affect our eyes than our ears. Also, visual forms are more varied than sounds, and more expressive, saying more in less time. Love, it is said, was the inventor of drawing. It might also have invented speech, though less happily. Not being very well pleased with it, it disdains it; it has livelier ways of expressing itself. How she could say things to her beloved, who traced his shadow with such pleasure! What sounds might she use to render this movement of the magic wand? ('Essay' 248, cited in *OG* 234)

Neither Rousseau nor Derrida here identifies the precise origin of this tale of the invention of drawing, though a note by Victor Gourevitch in his edition of the 'Essay on the Origin of Languages' traces it back to Pliny the Elder who, in *Natural History* XXXV, speaks of a young Corinthian girl named Butades who would have invented the art of drawing by tracing the outline of her lover's face on a rock ('Essay' 248 n. 349). But Rousseau would have probably had in mind not only the story from Pliny but the many pictorial representations of Butades in the mid-eighteenth century. In *Memoirs of the Blind*, in fact, Derrida comments on two of these representations (Joseph-Benoît Suvée's *Butades or the Origin of Drawing* and Jean-Baptiste Regnault's *Butades Tracing the Portrait of Her Shepherd or the Origin of Painting*) in order to show how, in this tradition, 'the origin of drawing [. . .] give[s] rise to multiple representations that substitute memory for perception' (49–51). In other words, Butades can trace the outline or shadow of her lover on the rock or wall behind him 'only on the condition of not seeing, as if drawing were a declaration of love destined for or suited to the invisibility of the other'. What is essential here is that, for Derrida, the shadow being traced is already 'detached from the present of perception, fallen from the thing itself', already a kind of 'simultaneous memory', that is, at once an immediate perception of the shadow and *already* a memory of the absent lover. If one had any doubts about Derrida's intentions in *Of Grammatology*, this passage alone would be enough to dispel them. Though the outline of the lover would be as close as possible to the lover himself, the gap or difference between the two is enough to call into question the possibility of what Derrida, parsing Rousseau, calls an 'immediate sign'. After analysing these two representations of Butades and the origin of drawing, Derrida in *Memoirs of the Blind* goes on to cite the very same passage from the 'Essay on the Origin of Languages' he had cited back in *Of Grammatology* and he sends the reader in a footnote back to that earlier analysis.

Now, after citing Rousseau in the passage of *Of Grammatology* that we have been reading here, Derrida picks up his own commentary, weaving critical questions about this 'language of gesture' into his paraphrase of Rousseau. According to Rousseau, he writes, '[t]he movement of the magic wand [this is, of the stick Butades uses to draw her lover's outline] that traces with so much pleasure does not fall outside of the body [*ne tombe pas hors du corps*]. Unlike the spoken or written sign, it does not cut itself off from the desiring body of the person who traces or from the immediately perceived image of the other'. The distance between the wand of Butades and her lover, or between the shadow of her lover and the lover himself, would thus be, Derrida adds, 'almost nothing', as the lover is 'almost present in person in his *shadow*'. But this *almost nothing* is, of course, not nothing, and this *almost present* is not presence. If Butades is indeed 'very close to touching what is very close to being the other *itself*, close by a minute difference [. . .] that small difference – visibility, spacing, death – is undoubtedly the origin of the sign and the breaking of immediacy' (*OG* 234). Rousseau's account of the language of gesture and his return to an 'archaeological moment' would thus be an attempt to think the sign by 'beginning from its limit', and 'this limit – of an impossible sign, of a sign giving the signified, indeed the thing, *in person*, immediately – is necessarily closer to gesture or glance than to speech'. What is marked off here by Derrida between hyphens is enough to call into question the rigour of Rousseau's distinction between gesture and speech and his claim that gesture can really be characterized in terms of 'liberty', 'immediacy', 'proper presence', the 'selfsameness of presence' and so on. For what Derrida characterized earlier in Rousseauian terms as an 'immediate sign' is now called, in his own voice, it seems, an 'impossible sign', that is, we might speculate, a sign that is possible only as impossible, that is, only as an illusion, phantasm or lure. When the signifier purports to give immediate access to the signified, when the sign – which cannot be thought without difference and articulation – claims to give immediate access to the thing itself, *in person*, then we know we have on our hands the phantasm of an original purity or presence that Derrida will attempt to draw attention to, make explicit, and, so to speak, deconstruct (*OG* 233–5).

PEGGY KAMUF, THE EYE AT THE CENTRE OF LANGUAGE (*OG* 238; *DG* 338–9)

So, how would this other way of inhabiting look? Not only how would it appear, but also how would it look at or look out upon the world it inhabits? The question is purposely ambiguous because, as we will see, the difference must also register as a difference for the eye, for looking and seeing, therefore. To inhabit in a certain deconstructive way – which is to say, an *ecographical,* if not *ecological,* but let us say, somewhat pleonastically for the moment, a *habitographical* way – may indeed mean something as obvious as opening an eye, as if upon waking from a long slumber.

I return to my hypothesis, namely that an important link in the signifying structure of Rousseau's text as read or produced by Derrida is a thinking of in-habitation in general and that this thinking is given a certain impetus by the particular situation accorded within that structure to 'l'habitation des femmes' (*OG* 155). In this hypothesis and without suspending its sexual significance, that phrase can also come to stand as a general designator of the exterior and inhabited space of others, everything that an economy of pure auto-affection – as represented, for example and perhaps par excellence, by Rousseau's self-awakening imagination – only imagines it can dispense with, which is to say, with everything. For the imagination to *s'éveiller,* awaken itself 'in the strongly reflexive sense' that Derrida says one must hear in Rousseau's language at that point (*OG* 187; *DG* 265), nothing can have come from an exteriority to space it out in a difference from itself – asleep/awake, virtual/actual, passive/active. This is at least what Rousseau means to say and what he declares. Derrida's productive reading, however, which plots the disjunction between the text's declarations and its descriptions, is able to open up gaps in the very reflexivity that declares a dispensation from inhabiting the exterior space of a world with others.

Indeed, this reading is stitched together by innumerable such moments of disjunction, but only two will interest me for the moment. Across a distance of fifty pages in the reading of the 'Essay on the Origin of Languages', they appear to wink at each other with their deployment of a similar figure, that of an eye, a single eye, opening onto an outside. Not only is it the same figure, but each is called up by a same dynamic in the 'Essay', which is the declared metaphoric origin of language.

In the first passage, the disjunction is plotted between, on the one hand, what Rousseau declares to be and wants to think as a distinction between passion and need and, on the other, what he describes as their unity in a supplementary differance. This disjunction is shown up by the 'Essay''s description of the advent or awakening of writing, which it situates, incoherently according to its own thesis, both before and after the birth of speech, as the instrument of both passion and need. Derrida explicitly compares this awakening of writing to that of the imagination as Rousseau had earlier described it:

How is writing, like pity for example, in nature and outside it? And, like that of the imagination earlier, what does the awakening [*l'éveil*] of writing mean if the latter belongs neither to nature nor to its other?

Writing precedes and follows speech, it comprehends it. [. . .] The first allusion to writing stands out of reach of all *distinction*, if not of all differance of need from passion. The advantage [*intérêt*] of writing demands a new conceptuality.

What happens is that the metaphoric origin of speech opens an eye, one could say, at the centre of language. And the passion that draws out [*arrache*] the first voices is related to the image. The visibility inscribed on the act of birth [*acte de naissance*: birth record or certificate] of the voice is not purely perceptual; it is signifying. Writing is the eve [*la veille*] of speech. (*OG* 238; *DG* 338–9, trans. mod.)

If one follows the parallel that Derrida signals between imagination and writing, then it is not merely a comparison that is put in place – writing awakens *like* imagination – but rather a substitution: imagination, which is to say writing, awakens as or through the inscription of an image that is not purely an object of perception because it also begins to signify something other than itself, a trace of another from outside the orbit of self-reflexive self-awakening. The inscription of the image-trace awakens also, originarily, in a transitive sense, even a violent one: 'Et la passion qui *arrache* les premières voix a rapport à l'image'. When set in proximity, as here, to an assertion concerning the metaphoric origin of speech, one should hesitate to understand the transitive violence of *arracher* as 'merely' a metaphor: to tear out, to rip out, said in particular of eyes, teeth, limbs, as well as figuratively of the heart, of confessions, of whatever is taken or given up only with great difficulty and pain. The awakening of writing, *l'éveil de l'écriture*, has thus a transitivity, which Derrida again conveys and even more clearly with his own striking image that 'opens an eye at the centre of language'. It is not that an eye opens there, of itself, but rather it is opened, forced or held open by the action of the metaphoric image-trace inscribing visibility on the birth certificate of speech. To this dense metaphoric pattern is added one more turn with the last phrase quoted: 'Writing is the eve, *la veille*, of speech', that is, also, writing *watches over*, *surveys* or *surveils* speech from that eye it opens at the centre of language; this metaphoric eye keeps watch – both in place of and on the lookout – *for* another, from a space that can never be located simply inside or outside the purview of the speaking subject.

Let us take a quick look at the other passage where a second occurrence of the image of the open eye echoes or rather winks at the first one. It comes as Derrida is introducing Rousseau's famous example, which will illustrate how it could happen that figurative speech preceded literal language or proper meanings. This example or this allegory begins: 'Upon meeting others, a savage man will initially have been frightened. His fear will have caused him to see these men as bigger and stronger than himself; he will have given them the name *giant*' ('Essay' 254, cited in *OG* 276; *DG* 391, trans. mod.). Derrida's analysis of Rousseau's claim and demonstration is phenomenologically precise and displays considerable respect for the *philosophe*'s own phenomenological acuteness, which is by no means not the only time that *Of Grammatology* marks a degree of admiration for Rousseau's accomplishment. Despite that, this key moment in the Essay's elaboration of its claim for the metaphoric origin of speech is no less a moment, once again, of disjunction between declaration and description, which opens a gap for the lever of Derrida's reading. In question is not only the difference between proper and figurative signs, but also between the motives of expression (of affect) and of designation (of an object), between the interiority of feeling or passion and the exteriority of a space in which others loom up suddenly on the horizon of one's habitation. Derrida's reading draws out how Rousseau's argument and example, even as they assert the figurative origin of language, 'maintain the proper: as *archē* and as *telos*. At the origin, because the first idea of passion, its first representative, is properly expressed. At the end, because the enlightened mind settles on the proper meaning'. But in this drive of the proper, from origin to end, is lodged necessarily and irreducibly an 'improper' wildness, which Derrida figures once again as 'an eye opening onto the outside':

Because speech does not dispense with reference to an object, the fact that 'giant' can be the proper sign of fear does not prevent, on the contrary it implies that it is improper or metaphoric as sign of the object. It cannot be the idea-sign of passion except by giving itself as idea-sign of the presumed cause of this passion, by opening an eye onto the outside. This opening allows the passage of a wild metaphor. (*OG* 276; *DG* 390–1, trans. mod.)

Within Rousseau's narrative, this event of wild metaphor will have been overcome and corrected by experience and the true knowledge it imparts ('After many experiences, he will have recognized that these so-called giants being neither bigger nor stronger than him'). But still that eye must remain open and therefore so must the always-possible, indeed necessary passage of the 'improper', which is to say referentiality in its essential and original metaphoricity. This is what 'a whole naïve philosophy of the idea-sign' obliged Rousseau – who is in this regard merely exemplary – to try not to see, to obliterate even as his writing 'sees' and describes it with that eye opened in the middle of its language (*OG* 277; *DG* 392, trans. mod.).

FORBES MORLOCK, THE SUBJECT OF
READING-4 (*OG* 240; *DG* 341)

'As we noted above, I can close my eyes, I can avoid being touched by what I see and what is perceptible at a distance' (*OG* 240, trans. mod.).

Eyes open and on the pronouns. What we are noting here was voiced differently earlier: 'One can *more naturally* close one's eyes or distract one's glance than keep oneself from listening' (*OG* 235–6, trans. mod.). We, I, one. *Je, nous, on* – these are the speaking parts of *Of Grammatology*. 'One' articulates a position, which the text will not avow as its own: thus, 'it may be objected [*on pourra objecter*]' (*OG* 339 n. 3; *DG* 212 n. 3). Against 'one's' objection, 'we' prevails . . . and coerces and seduces. Including at least the writer and his writing, 'we' calls the reader in, announcing what has happened in the reading and, hence, what will happen/will have happened to the reader. *Nous soulignons*. In 'our' underlining, the conjunction of writer and reader (like that of writing and reading) is effected and embodied in the text. 'Ours' is not the 'we' of the text, but a 'we' of which, without the text, there would be none.

And against 'our' rule, 'I' is the exception, the singular subject we are following through *Of Grammatology*. Of course, our 'rule' is not a set of rules – there is no specific grammar of *Of Grammatology*. No grammar to reading it, even as we must distinguish its 'I'-less voice from that of, say, *Speech and Phenomena* or *Writing and Difference*. No grammar to writing it, even as Derrida would recall the difference of its writing for the rest of his life: much later, speaking in the first person, he remembers saying to Marguerite, his wife, in the summer of 1965, ' "You know, I think something has happened" [. . .]. It was a moment, I had the feeling of an exceptional moment in fact in my, in my work, as if everything that could follow would simply follow, exactly, whatever happened' (Derrida and Dick, *Derrida*, Special Features/Derrida Interviews/Eureka, trans. mod.).

Let's not stare too fixedly at pronouns. Who or what reads, who or what reads differently in *Of Grammatology*? is also a question of passion. 'Sound touches us, interests us, impassions us all the more because it *penetrates us*. It is the element of interiority because its essence, its own [*propre*] energy, implies that its reception is obligatory' (*OG* 240; *DG* 341). Reading is an activity of the ear as well as the eye. Its silent sound occurs to us (*nous arrive*) without ever being wholly conscious, voluntary, or intentional – like the vision of commentary.

Of Grammatology touches and is touched by, interests and is interested by, impassions and is impassioned by Rousseau's text, all the more because it penetrates and is penetrated by that text. We can pursue the language of the *propre* – the clean and the self-identical, the proper and the proximate – as long as we hold that in reading there is also pleasure and pain. As long as we hold that there is affect in auto-affection and sexuality in the experience of touching-touched (*OG* 165, 167). (All of which may return us to childhood and the pages on Melanie Klein (in the voice of Marguerite Derrida's translation) (*OG* 88 and 333 n. 37).)

The magic of being read to as a child, the frustration and exhilaration of reading Derrida – how are we to invoke proximity without intimacy? The love of holding, the violence of being held, the violence of holding, the love of being held. Reading is reflexive without reciprocity. The 'I' and the ear. Close. Intimate – the transgression of this intimacy forever troubling the grammatical persons of its readers.

FORBES MORLOCK, THE SUBJECT OF READING-5 (*OG* 267; *DG* 376–7)

Close reading. You're close.

Nearness, proximity, intimacy before or beyond identity. Too close.

In the transgression of a love too close, 'it is always *as if* I had committed incest [*c'est toujours* comme si *j'avais commis un inceste*]' (*OG* 267; *DG* 377). 'As if I had committed incest' – the expression *itself* would be *incest itself* if some such thing – *itself* – could *take place* . . . But that is to anticipate.

We are in Chapter 9 of the 'Essai sur l'origine des langues'. And at the birth of society, in the time of the festival. 'The festival *itself* would be *incest itself* if some such thing – *itself* – could *take place* [. . .]. One is always short of or beyond the limit, the festival, the origin of society, that present in which the interdict is (would be) given simultaneously with the transgression' (*OG* 267, trans. mod.). The step across the limit, literally the transgression, has always taken and can never take place.

Again an 'I' appears in a paraphrase, but just this once it is almost a quotation. Nearly, unacknowledged, another's 'I'. The very first word of this part of the book hundreds of pages before is 'I' – Rousseau's own 'I', one of the more than two hundred that appear across the text. 'Part II: Nature, Culture, Writing' begins with an epigraph from the *Confessions*: 'I felt as if I had committed incest [*J'étais comme si j'avais commis un inceste*]' (*OG* 95; *DG* 143; Rousseau, *Les Confessions* 197, trans. mod.). *C'est toujours comme si j'avais commis un inceste.* We have made the step from 'j'étais' to 'c'est toujours' – and from 'je' to 'je'. Two hundred pages on, *Of Grammatology* gets ever more incestuously close to the text it reads.

Part II and the book end with a quotation from Rousseau, the *Émile*, and more of his 'I's': 'One will say that I too dream; I admit it, but I do what others fail to do, I give my dreams as dreams, and leave the reader to discover where there is anything in them which may prove useful to those who are awake' (*OG* 316; Rousseau, *Émile* 351 note, trans. mod.). Are theirs now one 'I'? Or – which may be the same thing – has a waking reader come to dream?

To give one's dreams as dreams, to give one's quotations as quotations, to give oneself as Rousseau (or Derrida) is possible only in a time without incest. Derrida the reader can leave his own reader to discover . . . only in a time – that impossible time – when writing is not (too closely related to) reading.

How are we, as if at its end, to read *Of Grammatology*? How are we to break into, which is also to break with and begin again, its incestuous cycle?

CLARE CONNORS, *PRESQUE* (OG 253; DG 358)

'Comme toujours, c'est la limite insaisissable du *presque*' (As always, it is the ungraspable limit of the *almost*) (*DG* 358; *OG* 253). Derrida is here writing, once again and still, about the limen between nature and society in the 'Essai', and between the 'Essai' and the *Discours* in Rousseau's thought. The *Discours* wants to mark the beginning, and so it sharpens up its purity. The 'Essai' essays something slightly different: it wants to make us sense the beginning , involve us right up close in the movement of its birthing, really to feel it. A bit later, breaking with this *presque* quite brusquely, Derrida will articulate the hard fact that 'no continuity from inarticulate to articulate, from pure nature to culture, from plenitude to the play of supplementarity, is possible' (*OG* 255). But here, in one paragraph, he insists thrice on it with his italics. The acute angle of these italics seems to sharpen up this ungraspable limit to its finest point, so that as we read it, it yearns towards us and touches us keenly. I'd like to translate it as 'nearly': an approximation doomed always to fall just shy of what it approaches, that can – at almost the same time – also be heard as what is dearest, *most* near.

TIMOTHY CLARK, CLIMATE AND CATASTROPHE: A LOST OPENING? (*OG* 255–68; *DG* 361–78)

Of Grammatology has fed one what has become in the twenty-first century one of the greatest difficulties for an emerging environmentalist literary and cultural criticism: that while the degradation of the planet accelerates, the term most crucial to its defence, 'nature', has been increasingly criticized as incoherent. Jhan Hochman argues that in deconstructing the logocentric concept of nature in Rousseau and 'the "age" of Rousseau' Derrida only strengthened the attitudes implicated in environmental destruction (*OG* 97).

> Deconstruction, in *Of Grammatology*, participates in a conspicuously luxurious and over-generalized metaphysics at a time when the majority of the fifth [the nonhuman] world is suffering under leaden oppression and constant threat from the four worlds of culture. (Hochman, *Green Cultural Studies* 170)

Hochman's argument seems questionable. His real target seems to be a lax version of Derrida related to forms of constructivism and culturalism that engaged the natural world only in destructively blinkered terms, as merely as a 'construct' of culture. Nevertheless, to think of *Of Grammatology* in relation to the intellectual challenge posed by the environmental crisis may still cast it in a new light.

Let us to turn to Hochman first, however. At issue for him is partly the following passage:

> The supplement [human imagination, culture] to Nature is within Nature as its play. Who will ever say if the lack within nature is *within* nature, if the catastrophe by which Nature *is separated from itself* [producing culture] is still natural? A natural catastrophe conforms to laws in order to overthrow the law. (*OG* 258; the additions in square brackets are Hochman's, but the emphases are in the original)

Hochman argues that in using the term 'culture' to name a de-essentializing element always at work as a sort of 'catastrophe' in 'nature', a kind of 'arche-culture' akin to an 'arche-writing', Derrida made a strategic error, projecting a falsely reductive concept of nature. He continues:

> Though Derrida is perspicuous, on epistemological grounds, to maintain Nature and culture as not mutually exclusive – culture as part of and within Nature and Nature involved in culture – nature and culture can, and at times, should be thought of as distinct primarily for this reason: *while culture is a subset of worldnature, worldnature is not a subset of culture.* (169)

Hochman's summary of Derrida's reading of Rousseau is dubious. He seems to mistake Derrida's reading of the economy of the concepts of culture and nature in Rousseau's texts in favour of the direct and sweeping claim that Derrida argues 'for a parity between nature and culture' per se. He reads 'culture' in a narrowly anthropological/ empirical sense, as opposed to its engaging a realm of the 'artificial' beyond the human, and he overlooks how it relates to earlier sections of *Of Grammatology* on the *graphe* and arche-writing as structurally neces- sary to the existence and functioning of any kind of informational or energy exchange, such as the metabolism of all living things. Neverthe- less, might Hochman's environmentalist indignation, for all its crudity of argument, still suggest new questions of *Of Grammatology*?

In relation to this huge issue some elements of *Of Grammatology* can look different in potentially provocative ways. Put it this way: what if Derrida had chosen as his strategic focus not 'writing' but a workably analogous term that did not have 'writing's' initial and potentially misleading implication of an exclusively human/cultural reference, for example 'reproduction', 'replication' or 'duplication'? The characteristics of Derrida's 'writing' are also precisely those of biological, physical, informational or genetic systems, of cell-division, protein creation, DNA/RNA etc. In this respect the logocentric den- igration of 'writing' is also a fantasy of human autonomy at odds with its incalculable physical and informational embeddedness in tangled networks of chemical and energy exchange, both microbiological, chemical and meteorological – in effect an *'originary environmentality'*. In some ways 'originary environmentality' might seem a stronger term of deconstruction than 'originary trace'. Its immediate inference is multi-dimensional, a circle or environing sphere of relations, whereas 'trace' still suggests a residually linear figure, a trail, marked line or path. Of 'supplementarity' Derrida writes:

> [T]his property [*propre*] of man is not a property of man: it is the very dislocation of the proper in general: it is the dislocation of the characteristic, the proper in general, the impossibility – and therefore the desire – of self-proximity; the impossibility, and therefore the desire of pure presence. That supplementarity is not a characteristic or property of man does not mean only, and in an equally radical manner, that is not a characteristic or property; but also that its play precedes what one calls man and extends outside of him. Man *calls himself* man only by drawing limits excluding his other from the play of supplementarity: the purity of nature, of animality, primitivism, childhood, madness, divinity. (*OG* 244)

While arguing that 'the absolute present [and] Nature [. . .] have never existed' (*OG* 159) *Of Grammatology* also contains a latent if undeveloped argument that what Hochman terms '*worldnature*' be reconceived as the play of supplementarity – 'The supplement to Nature is within Nature as its play' (*OG* 258). Yet one must be wary here: what is actually at issue is more accurately 'what Rousseau terms "Nature"' and 'what Rousseau terms "catastrophe"', and the supplementary logic which these concepts both generate and follow despite themselves. Derrida's text shows that to try to posit nature as some stable, self-identical foundational presence is actually also to concede or affirm such nature as supplementary 'play'. By implication then, for any thinker to assert hard and fast distinctions, placing nature on the one side and culture on the other, is not a matter of 'scientific' fact or discovery, but rather of kinds of performative and juridical engagement, matters of decision that cannot be fully justified. It becomes, as Paul de Man writes of Rousseau's own 'social contract': 'a complex and purely defensive verbal strategy by means of which the literal world is given some of the consistency of fiction, an intricate set of feints and ruses' (de Man, *Allegories of Reading* 159).

Clearly, to view history as essentially a matter of human agency, with the non-human appearing only in the guise of context, instrument, aberration or the contingent, would be to project a dogmatic ontological/teleological cut-off point constituting the border of the human and non-human. This element of *Of Grammatology* challenges any dogma of human exceptionalism and autonomy, while also deconstructing basic divisions constitutive of academic disciplines. *Of Grammatology* could not in principle respect the nature/culture distinction that normally separates the domain of 'history' from natural history, let alone from biology, genetics and geology – a perspective complementing the attention given to the incest prohibition in Rousseau and Lévi-Strauss as marking an aporia in the opposition of natural and cultural. Derrida opens here a space – if only briefly and formally – for thinking some of the philosophical ramifications of the human understood as a function of an interplay of multiple contexts and non-human agencies, in effect, of a deconstructive environmental history. Nevertheless this element of its argument seemed only adumbrated and, as I will argue, seems even to have been later forgotten by Derrida himself.

John McNeill writes: 'modern history, written as if the life-support systems of the planet were stable, present only in the background of human affairs, is not only incomplete but is misleading' (362). 'Environmental history' is a still relatively recent and ill-fitting newcomer in the academy. Prominent examples are McNeill's *Something New Under the Sun: An Environmental History of the Twentieth Century* (2000), Robert Marks, *The Origins of the Modern World: A Global and Ecological History* (2002) or Alfred W. Crosby's *Ecological Imperialism: The Biological Expansion of Europe 900–1900* (1986). Environmental history situates the vicissitudes of human societies in terms of many underconceptualized material events and contingencies, many of them all the more decisive for not falling within 'history' in terms of a realm of human representations and decisions – the insights of systems ecology, the contingencies of diseases and disease resistance, the chances of geography and climate in the domestication of plants and animals. Environmental history has none of metaphysical features of the anthropocentric concepts of history criticized in *Of Grammatology*, being neither linear, nor teleological, nor a matter of tradition as the development or accumulation of knowledge or culture. The list of genuinely significant historical agents thus soon extends itself beyond the human in a rather bewildering way: cotton grass competes with us for water, wheat replaces the native flora over large portions of the earth, rivers facilitate the growth of sedentary lifestyles, smallpox 'discovers America' etc. – 'world history, if done properly [. . .] expand[s] the theme of interactions to include *all* actors, not just human ones' (Holtz 11). Environmental history suggests that the agency of the human is far more circumscribed and saturated with illusion than one might suppose. What looks on one time scale like unqualified success – people living longer, more and more material wealth, an expanding population, increased use of resources, territorial expansion – could even appear on a larger scale as the upward sweep of a curve indistinguishable in crucial ways from, say, those tracing the cycles of population growth and collapse in field voles. The planet in its finitude acquires the force of an uncanny machine of which we are a part. The effect is no longer to take the opposition of 'culture' on one side and 'nature' on the other and to argue about the point or line of their differentiation, but to question the coherence of making any such distinction in the first place, and the anthropocentric fantasy that sustains it.

Environmental history of a kind is one of the stakes in the reading of Rousseau which Hochman does not pick up in the extract he quotes ('The supplement [human imagination, culture] to Nature is within Nature as its play. Who will ever say if the lack within nature is *within* nature, if the catastrophe by which nature *is separated from itself* [producing culture] is still natural?'). In fact, the 'catastrophe' referred to is not at all about 'culture' intervening in some previously intact state of nature. Rousseau is actually referring to a natural catastrophe, like an earthquake or hurricane. As part of his philosophical fable about a state of nature, Rousseau postulates that in earlier times the earth had had no seasons and existed in the stable condition of a perpetual spring. Only with a tilting of the planet's axis relative to the plane of its orbit did the seasonal variations of climate emerge. It was exposure to changes and extremes of weather which awakened human society out of the slumbers of a hypothetical barbaric state in whose equable climate no one would have been disposed to change. Derrida writes:

> The catastrophic origin of societies and languages at the same time permitted the actualization of the poetical faculties that slept inside man. Only a fortuitous cause could actualize natural powers which did not carry within themselves a sufficient motivation for awakening to their own end. Teleology is in a certain way external; it is this that the catastrophic form of archaeology signifies. (*OG* 257)

The passage quoted by Hochman started at this point. Derrida traces how Rousseau's reading/invention of the catastrophe props up the seeming coherence of his 'archeo-teleogic definition of nature' and human nature (*OG* 197). If, for Rousseau, the origin is truly a condition of self-presence then it should require no supplement, so the emergence of human culture, rationality etc., could arise only from an external intervention or catastrophe. By use of such an intervention Rousseau navigates the space between the two seemingly contradictory conceptions of nature in his work – between the concept of nature as origin and the teleological concept of a fully realized human nature achieved through culture and education, as in *Émile ou de l'éducation* (1762). For Rousseau climate, geography, etc. are understood as the making active of the previously merely potential – the human norm is already there, latent: it is a case of the various conditions which come to activate it. Derrida's argument of the supplement, however, must instead see the human as a function of the play of such contingencies – they would be far more than mere occasions. 'The supplement can only respond to the nonlogical logic of a game. That game is the play of the world' (*OG* 259).

This opens another issue that places Derrida's thinking within the horizon of environmentalist questions. With its meta-anthropological focus, *Of Grammatology* is striking for its projection of global contexts, its sense of the planetary or world history, of humanity as a species. Nevertheless, it does not encompass the crucial issue underlying so much environmental politics, that of the finitude of the earth. What is one to make of the fact that Derrida never engaged with what is surely the most significant event of the Twentieth Century – the emergence of the human species as a geological force, massively if often unwittingly changing the material fabric and operation of the planet in numerous ways? McNeill writes:

In time, I think, this will appear as the most important aspect of twentieth-century history, more so than World War II, the communist enterprise, the rise of mass literacy, the spread of democracy, or the growing emancipation of women. (McNeill 40)

Environmental feedback effects such as climate change have been making human actions and projects increasingly resemble communication in an imponderable echo chamber which immediately distorts, blurs or misconstrues what was said or meant, drowning it in the increasing volume of its own noise. Technology and energy use become skewed by meteorological, chemical and geological side-effects working according to their own incalculable logics. Non-human agency intervenes increasingly with all kinds of deconstructive effects.

What is both opened and then closed in Derrida's reading of Rousseau is how the line drawn between the human and its others is disputable and variable, as is the line between that causality which lies in the domain of human intentionality in some form (intention, cultural conflict and misunderstanding, etc.) and natural causality (climate, disease, the behaviours of other animals). Perhaps, because Derrida's thinking largely took the form of close textual readings that worked by extrapolating/undermining the thinking of others, he necessarily reproduced in choice of subject-matter and field the demarcations between the disciplines enacted in those texts, even if his thought implicitly undermined the borders maintaining their disciplinarity. *Of Grammatology*, in its close readings of Lévi-Strauss and of Rousseau, works within the terms of anthropocentric conceptions of history in practice even while thoroughly undermining them in thought.

Oddly, Derrida's later work also seems to forget and even foreclose the conceptual opening made in the 1960s. The later more 'politically', 'ethically' focused work may now seem relatively limited for the way it overlooks any reference to environmental issues. The supposed ten plagues facing humanity given in *Specters of Marx* make up a list entirely confined to human-human interactions (81–3). Derrida may see human acts and thoughts as bearing an internal, non-accidental relation to their technological prostheses – the postal system, technologies of the sign, email, TV, etc. – but not, oddly, to their geographical or meteorological ones, or those relating to interactions with agencies in the natural world – for instance, to cite some of an innumerable list, the plants and conditions informing agriculture as a system of protention and retention enabling human self-domestication; the domestication of other animals as part of that society (or, arguably their domestication of us?).

Derrida's limitation of scope re-emerges in 2002 in the account of deconstruction as what 'is happening' in *The Beast and the Sovereign* seminar – 'crises, wars, phenomena of so-called national and international terrorism, massacres that are declared or not, the transformation of the global market and of international law'. Derrida's remains an anthropocentric and blinkered account of 'the rhythm of what is happening in the world' (76). In effect, *Of Grammatology* opened a space for a deconstructive conception of the constitutive place of non-human agency in the human sphere, only for it to be closed again.

Another *Of Grammatology*, let us imagine, would have moved in another more 'ecological', direction, anticipating by twenty or more years the attention to the ethical challenge of the non-human animal in Derrida's work, and giving it a sensitivity to environmental questions which his oeuvre was never in fact to develop.

SARAH WOOD, THE *POINT D'EAU* OR THE WATER-HOLES THAT ARE IMPERCEPTIBLY PRESENT IN WRITING (*OG* 262–3; *DG* 370–1)

Reading a page from Rousseau's 'Essay on the Origin of Languages', late in *Of Grammatology*, Derrida finds 'presence at work, in the process of presenting itself' (*OG* 263). This could be considered surprising. Isn't deconstruction supposed to be about the impossibility of presence? But such a thing cannot be foretold. What Rousseau's page describes happens without those involved noticing. Derrida notices Rousseau noticing this. It happens at the 'point d'eau', the watering-hole (*DG* 369). The *point* part returns a few pages later, at (and referring to) 'a point in the system where the signifier can no longer be replaced by its signified, so that in consequence, no signifier can be so replaced, purely and simply' (*OG* 266; *DG* 376). The point of no pure and simple substitution is the point at which substitution must happen: each of us must live this, it is the movement of living. That's also the point where reading becomes necessary, and impossible to stop – where the 'fundamental signified, the meaning of the being represented, even less the thing itself, will never be given us in person, outside the sign or outside play' (*OG* 266). That's what gets everything moving. But it is still coming in the passage about the water-hole.

In the passage where Rousseau describes the *point d'eau*, there is, Derrida notes, presence 'at work, in the process of presenting itself'. It's an historic moment – the beginning of language, society, nation – but Rousseau has to guess and imagine it because what's happening is necessarily indecipherable. Derrida quotes the whole episode, when the young men and women come to the *point d'eau*, for the beasts to drink or to get water for the household, and their eyes 'begin to see with increased pleasure' (*OG* 262). They begin to feel an 'unknown attraction'. *What* they see, *what* they are attracted to, Rousseau's text does not say. The object is not the point. It is not present as an object: a surreptitious movement of desire takes the young people by surprise. The sentences where it happens are worthy of a *point d'ironie*, but if the irony were more marked, the force of history would be less apparent. Derrida called *Of Grammatology* 'a history book through and through' (Derrida, 'This Strange Institution' 54). He reminds us that history is not transparent, not while it is happening and not later. It is not a matter of the phenomenal manifestation of structural change. It involves, like the story of the origins of society and language told by Rousseau, 'presence at work, in the process of presenting itself. This presence is not a state but the becoming-present of presence' (*OG* 263). It cannot be historicized. And for this to happen (if that is the word), for history to be read, and written, one needs a sense of the unprecedented (a belief in true fiction of the kind Rousseau writes) and an ear for the pleasure and desire that touch and sometimes preoccupy language. Cadence, tone, accent, rhyme, consonance: Derrida says in 'Edmond Jabès and the Question of the Book' that 'there could be no history without the gravity and the labour of literality' (78). He also insisted that for him 'writing models itself on voice. Interior or not, the voice always stages itself, or is staged' ('From the Word to Life' 2).

Rousseau says: 'Imperceptibly, water becomes more necessary. The livestock become thirsty more often. One would arrive in haste and leave with regret'. There is, it seems, no particular awareness of the momentous 'first ties' that are being formed. Nobody recognizes what Rousseau identifies as 'the first rendezvous of the two sexes' because there is no precedent for what is happening. The lack of understanding (even of misunderstanding) is poignant. Rousseau's story is beautiful, in its narrative movement and in its language. Derrida introduces it as beautiful.

He says: 'Let us read this page, no doubt the most beautiful in the *Essay*'. Something is happening at the surface of the young people's daily life and at the surface of Rousseau's language. But it effaces itself. The text doesn't have the crystal transparency that the *Confessions* insist characterized Rousseau's relationship with himself, in the famous passage where he says: 'never throughout the whole of my life has my *heart*, as *transparent* as *crystal*, been able to hide for a single moment any feeling of any intensity that has taken refuge there' (*Confessions* 436). Well, at the water-hole, where eyes 'accustomed to the same sights since infancy' begin 'to see with increased pleasure', the protagonists remain opaque to themselves and each other. They think of the water, the necessity of water, the need to go to the *point d'eau* time after time in a time without time, in 'that happy age' when 'nothing marked the hours' (*OG* 262). 'Happy age' is *âge heureux*, from the Greek adverb *eu*, meaning 'happily, luckily, properly, well'. Something splashes about on the page: not water, not the signifier *eau*, but the vocable *eu* or sometimes *ue*. It has no determined place in the world or on the page. The beautiful impression that strikes Derrida is not the conscious strategy of an aesthetic 'ear' for the harmonies of language. It relates to the mysteries of writing. By what divining does the writer choose and place words? By what intuition does the reader lend them tone and accent? Perhaps the point here is the mysterious force of a certain mobilizing elation, a *eugraphia* that works magic. For example *eau*, water, gives rise to the 'fires [*feux*] of love' (*OG* 262; *DG* 371).

Derrida invites us to a page, and even if it is 'no doubt the most beautiful in the *Essay*', the page is a dry place, one of the 'li*eux* arides' where it is necessary, according to Rousseau, to 'rejoin one another [*se réunir*]' (*DG* 371) and dig wells (*creuser*). With the help of Cixous, especially her readings in *Portrait of Jacques Derrida* and *Insister*, one gets the confidence to insist too: the iterated letter or vocable in writing is not ornament or accident but a repetition that unbeknownst and without the accustomed trappings of scholarship, may be recognized in time as itself what Derrida's commentary on Rousseau calls 'the movement of a birth, the continuous advent of *presence*'. It's a movement that defies narration from a single point of view because of the particular relation it has to the experience of continuity and discontinuity. Derrida explains that before the festival at the waterhole, where 'ardent youth' will lose its wildness, dance and sing and fall in love, people are 'in the state of pure nature' with 'no *experience* of the continuous' – they are unaware. Afterwards, 'the experience of the *discontinuous* begins'. A lot depends on Derrida's emphasis here: it's not the words exactly. The change is a matter of how things are experienced as well as what is experienced. We all know how it is: one is changed, and the world is changed. How on earth do you measure this or give a synopsis of it?

The *point d'eau* is the 'true cradle of nations'. The digging of wells is the 'origin of societies and languages in warm countries'. It happens among the young of both sexes, girls who fetch water (*eau*) for the household, boys who 'water their herds'. Cixous emphasizes Derrida's lifelong youth, and to read him, I would say, it is important to retain the eyes and heart of the young person who is capable of seeing and being touched by 'novel objects' and able to feel, keenly, 'the pleasure of not being alone' which is so strangely important in the solitary activity of reading. One should note also that there are animals there at the dawn of language, human society and the erotic experience of sexual difference. The animality of the letter guides us to the waters of writing. There is a herd of vocables coming to drink. Rousseau's repetition of the vowel-vocable *eu* recalls for us the limit where, Derrida says, according to Rousseau's imaginary history, 'language [*langue*] is instituted [*instituée*] but still remains pure song, a language of pure [*pure*] accentuation, a sort of neume [*neume*]' without the articulation of consonants (*OG* 262; *DG* 370). A faint lowing across the words. I would have liked to have sung *eu* for you here, or mooed it, but the French sound does not carry well into English. *Eheu!* I have had to point it out, and emphasize the importance of certain words in *eu*: (*se réunir*) gather; (*creuser*) to dig; (*berceau des peuples*) cradle of nations; (*langue*) language; (*jeunes*) young; (*abreuver leurs troupeaux*) watering the animals; (*yeux*) eyes; (*coeur*) heart; (*nouveaux*) new; (*seul*) alone.

The harmony and togetherness of form and content that are associated with close reading are not there in my reading. It doesn't work, feels a little dry, messy, but perhaps the gathering at the spring-fed pool will be enough.

Rousseau's account of water becoming 'more necessary' is a story of the constitution of the object and its value, told with both irony and a kind of naivety. At the water-hole 'eyes, accustomed to the same sights [*objets*] since infancy, began to see with increased pleasure. The heart is moved by these novel objects' (*OG* 262; *DG* 371). The *jet* of *objets* in this context suggests *jets d'eau*, the gushing of springs, the playing of fountains, splashing against (Latin: *ob*) the eyes, against the heart. The word 'object' and Rousseau's emphasis on the water-hole as the birthplace of exogamous love takes me back to Melanie Klein, Fritz and the animated letters of Fritz's writing-fantasies. Fritz reads – I interrupt myself here to ask whether 'reads' is the right word. Is 'reading' the right term for this investment of letters as pictures, as *marks*, in the most unprincipled way? Questions that some readers will be quicker to answer than others . . . Fritz reads these letters without regard for their function as parts of the signifier.

He escapes the dead hand of 'good writing', the kind of writing that anticipates its own proper reading. There are all sorts of jets and wells and pools in writing: holes dug, scraped, written where water comes and where people come together and surprising things start to happen. For Fritz 'the pen was also a boat, the copy-book a lake' (*OG* 333 n. 37). These elaborations of 'picture-script' are, Klein maintains, 'still active in the phantasies of every individual child'. They mark *Of Grammatology*, and Rousseau's 'Essay on the Origin of Languages', apart from scholarship, the history of ideas, literary criticism and other arid places.

CHAPTER 4

FROM/OF THE SUPPLEMENT TO THE SOURCE: THE THEORY OF WRITING

SEAN GASTON, KAFKA, LITERATURE AND METAPHOR (*OG* 271–2; *DG* 383–4)

In the midst of his reading of Rousseau, Derrida offers a brief and unexpected reflection on 'literary modernity' (*OG* 272). After noting that Rousseau sees language as 'originarily metaphorical', Derrida quotes from the 'Essay on the Origin of Languages': 'Just as the first motives that made man speak were passions, his first expressions were Tropes. Figurative language arose first, proper [or literal] meaning was found last' (*OG* 271; 'Essay' 253). Derrida then turns to 'literary modernity' and its attempts 'to mark literary specificity against subjugation to the poetic, that is to say to the metaphoric' (*OG* 272).

Derrida raises the question here of 'la spécificité littéraire' (*DG* 383), of the claim to a particular or unique identity for literature that is defined by its resistance to the metaphorical and the figurative. He goes on to note: 'This modern protestation can be triumphant or, in Kafka's manner, denuded of all illusion, despairing, and no doubt more lucid' (*OG* 272). Derrida cites a passage from Kafka's journals from 1921 in which he laments that writing is dependent on metaphors:

From a letter: 'During this dreary winter I warm myself by it'. Metaphors are one thing which makes me despair of writing [*Schreiben*]. Writing's lack of independence: it depends on the maid who tends to the fire, on the cat warming itself by the stove, even on that poor old human being warming himself. These are all autonomous activities, ruled by their own laws; only writing is helpless, cannot live in itself, is a joke and a despair. (trans. mod.)

It is worth noting that Blanchot had cited this passage from Kafka's diary in *The Space of Literature* (1955), though he omitted the first two lines on metaphor (72). This omission suggests that Kafka's despair is prompted by 'writing's lack of independence' in relation to objects in reality and their 'autonomous activities': the maid tending the fire, the cat warming itself by the stove. As Blanchot observes before quoting Kafka, 'doesn't the humblest reality of the world have a solidity lacking in the strongest work?' (72). Blanchot's name does not appear in *Of Grammatology*, which is surprising, not least because in *The Book to Come* (1959) he had observed that Rousseau was 'desperate to write against writing', associating it 'with a power of strangeness under the threat of which he will little by little lose all stable rapport with a self' ('Rousseau' 42–3; cf. Derrida, *Ear of the Other* 77–8).

Before quoting from Kafka's journal, Derrida offers his own remarkably condensed analysis of this passage:

This modern protestation can be triumphant or, in Kafka's manner, denuded of all illusion, despairing, and no doubt more lucid: literature which lives by being outside of itself, in the figures of a language which from the start are not its own, would die as well by returning to itself in the nonmetaphor [*la littérature qui vit d'être hors d'elle-même, dans les figures d'un langage qui d'abord n'est pas le sien, mourrait aussi bien de rentrer en soi dans la non-métaphore*]. (*OG* 272; *DG* 383, trans. mod.)

Literature only lives by being 'outside itself'. Literature lives 'by being outside of itself' through its dependence on metaphor. 'Metaphor' here describes the 'figures of a language' that cannot *belong* to literature, that have never belonged to literature as a figure or language of its own. According to Derrida, 'literature' can only remain alive by maintaining a relation to what will always keep it 'outside of itself'. If it returns to itself through the non-metaphor, the literal, the proper, the literal or proper relationship between 'literature', 'reality' and 'language' – if there is one – it will cease to be literature. The joke and the despair, the restraint and the possibility of literature, Derrida suggests that metaphor never allows literature to claim itself as a *pure absence* in relation to reality and language: it is always more and less than language.

FORBES MORLOCK, THE SUBJECT OF READING-6
(*OG* 275–6; DG 390)

'If fear makes me see giants where there are only men, the signifier –
as the idea of the object – will be metaphoric, but the signifier of my
passion will be literal. And if I then say, "I see giants," that false
designation will be a literal [*propre*] expression of my fear. For in
fact I do see giants and there is a sure truth there, [. . .] analogous to
what Descartes analyzes in the *Regulae*: phenomenologically, the
proposition "I see yellow" is unexceptionable, error becomes possible
only in the judgement "the world is yellow"' (*OG* 275–6; *DG* 390,
trans. mod.).

We have come full circle.

Catachresis – the metaphor of an 'I' of which there is nothing
propre, nothing literal, no letter.

And if I then say 'I see giants', that false designation will be a
literal expression of my fear. For in fact I *do* see giants – Rousseau
and Derrida are giants – and *there is* a sure truth there.

How am I, are we, is one, ever to read *Of Grammatology*?

FORBES MORLOCK, THE SUBJECT OF
READING-7 (*OG* 277; *DG* 393)

Absolute fear would then be the first encounter of the other as *other*:
as other than myself and as other than itself. I can answer the threat
of the other as other (than myself) only by transforming it into
another (than itself), through altering it in my imagination, my fear,
or my desire. 'Upon meeting others, a savage man will *initially* be
frightened [*se sera* d'abord *effrayé*]' (*OG* 277; *DG* 391, trans. mod.;
quoting Rousseau, 'Essai' 381).

As if themselves staging the first encounter of the other as other,
Derrida's words continue until they meet another's, Rousseau's.
Another, first encounter. Here – as everywhere – is the question of
reading. The book that is so famous for articulating (and disarticu-
lating) a science of writing cannot stop exploring the question: what
is reading? Its heterogeneous parts are bound by this question and its
practice – but these seem hardly to be spoken of in the literature of
writing. Unlike writing, reading is so hard to speak of.

We may imagine that we can close our eyes to it and choose not
to read – as we can decide not to paraphrase or explicate, to offer

a commentary or an interpretation. A reading, though, cannot be decided. It is always too late to ask the question: what is reading? because reading – whatever it may be – is not entirely conscious, voluntary or intentional. It has always, *initially*, happened. In the surprise of that encounter, the subject of reading has yet to be decided. Like Derrida and Rousseau, the subject of reading – he, she, it, I, one – is a savage man. We read in absolute fear.

The threat of the other as other is always also a matter of the ear, which cannot close. The 'I' and the 'eye', the 'je' and the 'jeu' – the play cannot be stopped. A reading alters faithfully. It is equal to, but never the equivalent of, the text it reads. We may learn that all readers are equal afterwards, but reading is equal to what it reads from the first.

PEGGY KAMUF, ON NAÏVETÉ (*OG* 296–7; *DG* 417–18)

This eye, then, would not be naïve. What does that mean? Naïveté lives – if it can be called living – in an imagined, imaginary space, a space presumed to be native or natural (naïve is likewise derived from *nativus, natus*: born), one that is just there, given, self-evident. 'Naïf', says the *Dictionnaire Littré*, is 'what simply retraces the truth or nature, without artifice and without effort'. To point to a naïve philosophy of the idea-sign is thus almost redundant if it means a thinking of the sign as representation of a given – natural or true – presence. And of course this *is* what Derrida means, but I want to insist on the dimension of naïveté as an imaginary space presumed to be uninhabited and uninscribed – a natural space that is simply given according to a naïve or native ecology, if you will, of representation. In this sense, naïveté is a place in which one may live *as if* in a nature untouched by artifice and effort, which are, again naïvely, thought to be proper to man. Naïveté, then, would be something like the proper name of unthinking and unthought in-habitation, whether one situates its representations in a natural ecology or a political economy. Here, for example, is Derrida drawing out the links between linguistic and political representation, which he will read through *The Social Contract* and *The Letter to d'Alembert* (the latter being perhaps Rousseau's most virulently misogynistic work, a fact I mention not just in passing):

All Rousseau's thinking is in a sense a critique of representation, in the linguistic sense as much as in the political one. But at the same time – and here the entire history of metaphysics is reflected – this critique *lives in the naïveté* of representation. It supposes that representation both follows on a primary presence and restitutes a final presence. No one tries to figure anything out about presence and representation within presence. By criticizing representation as loss of presence, by expecting from it a reappropriation of presence, by making of it an accident or a means, one *installs oneself in* the self-evidence of the distinction between presentation and representation, in the *effect* of this split. One criticizes the sign *by installing oneself in* the self-evidence and the effect of the difference between signified and signifier. That is to say, *without thinking* [. . .] the productive movement of the effect of difference: the strange graphic of differance [Derrida emphasizes only 'effect']. (*OG* 296; *DG* 417–18, trans. mod.)

I cite this long passage not because its argument is unfamiliar; on the contrary, it follows the central nerve of *Grammatology*'s argument regarding representation, the metaphysics of presence and Rousseau's repetition of its unthinking assumptions. Rather, I want to stress how determining for Derrida's thought here are the figures – but perhaps it would be better to call them wild metaphors – of *living-in* and *installing-oneself-in*. These are what one could call modes of in-habitation that, when they naïvely take up residence in self-evidence, when they, as Derrida puts it, *live in* naïveté, cannot begin to think (from) where they are. This is certainly not to reinforce some idea about a deconstructive mode of thought as hyper-sophistication of artifice that confounds common sense; once again on the contrary, it takes a lot of artifice, albeit naturalized as self-evidence, not to see with that eye opening onto the outside, the eye that, from wherever one speaks, is forced to open at the centre of speech: 'For the voice has always, already been invested, set in motion, called up, and marked in its essence by a certain spatiality' (*OG* 290; *DG* 409–10, trans. mod.).

ANN SMOCK, THEATRE WITHOUT THEATRE
(*OG* 302–13; *DG* 428–41)

Rousseau proposes a theatre with no theatre to it. 'A stage without a show: without *theater,* with nothing to see' (*OG* 306). Derrida explains this odd idea of theatre minus the show: visibility, for Rousseau, separates the living voice from itself and infects it with death. As spectacle, *theatre* is akin to *theorems* – which need only be looked at and make no reference at all to a spoken language, a live voice.

It is true that a theatre audience *hears* the actors it sees addressing it; theatre ties visibility to speech again, and for this reason it looks superior – potentially, at least – to the standard situation where the public is addressed mainly in writing, via books, Rousseau says, and rarely any more out loud. What has become of the space for us to hear each other? 'Dans quel *espace* pourra-t-on encore *s'entendre*?' Derrida asks, adopting Rousseau's perspective (*DG* 429; *OG* 304). Maybe theatre, since it joins visibility to speech again, could make room for us to hear one another once more – to communicate directly among ourselves, entering fully into our mutual accord.

What Rousseau has in mind for the theatre, then, is a continuation of the unanimous assembly of citizens: 'the lyrical aspect of the general will', as Starobinski puts it (*OG* 306; Starobinski, *La transparence* 119). The spectators will be their own show: 'Make it so that each sees and loves himself in the others so that all will be better united' (*Letter to d'Alembert*, cited in *OG* 307). But for the sake of the public joy this theatre would be the site of, all the theatre must be drained out of it. 'What will be shown in [these entertainments]? Nothing, if you please' (*OG* 307).

It is best to stage nothing, because any scene is a re-presentation. Theatre, Derrida shows, provokes the same hostility in Rousseau that representative politics do. No sooner is there a play than the play of replacement and repetition has already taken over — the weird economy of the supplement, the shoring up of presence by an auxiliary deficiency. Immediate, unadulterated communication is doomed.

This means that theatre is its own sickness. Derrida's analysis shows Rousseau purging it of itself. And he locates the unlikely project of 'a stage without a show, without *theater*' within Rousseau's more general commitment to being as a presence originally and naturally at one with itself, having no give, no slack, no *play* to it at all, unless by a misfortune afflicting it from outside. Rousseau tries to keep the contaminating outside out. He guards being against all the risk and expenditure, all the gambling implied in the French word *jeu*, as if presence didn't depend on the outside within it that puts it in play and exposes it to death.

But the thought of a theatre without theatre, and Rousseau's blithe proposal to put *nothing* on a stage could suggest a different angle.

As Derrida observes, Rousseau's propositions don't all *have* to be interpreted in exactly the way he himself most often seems to urge. Some admit of other readings which he did not pursue – at least not systematically. So his statement that – notwithstanding the dim view he takes of everything theatrical – theatre is more than appropriate to the life of a republic, indeed that republics are the birthplace of theatre and that the shows enjoyed by republican citizens (where practically nothing is staged) are the best, might support an intuition that if you got rid of all the theatre in theatre the result would not be no theatre, or some radically toned-down, harmless version of it, but theatre. Not 'theatre' with its lighting and sets, its gestures and speeches, exits and entrances but theatre: the space where a *nothing* shows.

The nothing that we are. The nothing natural or proper, the nothing true. This might be considered the truth of theatre.

'Man's nature is to have no nature', writes Philippe Lacoue-Labarthe in an essay on Rousseau akin to *Of Grammatology* and to Derrida's thought generally (Lacoue-Labarthe, 'La scène de l'origine' 43). Human beings are characterless and possess no qualities, just the actor's aptitude for appropriating any and all. For a repetition, replacing life, *conditions* it and this sheer adulteration gives us to live and be ourselves. To me the suggestion is very appealing that precisely this de-naturing (but not of anything or anyone) could show somewhere and be the occasion of public gatherings. I am glad to entertain the thought that people might meet up in numbers around this equivocal nothing, and not around some grander truth, and in its flickering, unbelievable light feel a common joy.

SEAN GASTON, PERIODICITY (*OG* 306–9; *DG* 432–6)

Derrida begins the section on 'The Theorem and The Theatre' by linking Rousseau's criticisms of algebra, as a written language that 'has always already begun to separate itself from speech', to Leibniz's theory of a universal non-phonetic language (*OG* 303–4). Leibniz's universal language, Derrida notes, takes on the status of a theorem of visibility: '*it is enough to look in order to calculate*' (*OG* 304). Derrida then digresses for eight pages before returning to Leibniz to account for writing as a kind of machine that entirely separates the representer from the natural order that links it to the represented (*OG* 312).

In this digression, Derrida turns to the relation between the visible, the voice and the politics of representation. Evoking his earlier readings of Artaud and Bataille, Derrida examines Rousseau's account of the festival as a 'theatre without representation' (*OG* 306). Derrida describes this movement as an attempt to escape the 'difference between the object seen and the seeing subject', or the visible presence of 'an object which is *present* to be seen'. However, this apparent escape from the old economy of the presence of a represented object only elicits another, more profound, 'metaphysics of presence'. The festival without representation relies on a self-proximity in which 'the representative differance will be effaced in the self-presence of sovereignty' (*OG* 306). Derrida treats the attempt to go beyond the presence of the subject-object relation and the visible as a determined calculating on absence or the evocation of a sovereign pure possibility. Part of what makes *Of Grammatology* so significant is that it not only reinforces the critique of the metaphysics of presence that Heidegger had already identified but also questions the ruses and traps of escaping presence through an assured or absolute calculation on a pure absence.

In these last pages of the work Derrida offers an alternative to this sovereign calculating on absence. Tracing a number of terms in Rousseau, Derrida describes these terms in *and* as a series *of* intervals:

> Thus the North, winter, death, imagination, representation, the irritation of desires – this entire series of supplementary significations – does not designate a natural place or fixed terms: rather a periodicity. Seasons. (*OG* 309)

This periodicity of seasons as a regular irregular series of intervals can be seen as an anticipatory footnote to the passage in *Glas* (1974) where Derrida evokes a quasi-Hegelian saturnalia – a saturnalia that cannot be contained by Rousseau's chaste festival – in which the 'season disorder' (*mal de saison*) opens a gap that threatens any assured re-appropriation or final harvest (*Glas* 233a). In *Of Grammatology*, Derrida describes this excess of the festival in terms of a seasonal disorder *of* and *as* the order of 'time itself':

> Seasons. In the order of time, or rather like time itself, they speak the movement by which the presence of the present separates from itself, supplants itself, replaces itself by absenting itself, produces

itself in self-substitution. It is this that the metaphysics of presence as self-proximity wishes to efface by giving a privileged position to a sort of absolute now, the *life* of the present, the living present. (*OG* 309; *DG* 436)

PEGGY KAMUF, HABITATION IN GENERAL
(*OG* 290–1; *DG* 410–11)

Let us return to the quotation interrupted at the phrase 'inscription as habitation in general' (*supra* Kamuf, 114–15). As promised, here is the fuller context from *Of Grammatology*'s final chapter:

If one thinks, finally, that the scriptural space is linked, as Rousseau intuited, to the nature of social space, to the perceptive and dynamic organization of technical, religious, economic space and so forth, one has an idea of the difficulty of a transcendental question about space. A new transcendental aesthetic should let itself be guided [. . .] by the possibility of inscription in general, which does not befall like some contingent accident an already constituted space, but produces the spatiality of space. We say inscription *in general* so as to indicate clearly that we are not talking about only the notation of a ready speech representing itself, but inscription in speech and inscription as always already situated *habitation*. A transcendental question about space concerns the prehistoric and precultural layer of spatio-temporal experience that provides a unitary and universal ground for every subjectivity, every culture, from on this side of the empirical diversity, the proper orientations of their space and their time. Now, if one lets oneself be guided by inscription as habitation in general, the Husserlian radicalization of the Kantian question is indispensable but insufficient. [Here, I will skip Derrida's very succinct summary of why it is both indispensable and insufficient so as to pick up the passage ten lines further down.] If the space-time we inhabit is *a priori* the space-time of the trace, there is neither pure activity nor pure passivity. This pair of concepts [. . .] belong to the origin myth of an uninhabited world, a world alien to the trace: pure presence of the pure present, which one may indifferently call the purity of life or the purity of death. [. . .] By breaking with linear genesis and by describing correlations among systems of writings, social structures, and figures of passion, Rousseau opens his questions in the direction we have just indicated. (*OG* 290–1; *DG* 410–11, trans. mod.)

That Rousseau could open the questions in this direction testifies once again to the operation of that eye opened at the centre of the language of his text, even if it is so largely despite what he wanted to say and to mean. This eye keeps watch for the other inhabitants of a same space not all of whom are giants or men, that is, not all of whom are beings comparable to or the same as himself; for some are undoubtedly women, some, apparently not human at all, neither women nor men, can approach or flee humans as they will; some cannot flee but are held captive, either for enforced labour or enforced reproduction in view of human food production, some are rooted in place, some fly or flow through space, some appear to be inanimate, and they alone do not seem to experience what is called death, although they can undergo transformation, disintegration, even disappearance; the disappeared ones, whether animate or inanimate, do not ever return as they were before, before death or destruction; yet because they can leave marks, the habitation is an archive, ever changing, of retention and protention, a ground for the inscription of all those who come to inhabit it, whether they are born there, or migrate there, or fall somehow to this piece of ground from out of the air; as we read, a habitation is space of *general* inscription: 'the possibility of the gramme structures the movement of its history according to rigorously original levels, types, and rhythms' (*OG* 84).

PEGGY KAMUF, 'FROM SOMEWHERE WHERE WE ARE' (*OG* 309, 162; *DG* 436, 233)

So, Rousseau opens the question of habitation in general as the ground of inscription, including his own strange description of himself isolated in the midst of habitations of men gathered in cities, towns, nations, to which this Citizen of Geneva is forever ready to prescribe laws and practices. The strangest prescriptions, perhaps, are those consigned to his open *Letter to d'Alembert* in 1758, which responds energetically to d'Alembert's article on Geneva in the *Encyclopedia*. More or less in passing, d'Alembert had deplored the ban on theatrical spectacles in Jean Calvin's adopted home town. Thereupon, convinced that d'Alembert's remark was meant above all to gratify women who sought more opportunity to put themselves on public display, Rousseau unleashes a misogynistic fury, lacing it with fairly ludicrous recommendations on how to supplement the lack of theatre, the institution which has inevitably had, Rousseau asserts, such a corrupting effect on women's morals and, consequently the morals of any city that tolerates it. Unless I am mistaken, this strange text is not cited in *Of Grammatology* until very near the end, in the next to the last section of the last chapter, 'The Theorem and the Theater', where it undergoes a succinct but probing X-ray of some of its more striking symptoms. One of these, however, Derrida merely points to, almost without comment. It is included in a note in which Rousseau imagines the kind of misimpressions of its author's tastes readers of this very text are liable to form. He anticipates three such misapprehensions, but as Derrida points out, he corrects two of them and 'makes only one exception to his disclaimers'. Rousseau writes, then:

> Based on this work, people will not fail to say: 'This man is crazy about dancing'. I am bored by dancing. 'He cannot bear the drama'. I love drama with a passion. 'He has an aversion for women'. On this point, I will be only too well justified. (*OG* 309; *DG* 436, trans. mod.; citing *Lettre* 120 note)

I will let my reading hypothesis come to rest *there*, on Rousseau's confession of a justifiable aversion for women, for 'l'habitation des femmes', which Derrida asks his readers to remark, without too much risk of misapprehension, so it may then be reframed within the immense *general* in-habitation that is *Of Grammatology*.

More than forty years have passed since this text first affirmed its principle: 'One must begin *somewhere where we are*' (*OG* 162; *DG* 233, trans. mod.). Today, it is still time to begin *there*.

BIOGRAPHICAL NOTES – INTERVALS

DEREK ATTRIDGE

I honestly can't remember when I first encountered *Of Grammatology* – it's one of those works one feels one has always lived with. The truth, however, is that I spent many years doing research (on Elizabethan poetry and questions of prosody) before I started to take a serious interest in Derrida, though I was well aware of his work thanks to conversations during my graduate student years with a research fellow at Cambridge, Jonathan Culler. My heavily annotated copy of Gayatri Spivak's translation of *De la grammatologie* is the third printing of 1978, so I guess my purchase took place a year or two after that date, and I suspect it was with the encouragement of two new colleagues at the University of Southampton who arrived around that time, Maud Ellmann and Robert Young, that my careful reading occurred. I began teaching an advanced class on *Finnegans Wake* at about the same time, and the two experiences fed into and enhanced one another, permanently transforming my intellectual life.

GEOFFREY BENNINGTON

I had read a very little Derrida in 1976–77, as a third-year under-graduate spending a year teaching in France, led to him from structuralism via Barthes and *Tel Quel*. I returned to Oxford in the Fall of 1979 determined to bring the revolution with me, and duly met the editors of the *Oxford Literary Review* who were already building the barricades. My first true read through of *De la grammatologie* (a copy bought, I believe, at Compendium Books in Camden) took place only in the summer of 1978, after graduation, as I embarked on graduate work in the French eighteenth century: I imagined the move from undergraduate to graduate status as one of becoming a professional, and now being a professional, it seemed important actually to read and understand the thinkers whose names I had brandished happily up until then. I took many careful pages of notes I still have but never consult, carefully underlined in pencil passages I thought were important, and made tentative marginal annotations (some of which I have subsequently erased out of embarrassment). My reading-experience was that vivid mixture of excitement and panic that I later realized just is the experience of reading. This is probably the text of Derrida's I have read most often, and certainly the one I can most readily quote from memory, and contains one of my favourite sentences of Derrida's, for its inner parenthetical remark anticipating its own end: 'La "rationalité" – mais il faudrait peut-être abandonner ce mot pour la raison qui apparaîtra à la fin de cette phrase – qui commande l'écriture ainsi élargie et radicalisée, n'est plus issue d'un logos et elle inaugure la destruction, non pas la démolition mais la dé-sédimentation, la dé-construction de toutes les significations qui ont leur source dans celle de logos' (*DG* 21).

TIMOTHY CLARK

I'm personally uncomfortable with the request to narrate my first encounter with *Of Grammatology*. This has about it the feeling of a cult of academic celebrity ('little did I know, when I first met John back in 1977, auditioning for a small part . . .'), or of the suffocating monumentalization already informing too many similar books in memory of Derrida. For the record, I first heard of the book in 1978, while deciding what further course to take in my 'English Literature and Language' degree at Exeter College, Oxford University. I chose the controversial option on literary theory. My tutor, Jonathan Wordsworth, expressed his annoyance at this choice but gave me the phone number of an academic who would advise on the course and on summer reading. This turned out to be his ex-wife, Ann Wordsworth. What books should I read? 'Well, *Of Grammatology* I suppose . . .'.

CLARE CONNORS

There was no *coup de foudre* for me, more a series of *après coups*. I first began to read *Of Grammatology* as a first-year undergraduate in Oxford in 1991, at the suggestion of my tutor Robert Smith. In the conservative, predominantly historicist culture of the Oxford English faculty, reading Derrida (and this was the first of Derrida's texts I'd encountered) had the easy glamour of rebellion about it. But it was such hard work! I read slowly, pegging away, looking up words (what's an exergue? What's cuneiform mean?), baffled by all the proper names I didn't know, all the other writers quoted. It was stymieing: for the first time I couldn't write my weekly essay. Every sentence I wrote failed to match or meet what I'd been reading, seemed to need hedging and qualifying. Only later, on re-reading, did I start to feel the rhythm of the writing more, and to understand the book's generosity as well as its exigent rigour. That was also when I first took notice of the so-helpful sentence that begins 'we must begin *wherever we are*' – a phrase from which I continue to take courage.

PAUL DAVIES

The Derrida texts I read first in the early to mid-1980s were *Speech and Phenomena*, 'Violence and Metaphysics' and '*Ousia* and *Grammē*'. I had been told that *Of Grammatology* put these and other seemingly secondary readings into the context of a primary philosophical project. I remember a walk in Umbria in 1983 with an American 'Orthodox' Heideggerian who, with the first part of the book in mind, asked me gloomily whether I thought Derrida might not be 'the thinker to come'. I bought copies in London, the French from Grant and Cutler, the English translation from Compendium, but I'm not sure I really read the book properly until after Derrida had made some quizzical remarks about its style and about attempts to apply or develop it. I remember discussing its treatment of language and linguistics in a presentation in Memphis in 1987–88, trying to write something first in an apartment overlooking Lake Michigan in Chicago and then in Robert Bernasconi's apartment by the Mississippi: places and names, titles and ideas, once so new and set to become so familiar.

SEAN GASTON

A few weeks into my first year of studying at the University of Melbourne in 1987 I was fortunate to attend a lecture by Clifford Geertz as part of an exceptional course in the History Department, 'European Hegemony 1600–1800', run by the late Greg Denning. This led me eventually to a footnote in *The Interpretation of Cultures*

on the work of Paul Ricoeur. Over the next two years, not least thanks
to the encouragement of Peter Otto in the English Department,
I slowly followed a trail of footnotes – from a footnote in the third
volume of Ricoeur's recently translated *Time and Narrative* to
Levinas's 'The Trace of the Other', collected in Mark Taylor's
Deconstruction in Context, to Derrida's 'Violence and Metaphysics'.
Among the students in the English Department, *Of Grammatology*
was a much discussed if little read book. I recall standing for an hour
in the library passionately arguing about *Of Grammatology* with
someone until, at last, we both acknowledged that we had not read a
single word of Derrida's work. I bought my own copy on 15 January
1991. By March of that year I was in Paris and on page 44 there is
a note in pencil: 'March 15 Paris: I met Derrida today'. I would be
preoccupied for the next few years by a passage that appears early
in the text in parentheses: '(*Aufhebung* is, more or less implicitly, the
dominant concept of nearly all histories of writing, even today. It is
the concept of history and of teleology)' (*OG* 25).

CHRISTOPHER JOHNSON

My own copy of *De la grammatologie* is dated 5 May 1984, but
I must have started reading it a few years before this. I was nearing
the end of a three-year term in Paris, first as an *auditeur libre* at
the École Normale Supérieure, then as a *lecteur d'anglais* at the
Université de Paris X-Nanterre. While at the École Normale I was
fortunate enough to be invited to the seminars Derrida offered to
Yale postgraduates and other foreign-language students, which were
held in his office at the École. *De la grammatologie* was a formative
text for me – everything I have done since that period has been more
or less influenced by it. The text was an important point of reference
for my doctoral thesis on Derrida, which became my first book.
When I was asked to write a short book explaining Derrida to a
general readership, I chose *De la grammatologie* as the text I thought
best exemplified some of the essential features of his thought. Reading
De la grammatologie also inspired me to read other contemporary
French thinkers. Derrida's reading of Lévi-Strauss, for example,
made me want to find out more about the wider intellectual context
of *De la grammatologie*, which led to a monograph on Lévi-Strauss
and structuralism. Finally, I was fascinated by the way *De la grammatologie* referenced different developments in post-war science and

technology – for instance, evolutionary theory and cybernetics – which enabled new ways of thinking the human. This has become the subject of my most recent research on French cybernetics and the pre-historian André Leroi-Gourhan.

PEGGY KAMUF

I have recounted once in print already the first time I saw *De la grammatologie* (in 1971, during graduate study at Cornell in Romance Studies, a young professor held a copy out to the neophytes and said 'You must read this'). So I don't want to repeat the same story. But there are so many stories that were set in motion for me by reading – trying to read, struggling to read – this book. First, there was the luck of timing: I was just beginning doctoral studies, which had not been a long-hatched plan but a mad decision after another life and another plan had suddenly been cut short. I was starting again from nothing and nowhere, it seemed. Did I notice then, on page 233, the sentence that begins 'One must begin *somewhere where we are* . . .'? I can't recall, but today it gives me great pause to think about this extraordinary affirmation with which Derrida *departed from* a whole tradition of philosophy – but also of the most everyday thinking – that dismisses as inessential the experience of all of life's accidents. Secondly, there was Rousseau and the reading of Rousseau: *De la grammatologie* inducted me into an enduring attraction for Rousseau's work, which also set the course I followed through a doctoral dissertation and beyond. Thirdly, there was the idea that the most serious things comprise what Derrida understands as play, that is, risk, chance, movement, uncertainty. 'Rousseau puts play out of play' one reads on page 439, as if he or anyone else could simply choose that, as if the play of the world would just respond to someone's desire. Sure, who wouldn't want to put play out of play? That is the purest desire. But, then, there is still necessity and *De la grammatologie* taught me to remember necessity.

IAN MACLACHLAN

During my undergraduate year in France in the early 1980s, a route through various literary-theoretical titles in the Seuil 'Points' series (Barthes, Genette, Todorov) had led me to Tel Quel's *Théorie d'ensemble* and Derrida's *L'Écriture et la différence*, both of which seemed terribly glamorous and also more or less impenetrable to me (there being a close correlation between these two qualities, no doubt). A couple of years later, as I was embarking on doctoral work on Roger Laporte, I picked up a second-hand copy of *De la grammatologie*, the first part of which, in its exploration of writing and the idea of the book, seemed to connect more readily with the recent French literature and theory I'd been reading, and it sent me back to certain essays in *L'Écriture et la différence* and forward, particularly to *La Dissémination* and *La Carte postale*. 'L'écriture avant la lettre' remains the part of *De la grammatologie* that I return to most often (as here, in fact).

J. HILLIS MILLER

I read the first version of Part I of *De la grammatologie* when it came out in the journal *Critique* (December 1965–January 1966). Eugenio Donato, then my colleague at Johns Hopkins, first told me about Derrida and advised me to read him in *Critique*. Donato, a remarkable scholar, kept up with the latest developments in Paris. I then bought and read the book itself. My copy is inscribed with my name and, below that, 'Paris/Feb. 5, 1968'. My copy of *L'écriture et la différence* says 'Paris/Feb. 6. 1968'. Why one day later? Did I go back the next day and buy the second book? *L'écriture et la différence* contains of course the French original of the lecture Derrida gave at the Hopkins symposium of 1966. I have no memory of what I was doing in Paris on 5 February 1968, or on 6 February for that matter. When I got home to our house in Roland Park in Baltimore, I read *De la grammatologie*, bit by bit, in the early mornings, at a table in a bright sun-porch behind our kitchen. Passages here and there are marked in red pencil, though why just those sentences is no longer entirely clear to me. The book is pretty battered, with the cover held on by scotch tape. I was, as they say, 'bouleversé' by *De la grammatologie*, as I had been by the preliminary version in *Critique*, and by my first encounter with Derrida at the famous Hopkins symposium on 'The Languages of Criticism and the Sciences of Man' on 18–21 October 1966. My 'overturning' was drawn out over several years. I can hardly yet say that I am not inhabited by logocentric ways of thinking. Who can? In any case, what Derrida says in *Of Grammatology* overturned all my Pouletian assumptions about 'criticism of consciousness', the idea, that is, that all the works of a given author form a whole based on a unique *cogito* and transmitted in the act of reading from the consciousness of the author to the consciousness of the reader by way of representational language (that is, written language transparently representing consciousness). I could see, on those sunny mornings, that either Poulet or Derrida might be right, but not both. Reading *De la grammatologie* was a crisis in my life, a sharp division between before and after.

FORBES MORLOCK

My earliest memory: an afternoon, my sophomore dorm room, reading my first bit of the book – perhaps even Spivak's introduction – and thinking with excitement, 'This is harder than Hegel'. Derrida was teaching on campus, de Man's students were giving brilliant courses on Rousseau, but the reading was for a course on the pre-Socratics and poststructuralism taught by a classics professor in the philosophy department. I can't remember whether the whole book was assigned. I read it all: an essay question referred to 'the logic of the supplement' and I felt I had to try to find the words – if they were Derrida's – in the text. It feels like I have been looking for and finding things – often not together – in it ever since. Everything is there. Today my copy of the white Minuit edition is one of the very few books it gives me pleasure just to hold, open or closed.

MICHAEL NAAS

Though I first began to read *Of Grammatology* in 1985 as a second-year graduate student at SUNY Stony Brook, it was not until the academic year 1988–89 that I really began to *study* it. That was the year I was fortunate enough to spend a year in Paris, thanks to a fellowship from the French government, writing my dissertation and attending every Wednesday afternoon Derrida's seminar at the École Normale Supérieure. To prepare for that seminar – and to make sure I would arrive early enough to get a seat! – I met several hours in advance at a café just a block away from the seminar with two good friends from Stony Brook, James Clarke and Steve Michelman. We met there to discuss Derrida's ongoing seminar on friendship but also to read together, line by line, *Of Grammatology*. That little café on the rue d'Ulm just south of the Pantheon thus became for us all a site of friendship and intense study of this important work.

More than two decades later, those weekly meetings around *Of Grammatology* in anticipation of Derrida's seminar on 'the politics of friendship' remain for me a model of what is best in philosophical dialogue and what is most valuable, though also most fragile, in friendship. I have been breathing the air and living off the memories of those days ever since.

JEAN-LUC NANCY

Dans les années soixante, nous lisions beaucoup la revue *Critique*. Elle offrait beaucoup moins qu'aujourd'hui des numéros thématiques, mais c'était l'actualité de la pensée – en tous les sens possibles – qui passait par là. Un jour j'ai vu l'article de Derrida qui était la première version du premier chapitre de la *Grammatologie*. J'ai su tout de suite que ce qui m'avait déjà frappé dans la *Voix et le phénomène* se confirmait: il y avait là un penseur vivant qui me faisait entendre la voix vivante, présente (je fais exprès de le dire dans des termes qu'on croit le plus souvent irrecevables pour lui! . . .) du travail philosophique. Ni Deleuze, ni Lévi-Strauss ne m'avaient donné cette impression très particulière. L'écriture', je la recevais tout de suite comme 'notre' question. Elle nommait un souci envers le 'sens' que je ne savais pas exprimer. L'année suivante, je rencontrais Lacoue-Labarthe, à Strasbourg. Nous avions lu, entendu, perçu la même chose, la même *actualité*. Et puis ce fut 68. Derrida n'était pas un 'soixante-huitard', mais il ne savait pas à quel point, en fait, l'ouverture de sa pensée était aussi celle de cet 'au-delà' soudain présent en 68.

(In the 1960s we'd often read the review *Critique*. It had far less in the way of themed issues than nowadays, but its pages contained what was current in thought, in every possible sense. One day I saw the article by Derrida that was the first version of the first chapter of *De la grammatologie*. I knew immediately that it confirmed what had already struck me in *La Voix et le phénomène*: here was a living thinker in whom I could hear the living, present voice (I'm deliberately saying it in terms that are often thought to be unacceptable to him! . . .) of philosophical work. Neither Deleuze nor Lévi-Strauss had given me that very specific impression. 'Writing' was something that I took on board straightaway as being 'our' question. It named a concern with 'sense' that I didn't yet know how to express. The next year, I was to meet Lacoue-Labarthe, in Strasbourg. We had both read, heard, perceived the same thing, the same sense of *what was current*. And then it was '68. Derrida wasn't a so-called *soixante-huitard*, but he didn't realize the extent to which, in fact, the opening of his thought was also the opening of the 'beyond' that was suddenly present in '68.)

NICHOLAS ROYLE

I first saw Derrida's *Of Grammatology* on a display shelf in Blackwell's bookshop, Broad Street, Oxford, when I was an undergraduate, probably in 1977. I was very struck by the beautiful, ancient-looking (but in fact nineteenth-century) image of Nikka's *kakemono* or hanging scroll ('The artist's seals and emblems of longevity') on the cover. But the book was already a not very obscure object of desire to me: it was in the air, it what was being talked about by those with whom I had the good fortune to come into contact in my early years at Oxford, especially those involved with the *Oxford Literary Review*. The book was expensive and, inevitably, too new and strange to be regarded as having any relevance to undergraduate study. More than once I took it down from the shelf and looked at it, but I never bought a copy. Then one night in the college bar I saw it, evidently left behind by someone, along with a couple of other books. (One of these was Blanchot's *Death Sentence*, I don't recall the other.) The evening went by and no one came to collect them. I stole it, I confess. If the original owner should ever happen to read these words, please let me know and I will gladly provide a replacement. (The tome I nicked is now in a quite forlorn and battered state, alas, its spine broken in several places, its margins much pencilled.) Reading *Of Grammatology* was thus, from the first, a guilty pleasure, inevitably redolent of the links between theft and autobiography I would come to find confirmed in Rousseau, Augustine and Derrida himself. But I must also confess I didn't read this astonishing work straightaway. As with Freud's *The Interpretation of Dreams*, I waited, I deferred, all the while feeling that it was one of the only books I *had* to read.

ANN SMOCK

I first encountered *De la grammatologie* as a French literature student in the seminar of Jacques Ehrmann in 1967. The book had just appeared in France. In his excitement, Ehrmann abandoned the programme of study he'd announced, and launched into a reading of the second part of *Grammatology* with us. I cannot claim to have been anything like equal to this experience. But I admired Jacques Ehrmann more than anyone else I encountered at Yale, and it was through his vehemence, mixed with the agitation and uncertainty about literature and literary studies he shared with me and all my fellow students in the middle of the Vietnam War, that I got a glimmer of a reason – not a justification, but a motive – for remaining a student all my life and sticking for good with the demands writing can make of a person.

MICHAEL SYROTINSKI

My own copy of *De la grammatologie*, now rather fittingly coming apart at the seams as a book from many years of reading and re-reading, is dated 21 October 1982, New Haven (I might add that I have only just purchased my own copy of Gayatri Spivak's English translation, dated 28 June 2010!). I had gone to Yale as a graduate student mainly because of Paul de Man and Jacques Derrida. It was only once I was there that I fully appreciated my good fortune to be present during the golden years of 'deconstruction in America', and to be taught by Derrida and de Man, but also J. Hillis Miller, Geoffrey Hartman, Harold Bloom, Shoshana Felman, Barbara Johnson, Ellen Burt, Andrzej Warminski and Kevin Newmark. It was an exhilarating and life-changing time for me, and I would confidently predict that we will never again see such a community of like-minded theorists and critics in one place. My favourite memory of *De la grammatologie* was during one of Ellen Burt's graduate seminars on Rousseau. Wanting to look for a particular passage in Derrida's text, but having forgotten to bring her own copy to class, she asked to borrow one. I passed her my copy to look at. She began thumbing through it, but was quickly disoriented by my many notes scribbled in the margins. She gave up, and passed it back to me with a wry smile: 'Ce n'est pas le même livre' (It's not the same book). *Différance* indeed!

JULIAN WOLFREYS

In 1983, a first-year undergraduate, I had heard the name 'Derrida' in lectures. At the end of a seminar, I asked a tutor who Derrida was, and where I might begin reading Derrida. He suggested that though

I wouldn't be able to make much sense of it, I should start with *Of Grammatology*. I found a copy in The Public House bookshop, Brighton, owned and run by an American, Richard Cupidi. It was filled with alternative press publications, avant-garde jazz records and university presses specializing in 'theory' and radical politics. Though the bookshop has gone, the bookshop sticker is still hanging on to the back cover. The book was and remains a *carrefour* in every sense – X marks the spot. I frequently thought, repeatedly, I'd begun reading *Of Grammatology*, in Brighton, Northampton, MA, Hamburg and South Pasadena, just to recall some of the locations in which the book has lived, but though I've a feeling I haven't, I still have hopes of doing so.

SARAH WOOD

I can't locate my reading of *Of Grammatology* biographically. My copy is inscribed with my name, college and 1984 – my second or third undergraduate year. I found the book in the Norrington Room under Blackwell's. But *Of Grammatology* never became a complete single thing to me. It remains in the offing. What *was* it about? It seemed to me to face France, and to open on to three major oeuvres then unknown to me: Saussure, Lévi-Strauss and Rousseau. I can't pretend, still, to have 'got' it – not even the 'principles of reading' that were pointed out to me one day in a tutorial (*OG* 158). The passage my tutor read out to me emphasized the necessity of knowing how to decipher and reproduce the conscious, voluntary, intentional aspects of texts. *Of Grammatology* called this kind of commentary a guardrail. The traditional critical skills I had come to university to learn promised some protection for the rather wild readings I'd begun, having read some Derrida and more English poetry, to write. But I wondered about the risks of critical production 'developing in any direction at all' and saying 'almost anything'. Where did the risks come from? From writing itself? And was that force really in my most unqualified keeping? If the future could 'only be anticipated in the form of an absolute danger' (*OG* 5) what guardrail could possibly protect reading and critical production from what was coming? It was some years before it occurred to me that it might be anticipation, seeing ahead, that would have to go.

CONTRIBUTORS

Derek Attridge, Professor of English, University of York
Geoffrey Bennington, Professor of French and Comparative Literature, Emory University
Timothy Clark, Professor of English, University of Durham
Clare Connors, Lecturer in Literature, University of East Anglia
Paul Davies, Reader in Philosophy, University of Sussex
Sean Gaston, Reader in English, Brunel University
Christopher Johnson, Professor of French, University of Nottingham
Peggy Kamuf, Professor of French and Comparative Literature, University of Southern California
Ian Maclachlan, Fellow and Tutor in French, Merton College, Oxford
J. Hillis Miller, Distinguished Research Professor of Comparative Literature and English, University of California at Irvine
Forbes Morlock, Lecturer in English, Syracuse University (London)
Michael Naas, Professor of Philosophy, DePaul University
Jean-Luc Nancy, Professor of Philosophy (Emeritus), University of Strasbourg
Nicholas Royle, Professor of English, University of Sussex
Ann Smock, Professor of French (Emerita), University of California (Berkeley)
Gayatri Chakravorty Spivak, University Professor, Columbia University
Michael Syrotinski, Professor of French, University of Aberdeen
Julian Wolfreys, Professor of Modern Literature and Culture, Loughborough University
Sarah Wood, Senior Lecturer in English, University of Kent

NOTES

INTRODUCTION: PUNCTUATIONS

1. *The Languages of Criticism and the Sciences of Man: The Structuralist Controversy*, ed. Richard Macksey and Eugenio Donato (Baltimore: Johns Hopkins Press, 1970), 267. This is part of Derrida's response to Jean Hyppolite after delivering his paper 'Structure, Sign and Play' in 1966 at Johns Hopkins University.

2. Sean Gaston, 'An Inherited Dis-Inheritance', in *Derrida, Literature and War: Absence and the Chance of Meeting* (London: Continuum, 2009), 15–33.

3. Our title is taken from Derrida's 1980 paper, 'Punctuations: The Time of the Thesis', in *Eyes of the University: Right to Philosophy 2*, trans. Kathleen McLaughlin (Stanford: Stanford University Press, 2005), 113–28. On the response to the work as a series of intervals and moving gaps, see Sean Gaston, 'A Series of Intervals', in *Derrida, Literature and War*, 1–11; *The Impossible Mourning of Jacques Derrida* (London: Continuum, 2006). See also Geoffrey Bennington's notion of scattering in *Deconstruction is not what you think . . . and other short pieces and interviews* (e-book, 2005), 22–3.

4. Jacques Derrida, 'Cogito et histoire de la folie', *Revue de métaphysique et de morale* 68.4 (1964): 460–94; 'Violence et métaphysique: essai sur la pensée d'Emmanuel Levinas', *Revue de métaphysique et de morale* 69.3–4 (1964): 322–45, 425–73. Jacques Derrida, 'Force et signification', *Critique* 193 and 194 (1963): 483–99, 619–36; 'Edmond Jabès et la question du livre', *Critique* 201 (1964): 99–115; 'De la grammatologie I' and 'De la grammatologie II', *Critique* 223 and 224 (1965–66): 1016–42, 23–53; 'Le théâtre de la cruauté et la clôture de la représentation', *Critique* 230 (1966): 595–618.

5. 'De la grammatologie I': 1019.

6. 'De la grammatologie I': 1023. See also, *OG* 11; *DG* 21–2. Aristotle, *De Interpretatione*, ed. and trans. Harold P. Cooke (Cambridge, MA: Harvard University Press, 2002), I.16a 4–9. One can hear an echo of Derrida's interest here in his later paper, *États d'âme de la psychanalyse: L'impossible au-delà d'une souveraine cruauté* (Paris: Galilée, 2000); 'Psychoanalysis

Searches the States of Its Soul: The Impossible Beyond of a Sovereign Cruelty (Address to the States General of Psychoanalysis)', in *Without Alibi*, ed. and trans. Peggy Kamuf (Stanford: Stanford University Press, 2002), 38–80.

7. See for example, *On Touching – Jean-Luc Nancy*, trans. Christine Irizarry (Stanford: Stanford University Press, 2005).

8. Jacques Derrida, 'Nature, Culture, Ecriture: La violence de la lettre de Lévi-Strauss à Rousseau', *Cahiers pour l'Analyse* 4 (1966), 1–46. The issue was entitled: *Lévi-Strauss dans le dix-huitième siècle*. Derrida notes that this article was based on two sessions in his 1965–66 seminar at the École Normale Supérieure, devoted to 'Ecriture et Civilisation' (5). The Centre for Research in Modern European Philosophy, now placed at Kingston University, has made the full run of this journal available online. See also, Jacques Derrida, *The Beast and the Sovereign, Volume 1*, trans. Geoffrey Bennington (Chicago: University of Chicago Press, 2009), x.

9. Michel Deguy, 'Husserl en seconde lecture', *Critique* 192 (1963): 434–48; Gérard Granel, 'Jacques Derrida et la rature de l'origine', *Critique* 246 (1967): 887–905.

10. Jacques Derrida, 'La dissémination I' and 'La dissémination II', *Critique* 261 and 262 (1969): 99–139, 215–49; *Marges – de la philosophie* (Paris: Minuit, 1972); *Positions* (Paris: Minuit, 1972).

11. Geoffrey Bennington, 'Derridabase', in Geoffrey Bennington and Jacques Derrida, *Jacques Derrida* (Paris: Seuil, 1991), 10.

12. Jacques Derrida, 'Différance', in *Margins of Philosophy*, trans. Alan Bass (Chicago: University of Chicago Press, 1982), 22.

13. 'Différance', 8; 'La différance', in *Marges – de la philosophie* (Paris: Minuit, 1972), 8.

14. Jacques Derrida, 'Implications: Interview with Henri Ronse', in *Positions*, trans. Alan Bass (Chicago: University of Chicago Press, 1981), 3–4; 'Implications: entretien avec Henri Ronse', in *Positions*, 11–12.

15. Jacques Derrida and F. Joseph Smith, 'Jacques Derrida's Husserl Interpretation: Text and Commentary', *Philosophy Today* 11.2–4 (1967) 106–23.

16. Jacques Derrida, 'The Ends of Man', *Philosophy and Phenomenological Research* 30.1 (1969): 31–57.

17. Jacques Derrida, 'Structure, Sign and Play in the Discourse of the Human Sciences', in *The Languages of Criticism and the Sciences of Man*, 247–64. See also, *Writing and Difference*, 278–93.

18. Jacques Derrida, '"Ousia" and "Grammé": A Note to a Footnote in *Being and Time*', in *Phenomenology in Perspective*, ed. F. Joseph Smith, trans. Edward Casey (The Hague: Nijhoff, 1970 [1968]), 54–93; 'Freud and the Scene of Writing', *Yale French Studies: French Freud, Structural Studies in Psychoanalysis* 48 (1972 [1966]): 74–117; 'White Mythology: Metaphor in the Text of Philosophy', *New Literary History* 6.1 (1974 [1971]): 5–74; 'The Copula Supplement', in *Dialogues in Phenomenology*, ed. Don Ihde and Richard M. Zaner, trans. David B. Allison (The Hague: Nijhoff, 1975 [1971]), 7–48; 'The Purveyor of Truth', *Yale French*

Studies: Graphies, Perspectives in Literature and Philosophy 52 (1975):
31–113.
19. Jacques Derrida, *Speech and Phenomena: And Other Essays on Husserl's
Theory of Signs*, pref. Newton Garver, intro. and trans. David B. Allison
(Evanston: Northwestern University Press, 1973).
20. Jacques Derrida, 'Linguistics and Grammatology', *SubStance* 4.10
(1974): 127–81.
21. Jacques Derrida, 'The Ends of Man', in *Margins of Philosophy*, 111.
22. Jacques Derrida, *Du droit à la philosophie* (Paris: Galilée, 1990); *Who's
Afraid of Philosophy: Right to Philosophy 1*, trans. Jan Plug (Stanford:
Stanford University Press, 2002); *Eyes of the University: Right to
Philosophy 2*, trans. Jan Plug (Stanford: Stanford University Press,
2005). See also, Simon Morgan Wortham, *Counter-Institutions: Jacques
Derrida and the Question of the University* (New York: Fordham
University Press, 2006).
23. Jacques Derrida, *The Problem of Genesis in Husserl's Philosophy*, trans.
Marian Hobson (Chicago: University of Chicago Press, 2003), xvii–xix;
Edmund Husserl's Origin of Geometry: An Introduction, trans. John
P. Leavey, Jr. (Lincoln: University of Nebraska Press, 1989), 26, 46–51,
94; 'Violence and Metaphysics: An Essay on the Thought of Emmanuel
Levinas', in *Writing and Difference*, trans. Alan Bass (Chicago: University
of Chicago Press, 1978), 117. See also, *OG* lxxxix, 3–4, 8, 10, 14, 27–8;
'Parergon', in *The Truth in Painting*, trans. Geoff Bennington and Ian
McLeod (Chicago: University of Chicago Press, 1987), 20–1; 'Envois',
in *The Post Card: From Socrates to Freud and Beyond*, trans. Alan Bass
(Chicago: University of Chicago Press, 1987), 20; *Specters of Marx: The
State of the Debt, the Work of Mourning, and the New International*,
trans. Peggy Kamuf (London: Routledge, 1994), 17.
24. Jacques Derrida and Dominique Janicaud, 'Entretien', in *Heidegger en
France,* 2 vols (Paris: Hachette, 2005), II: 96.
25. Edward W. Said, 'The Problem of Textuality: The Two Exemplary
Positions', *Critical Inquiry* 4.4 (1978): 673. In an interview with Imre
Salusinszky from 1986, Said remarked: 'I never really cared for
the *Grammatology*. It struck me as a ponderous ineffective book'. At
the same time, he praises *Dissemination* and *The Origin of Geometry*,
Imre Salusinszky, *Criticism in Society* (New York: Metheun, 1987), 139.
26. 'The Problem of Textuality', 704; Michel Foucault, *The History of
Madness in the Classical Age*, ed. Jean Khalfa, trans. Jonathan Murphy
and Jean Khalfa (Abingdon: Routledge, 2006), 573; Jacques Derrida,
'Cogito and the History of Madness', in *Writing and Difference*, 31–63.
27. See Jonathan Culler, 'Text: Its Vicissitudes', in *The Literary in Theory*
(Stanford: Stanford University Press, 2007), 110–13.
28. Jacques Derrida, 'Afterword: Toward An Ethic of Discussion', in *Limited
Inc*, trans. Samuel Weber (Evanston: Northwestern University Press,
1988), 148. Jonathan Culler cites this passage in 'Text: Its Vicissitudes'.
29. Tribute is of course due here to the remarkable bibliographical work of
William R. Schultz and Lewis L. B. Fried in *Jacques Derrida: An Annotated Primary and Secondary Bibliography* (New York and London:

Garland, 1992). I have also found the JSTOR search engine helpful: www.jstor.org

30. Bernard Vannier, 'Et Pictural', *MLN* 84.4 (1969): 642.

31. Edward W. Said, 'Notes on the Characterization of a Literary Text', *MLN* 85.6 (1970): 766–7.

32. Carol Jacobs, 'Walter Benjamin: Image of Proust', *MLN* 86. 6 (1971): 925 n. 13; John Heckman, 'From Telling Stories to Writing', *MLN* 86.6 (1971): 879 n. 32.

33. Alan Bass, ' "Literature"/Literature', *MLN* 87.8 (1972): 853.

34. This was part of an email exchange on 27 April 2010 and I would like to thank J. Hillis Miller for his very kind and helpful response to an earlier version of this section of the introduction.

35. *The Languages of Criticism and the Sciences of Man*, 155–6, 294 (Derrida's comments); 265–72 (discussion after Derrida's paper); 95–6 (Donato on Derrida).

36. Ronald Paulson, 'English Literary History at The Johns Hopkins University', *New Literary History* 1.3 (1970): 559. One can also note in the British context the founding of the *Journal for the British Society for Phenomenology* in 1970. Derrida's work features in a number of early articles: Annette Lavers, 'Man, Meaning and Subject: A Current Reappraisal', *JBSP* 1.3 (1970): 44–9; Christopher Macann, 'Jacques Derrida's Theory of Writing and the Concept of Trace', *JBSP* 3.2 (1972): 197–200. See also, Stephen Heath, *The Nouveau Roman: A Study in the Practice of Writing* (London: Elek, 1972).

37. See also, J. Hillis Miller, 'The Geneva School: The Criticism of Marcel Raymond, Albert Béguin, Georges Poulet, Jean Rousset, Jean-Pierre Richard, and Jean Starobinski', in *Theory Now and Then* (Hemel Hempstead: Harvester Wheatsheaf, 1991), 13–29. Miller's article was first published in 1966.

38. Jean Rousset, *Forme et signification: essais sur les structures littéraires de Corneille à Claudel* (Paris: José Corti, 1962); 'Force and Signification', in *Writing and Difference*, 3–30.

39. Jean Starobinski, *Jean-Jacques Rousseau: la transparence et l'obstacle* (Paris: Plon, 1958); *Jean-Jacques Rousseau: Transparency and Obstruction*, trans. Arthur Goldhammer, intro. Robert J. Morrissey (Chicago: University of Chicago Press, 1988). Paul de Man, 'Rhétorique de la cécité: Derrida lecteur de Rousseau', *Poétique* 4 (1970): 445–75; 'The Rhetoric of Blindness: Jacques Derrida's Reading of Rousseau', in *Blindness and Insight: Essays in the Rhetoric of Contemporary Criticism* (New York: Oxford University Press, 1971), 102–41. See also, Paulson, 'English Literary History at The Johns Hopkins University', 662. Starobinski himself would respond in part to Derrida's reading of Rousseau much later. See Jean Starobinski, 'Note sur l'établissement du texte', in Jean-Jacques Rousseau, *Essai sur l'origine des langues, Œuvres complètes*, vol. V, ed. Bernard Gagnebin, Marcel Raymond and others (Paris: Gallimard, 1995), cci–cciii.

40. J. Hillis Miller, 'Geneva or Paris: Georges Poulet's "Criticism of Identification"', in *Theory Now and Then*, 54–5. In this collection of articles

Miller has combined two essays on Poulet that were originally published in 1963 and 1970. 'Geneva or Paris? The Recent Work of Georges Poulet' first appeared in the *University of Toronto Quarterly* 29 (1970): 212–28.

41. Georges Poulet, *Studies in Human Time*, trans. Elliott Coleman (Baltimore: Johns Hopkins University Press, 1956), 161–2, 169, 172. See also, Paul de Man, 'The Literary Self as Origin: The Work of Georges Poulet', in *Blindness and Insight*, 79–101. Derrida refers to Poulet in his notes, *Of Grammatology*, 338 n. 1.

42. J. Hillis Miller, 'The Still Heart: Poetic Form in Wordsworth', *New Literary History* 2.2 (1971): 298.

43. Richard Klein, 'Prolegomenon to Derrida', *Diacritics* 2.4 (1972): 29.

44. Jeffrey Mehlman, 'Introductory Note', *Yale French Studies* 48 (1972): 73–4.

45. Alexander Gelley, 'Form as Force: Jacques Derrida, *De la grammatologie*', *Diacritics* 2.1 (1972): 9–13.

46. Taken from Derrida's response to Jean Hyppolite's question, *The Languages of Criticism and the Sciences of Man*, 268. See also, Richard Macksey, 'Anniversary Reflections', in *The Structuralist Controversy: The Language of Criticism and the Sciences of Man – 40th Anniversary Edition* (Baltimore: Johns Hopkins Press, 2007), xii. See also, Jacques Derrida, 'Some Statements and Truisms about Neologisms, Newisms, Postisms, Parasitisms, and Other Small Seismisms', in *The States of 'Theory': History, Art and Critical Discourse*, ed. and intro. David Carroll, trans. Anne Tomiche (New York: Columbia University Press, 1990), 63–94.

47. Eugenio Donato, 'Structuralism: The Aftermath', *SubStance* 3.7 (1973): 25. See also, Jonathan Culler, *Structuralist Poetics: Structuralism, Linguistics and the Study of Literature* (London: Routledge, 2002 [1975]), 281–96.

48. Lacoue-Labarthe, Philippe, 'In the Name of . . .', in Philippe Lacoue-Labarthe and Jean-Luc Nancy, *Retreating the Political*, ed. Simon Sparks (London: Routledge, 1997), 58. See also, Janicaud, *Heidegger en France*.

49. *Della grammatologia*, trans. G. Dalmasso (Milan: Jaca, 1969); *Grammatologie*, trans. Hans J. Rheinberger and Hans Zischer (Frankfurt: Surkamp, 1974); *Kongen no Kanatani*, trans. Adachi Kazuhiro (Tokyo: Gendai Shichōsha, 1976).

50. Edward W. Said, 'Abecedarium Culturae: Structuralism, Absence, Writing', *Triquarterly* 20 (1971): 65–6, 67. This article was reprinted in Said's *Beginnings: Intention and Method* (New York: Basic Books, 1975), 279–343. See also, J. Hillis Miller, 'Beginning With a Text', *Diacritics* 6.3 (1976): 2–7; Eugenio Donato, ' "Here, Now"/"Always Already": Incidental Remarks on Some Recent Characterizations of the Text', *Diacritics* 6.3 (1976): 24–9.

51. Fredric Jameson, *The Prison-House of Language: A Critical Account of Structuralism and Russian Formalism* (Princeton: Princeton University Press, 1972), 183.

52. Jacques Derrida, 'Des Tours de Babel', in *Psyche: Inventions of the Other, Volume I*, trans. Joseph F. Gordon, ed. Peggy Kamuf and Elizabeth Rottenberg (Stanford: Stanford University Press, 2007), 191–225.

PREFACE: READING *DE LA GRAMMATOLOGIE*

1. I thank Eric Mazel for superb research assistance in preparing this essay for publication.
2. This conference has a quiet mythic status as a moment of origin. Many stories circulate. Derrida and Lacan were both present. In unpublished conversation Derrida told me that he was nervous and had written 'Structure, Sign, and Play', his paper for the conference, in one tense night in his hotel room. Many stories circulate.
3. The example is Martin McQuillan's, not Spivak's, as follows: 'Gayatri Chakravorty Spivak's work has opened many doors for post-colonial criticism and for the study of post-colonial writing within the academy. Along with Homi K. Bhabha and Robert Young (two other critics whose work would not have been possible without de Man's version of deconstruction) she has helped to install the insights of deconstruction into the intellectual project of post-colonial theory. Her writing could be described, following Johnson and Brooks, as a reading of race as a trope. Despite what racists (and some "materialist" post-colonial critics) believe, race is not a given, inscribed in the pigment of the skin. Rather, as a concept it has a textual history in which racism is precisely the logocentric gesture which mistakes the figural for the literal. To offer an example, the idea of Aryan (white) supremacy is not based upon any verifiable fact but on a tropological structure. Like Rousseau's discussions of the primitive who calls strangers "giants", the word "Aryan" is a metaphor for the "fear of difference" on the part of the speaker who identifies with this term and a metonym for a racist ideology employed by its adherents. Aryanism itself has a conceptual history, which cannot be dissociated from the history of Western philosophy. Here we might think of texts such as Plato's *Republic*, which makes reference to the lost Aryan people of Atlantis, or Friedrich Nietzsche's notion of the *Übermensch* (superman) in *Thus Spake Zarathustra*. While Spivak (the translator of Derrida's *Of Grammatology*) is not alone in this deconstruction of race (Henry Louis Gates and Paul Gilroy have also adopted similar de Manian arguments) she is one of the few post-colonial critics to pursue the rhetorical nature of race into the canon of European philosophy. In *A Critique of Postcolonial Reason: Toward a History of the Vanishing Present* (1999), which she dedicates to de Man, Spivak offers an extended analysis of Kant, Hegel, and Marx' (McQuillan, *Paul de Man* (London: Routledge, 2001), 118–19).
4. Now included in revised form in Gayatri Chakravorty Spivak, *A Critique of Postcolonial Reason: Toward the History of a Vanishing Present* (Cambridge, MA: Harvard University Press, 1999), 248–311.

5. John P. Leavey, Jr., 'Destinerrance: The Apocalyptics of Translation', in *Deconstruction and Philosophy: The Texts of Jacques Derrida*, ed. John Sallis (Chicago: University of Chicago Press, 1987), 33–43, provides a trajectory of this concept-metaphor in the works of Derrida.

6. Nayanika Mookerjee, *The Spectral Wound: Sexual Violence, Public Memories and the Bangladesh War of 1971* (Durham, NC: Duke University Press, 2011, forthcoming).

7. The frequent modifications of the translation are a result of the reading lesson of *Grammatology*. I proposed revising the translation at a moment of change of editorship and it came to no avail. In the event, an edition with the printing errors corrected, and in a squat format, was brought out as a 'corrected edition'.

8. This essay is in reference to Foucault's relationship to Freud; and locating this problematic was the mainspring of Derrida's general critique of Foucault: not enough compromisingly acknowledged entry into the subject to be obliged to handle the self-compromise. The implications of this criticism for bio-power and governmentality are immense.

9. *Epistémè* has been changed to 'episteme' because the subsequent translations of Foucault have made that form current.

10. Gayatri Chakravorty Spivak, 'Notes toward a Tribute to Jacques Derrida', in *Adieu Derrida*, ed. Costas Douzinas (London: Palgrave Macmillan, 2007), 47–60.

11. 'The mere animal, such as a dog, never represents [*vorstellen*] anything, it can never represent anything *for itself* [*vor*-sich-*stellen*]; to do so, the animal would have to perceive *itself*. It cannot say "I", it cannot say at all. By contrast man, according to metaphysical doctrine, is the representing [*vorstellende*] animal, to whom the ability to speak properly belongs [*dem das Sagenkönen eignet*]', Martin Heidegger, *What is Called Thinking?*, trans. Fred D. Wieck and J. Glenn Gray (New York: Harper and Row, 1968), 61. Translation modified.

12. Stathis Gourgouris, *Dream Nation: Enlightenment, Colonization and the Institution of Modern Greece* (Stanford: Stanford University Press, 1996).

13. I have discussed this book in detail in 'Responsibility – 1992: Testing Theory in the Plain', in *Other Asias* (Boston: Blackwell, 2008), 58–96.

14. I use 'size' in the sense of Derrida's 'Restitution of Truth to Size, de la Vérité en Peinture', trans. John P. Leavey Jr., *Research in Phenomenology* 8.1 (1978): 1–44. See also, Jacques Derrida, 'Restitutions of the Truth in Pointing', in *The Truth in Painting*, trans. Geoff Bennington and Ian McLeod (Chicago: University of Chicago Press, 1989), 255–382.

15. Barbara Cassin and Philippe Büttgen do not explain why they write: 'Derrida's "without condition" is grasped in the ethic of *desaississement*, of non-mastery, of the always-excessive event, in short of masculine hysteria', 'The Performative Without Condition: A University *sans appel*', *Radical Philosophy* 162 (2010): 31. An unfortunate empiricization, in line with all irresponsible confident diagnostic uses of psychoanalytic vocabulary.

16. 'And Catty, indifferent yet devoted companion through a season of solitary labor' (*OG* vii).

CHAPTER 1: THE END OF THE BOOK AND THE BEGINNING OF WRITING

1. The phrase 'dark [or hard] sentence' is found in Bible translations, signifying a difficult problem. Gnome (from Gr. γνωμη): thought, judgement, opinion.
2. Given the phrase 'signifier of the signifier': if the first (first here designated through the assumption of an unbroken linear progression dictated by the semantic and grammatical protocols of reading and writing) 'signifier' is A^1 and the second 'signifier' (sequentially) is A^2, then, in a movement that folds back on itself, wherein = is the signifier of equivalence, then:

$$
\begin{array}{ccc}
A^1 & = & A^2 \\
\| & & \| \\
A^2 & = & A^1
\end{array}
$$

The figure is given as a square or phantom gnomon, rather than as a line or in imitation or representation of a sentence, in order to make clearer iterability and doubling, and the way in which, in the phrase, re*pli*cation is caught up in, and shadows ex*pli*cation. The first model appears closed. Thus, it is necessary to modify it in the following manner:

$$
\begin{array}{ccc}
 & + & \\
A^1 & = & A^2 \\
\|+ & & +\| \\
A^2 & = & A^1 \\
 & + &
\end{array}
$$

which modification serves to signify both finite structure, within which we remain, and an endless motion or iterability, intimating an excess beyond representation. For even as equivalence is seen to be staged, one term or figure, being the double and supplement of the other, so addition is implied simultaneously to equivalence, for $A^1 + A^2$ equals both A^1 *and* A^2, and so on and so forth . . .

However, because one mark is neither the representation nor logical equivalent of the other, there is no true or absolute equivalence, other than in (the undecidability that informs) the operation of either term in a differential relationship, therefore (‖ determining incomparability), leaving us with the possibility that:

$$
\begin{array}{ccc}
A^1 & = & A^2 \\
\| & & \| \\
A^2 & = & A^1
\end{array}
$$

Every figure being both singular and iterable, it necessarily follows that no figure, while being a tropic double of every other figure, nonetheless is and remains in its singularity as incomparable with each and every other figure, no figure therefore being recuperable as an example, or exemplary of an economy of writing conventionally understood. Thus, a distance (| . . . |) is implied and revealed, which distance *qua* spacing is also, simultaneously, a determination of a displacement, displacement itself, absolute displacement, and, at the same time and additionally, a deferral, which maintains *both* singularity *and* iterability; différance, marking both the becoming-space of time and the becoming-time of space, institutes a 'norm', both finite and endless, which is also the determinant of a matrix (| . . . |), thus:

$$| \, | \, A^1 = A^2 | = | \, A^1 \pm A^2 | \, |$$

(equivalence in the first pairing signifying not absolute repetition but, instead, two possible and different values, as figured in the second pairing).

The projection and working of the matrix is remarked on the understanding that what takes place between is irreducible to a determinable or fixable signification, other than the recognition of différance as an open interval, indicated thus (,) whereby { $(A^1, A^2) =]\,A^1, A^2\,[$ } signifies an irreducible undecidability as the work of différance, even as meaning takes place, because the figure signifies, on the one hand, an ordered pair and, on the other hand, an open interval, within and as a result of which, representation and logic collapse into the abyssal taking-place, that we name, provisionally, deconstruction (as in the work, and supplement, of the copula 'of', in the phrase 'signifier of the signifier', which points in more than one direction).

CHAPTER 2: LINGUISTICS AND GRAMMATOLOGY

1. Derrida glosses this notion of being 'in a text already where we believe ourselves to be' (*en un texte déjà où nous croyons être*) (*OG* 162; *DG* 233) as being 'in the vertigo', in Catherine Malabou and Jacques Derrida, *Counterpath: Travelling with Jacques Derrida*, trans. David Wills (Stanford: Stanford University Press, 2004), 147.

CHAPTER 3: OF GRAMMATOLOGY AS A POSITIVE SCIENCE

1. Was this appeal to what is lacking in Leibniz not already made in 'Force and Signification', the opening essay of *Writing and Difference*? It is as though both that text and this one (*OG*) had to begin by distancing themselves from Leibniz, by mentioning him and by outlining or gesturing towards a reading that might take place elsewhere, perhaps in the future or in the footnotes? Let us indicate one of those possible futures. The Leibnizian project of the universal characteristic is twofold. On the one hand it requires an encyclopedia, the gathering of facts about each

thing that can be fed into a definition. On the other hand, it requires the manipulation of a symbolism and a mark that empowers thought to move across and above things, a genuine and genuinely rational process, the universalizable process of reason as such and as simple and as perfect as calculation. Thus what is at stake is both institution and invention where each in turn is configured empirically and conceptually. Empirically and historically, 'institution' brings to mind the Royal and National Societies, and the call for a reorganizing of science as a communal activity driven by a common purpose. Empirically, 'invention' means the bringing about of an actual script. Conceptually, 'institution' and 'invention' must broach the question of their possibility and their essence. What is essential in the instituting of knowledge and in the invention of a mark or script that guarantees truth? Leibniz frequently returns to these matters, indeed they make up a good deal of the content of the texts which offer sketches for the characteristic and reflections on a future in which it will be realized. In 'Psyche: Invention of the Other', and so in the year or two preceding the 'Why Leibniz?' question, Derrida refers parenthetically to a 'deconstructive activity' that might arise from a reading of these sketches and reflections. It would be one that would begin by deconstructing Leibniz's own distinctions between what is essential in invention and what a matter of (historical) chance or individual ingenuity. Again, it would be one that would read into the 'Characteristic' all those features supposedly necessarily excluded by its (logocentric) universality, all those features that trace iterability within universality.

2. The comments are taken from a discussion following Robert Bernasconi's paper 'Descartes in the History of Being: Another Bad Novel?' *Research in Phenomenology* 17 (1987): 97–8.

3. *Of Grammatology* would not have imagined such an age. Here, when Spinoza is named (71), it is with regard to the infinitism and immediacy of logos and so it is in a manner wholly compatible with what is said of the theological and metaphysical prejudices underwriting Leibniz's project.

4. In his engagements with Leibniz, Heidegger also raises the question of how a principle can be an event, an institution and an invention, the question that Derrida makes his own in 'Psyche: Invention of the Other'. But however much that text complicates Derrida's and deconstruction's relations with Heidegger and however much its tone and focus, in line with the 1987 worries about periodizing and epochalizing, differ from that of *Of Grammatology*, when it turns its attention to Leibniz it does so in a manner explicitly guided and authorized by *Der Satz vom Grund*.

BIBLIOGRAPHY

Abraham, Nicolas and Maria Torok, *The Wolf Man's Magic Word: A Cryptonymy*, trans. Nicholas Rand (Minneapolis: University of Minnesota Press, 1986).

Aristotle, *De Interpretatione*, ed. and trans. Harold P. Cooke (Cambridge, MA: Harvard University Press, 2002).

Badiou, Alain, '*Français*', in *Vocabulaire européen des philosophies*, ed. Barbara Cassin (Paris: Seuil/Le Robert, 2004), 465–73.

Bass, Alan, '"Literature"/Literature', *MLN* 87.8 (1972): 852–64.

Bennington, Geoffrey, *Deconstruction is not what you think . . . and other short pieces and interviews* (e-book, 2005).

—, 'Derridabase', in Geoffrey Bennington and Jacques Derrida, *Jacques Derrida* (Paris: Seuil, 1991).

—, *Interrupting Derrida* (London: Routledge, 2000).

Blanchot, Maurice, 'Kafka and the Work's Demand', in *The Space of Literature*, trans. Ann Smock (Lincoln: University of Nebraska Press, 1982), 57–83.

—, 'Rousseau', in *The Book to Come*, trans. Charlotte Mandell (Stanford: Stanford University Press, 2003), 41–8.

—, *The Step Not Beyond*, trans. Lycette Nelson (New York: State University of New York Press, 1992); *Le Pas au-delà* (Paris: Gallimard, 1973).

—, *The Writing of the Disaster*, trans. Ann Smock (Lincoln: University of Nebraska Press, 1995).

Cassin, Barbara, ed., *Vocabulaire européen des philosophies* (Paris: Seuil/Le Robert, 2004).

Cassin, Barbara and Philippe Büttgen, 'The Performative Without Condition: A University *sans appel*', *Radical Philosophy* 162 (2010): 31–6.

Crosby, Alfred W., *Ecological Imperialism: The Biological Expansion of Europe 900–1900* (Cambridge: Cambridge University Press, 1986).

Culler, Jonathan, *Structuralist Poetics: Structuralism, Linguistics and the Study of Literature* (London: Routledge, 2002 [1975]).

—, 'Text: Its Vicissitudes', in *The Literary in Theory* (Stanford: Stanford University Press, 2007), 99–116.

Deguy, Michel, 'Husserl en seconde lecture', *Critique* 192 (1963): 434–48.

Deleuze, Gilles and Félix Guattari, 'Introduction: Rhizome', in *A Thousand Plateaus: Capitalism and Schizophrenia*, trans. Brian Massumi (Minneapolis: University of Minnesota Press, 1987), 3–25.

de Man, Paul, *Allegories of Reading: Figural Language in Rousseau, Nietzsche, Rilke, and Proust* (New Haven: Yale University Press, 1979).

—, 'The Literary Self as Origin: The Work of Georges Poulet', in *Blindness and Insight: Essays in the Rhetoric of Contemporary Criticism* (New York: Oxford University Press, 1971), 79–101.

—, 'The Rhetoric of Blindness: Jacques Derrida's Reading of Rousseau', in *Blindness and Insight: Essays in the Rhetoric of Contemporary Criticism* (New York: Oxford University Press, 1971), 102–41; 'Rhétorique de la cécité: Derrida lecteur de Rousseau', *Poétique* 4 (1970): 445–75.

Derathé, Robert, *Rousseau et la science politique de son temps* (Paris: Presses universitaires de France, 1950).

Derrida, Jacques, 'Abraham, the Other', trans. Gil Anidjar, in *Judeities: Questions for Jacques Derrida*, ed. Bettina Bergo, Joseph Cohen and Raphael Zagury-Orly (New York: Fordham University Press, 2007), 1–35.

—, 'Afterword: Toward an Ethic of Discussion', in *Limited Inc*, trans. Samuel Weber (Evanston: Northwestern University Press, 1988), 111–54.

—, 'A "Madness" Must Watch Over Thinking', trans. Peggy Kamuf, in *Points . . . Interviews, 1974–1994*, ed. Elisabeth Weber (Stanford: Stanford University Press, 1995), 339–64.

—, *The Animal That Therefore I Am*, ed. Marie-Louis Mallet, trans. David Wills (Stanford: Stanford University Press, 2008).

—, *Archive Fever: A Freudian Impression*, trans. Eric Prenowitz (Chicago: University of Chicago Press, 1996).

—, *The Beast and the Sovereign, Volume 1*, ed. Michel Lisse, Marie-Louise Mallet and Ginette Michaud, trans. Geoffrey Bennington (Chicago: University of Chicago Press, 2009).

—, *La Bête et le souverain: Volume II (2002–2003)* (Paris: Galilée, 2010).

—, 'Circumfession', in *Jacques Derrida*, trans. Geoffrey Bennington (Chicago: University of Chicago Press, 1993).

—, 'Cogito and the History of Madness', in *Writing and Difference*, trans. Alan Bass (Chicago: University of Chicago Press, 1989), 31–63; 'Cogito et histoire de la folie', *Revue de métaphysique et de morale* 68.4 (1964): 460–94.

—, 'The Copula Supplement', in *Dialogues in Phenomenology*, ed. Don Ihde and Richard M. Zaner, trans. David B. Allison (The Hague: Nijhoff, 1975), 7–48.

—, 'De la grammatologie I' and 'De la grammatologie II', *Critique* 223 and 224 (1965–66): 1016–42, 23–53.

—, 'Des Tours de Babel', in *Psyche: Inventions of the Other, Volume I*, trans. Joseph F. Gordon, ed. Peggy Kamuf and Elizabeth Rottenberg (Stanford: Stanford University Press, 2007), 191–225.

—, 'Différance', in *Margins of Philosophy*, trans. Alan Bass (Chicago: University of Chicago Press, 1982), 3–27; 'La différance', in *Marges – de la philosophie* (Paris: Minuit, 1972), 1–29.

—, 'La dissémination I' and 'La dissémination II', *Critique* 261 and 262 (1969): 99–139, 215–49.

—, 'The Double Session', in *Dissemination*, trans. Barbara Johnson (Chicago: University of Chicago Press, 1981), 173–285.

—, *Du droit à la philosophie* (Paris: Galilée, 1990); *Who's Afraid of Philosophy: Right to Philosophy 1*, trans. Jan Plug (Stanford: Stanford University Press, 2002); *Eyes of the University: Right to Philosophy 2*, trans. Jan Plug (Stanford: Stanford University Press, 2005).

—, *The Ear of the Other*, ed. Christie McDonald, trans. Peggy Kamuf (Lincoln: University of Nebraska Press, 1988).

—, *L'Écriture et la différence* (Paris: Seuil, 1967).

—, 'Edmond Jabès et la question du livre', *Critique* 201 (1964): 99–115; 'Edmond Jabès and the Question of the Book', in *Writing and Difference*, trans. Alan Bass (Chicago: University of Chicago Press, 1978), 64–78.

—, *Edmund Husserl's Origin of Geometry: An Introduction*, trans. John P. Leavey, Jr. (Lincoln: University of Nebraska Press, 1989).

—, 'Ellipsis', in *Writing and Difference*, trans. Alan Bass (Chicago: University of Chicago Press, 1978), 294–300; 'Ellipse', in *L'Écriture et la différence* (Paris: Seuil, 1967), 429–36.

—, 'The Ends of Man', *Philosophy and Phenomenological Research* 30.1 (1969): 31–57; 'The Ends of Man', in *Margins of Philosophy*, trans. Alan Bass (Chicago: University of Chicago Press, 1990), 109–36.

—, 'Envois', in *The Post Card: From Socrates to Freud and Beyond*, trans. Alan Bass (Chicago: University of Chicago Press, 1987), 1–256; 'Envois', in *La Carte postale: de Socrate à Freud et au-delà* (Paris: Aubier Flammarion, 1980), 5–273.

—, 'Et Cetera . . . (and so on, und so weiter, and so forth, et ainsi de suite, und so überall, etc.)', in *Deconstructions: A User's Guide*, trans. Geoffrey Bennington, ed. Nicholas Royle (Basingstoke: Palgrave, 2000), 282–305.

—, 'Faith and Knowledge: Two Sources of "Religion" at the Limits of Reason Alone', in *Religion*, ed. Jacques Derrida and Gianni Vattimo, trans. Samuel Weber (Cambridge: Polity Press, 1998), 1–78; *Foi et Savoir, suivi de Le Siècle et le Pardon* (Paris: Seuil, 2000).

—, 'Force and Signification', in *Writing and Difference*, trans. Alan Bass (Chicago: University of Chicago Press, 1989), 3–30; 'Force et signification', *Critique* 193 and 194 (1963): 483–99, 619–36.

—, 'Foreword: Fors: The Anglish Words of Nicolas Abraham and Maria Torok', trans. Barbara Johnson, in Nicolas Abraham and Maria Torok, *The Wolf Man's Magic Word: A Cryptonymy*, trans. Nicholas Rand (Minneapolis: University of Minnesota Press, 1986), xi–xlviii; 'Fors: Les mots anglés de Nicolas Abraham et Maria Torok', in Nicolas Abraham and Maria Torok, *Cryptonymie: Le verbier de l'homme aux loups* (Paris: Aubier Flammarion, 1976), 7–73.

—, 'For the Love of Lacan', in *Resistances of Psychoanalysis*, trans. Peggy Kamuf, Pascale-Anne Brault and Michael Naas (Stanford: Stanford University Press, 1998), 39–69.

—, 'Freud and the Scene of Writing', trans. Jeffrey Mehlman, *Yale French Studies: French Freud, Structural Studies in Psychoanalysis* 48 (1972): 74–117; 'Freud and the Scene of Writing', in *Writing and Difference*, trans. Alan Bass (Chicago: University of Chicago Press, 1981), 196–231.

—, *The Gift of Death* and *Literature in Secret*, trans. David Wills (Chicago: University of Chicago Press, 2008); *Donner la mort* (Paris: Galilée, 1999).

—, *Glas*, trans. John P. Leavey Jr. and Richard Rand (Lincoln: University of Nebraska Press, 1986).

—, 'Geschlecht I: Sexual Difference, Ontological Difference', in *Psyche: Inventions of the Other, Volume II*, trans. Ruben Bevezdivin and Elizabeth Rottenberg, ed. Peggy Kamuf and Elizabeth Rottenberg (Stanford: Stanford University Press, 2008), 7–26.

—, 'Heidegger's Ear: Philopolemology (*Geschlecht* IV)', in *Reading Heidegger: Commemorations*, ed. John Sallis, trans. John Leavey Jr. (Bloomington: Indiana University Press, 1992), 163–218.

—, 'Heidegger's Hand (*Geschlecht* II)', in *Psyche: Inventions of the Other, Volume II*, trans. John P. Leavey Jr. and Elizabeth Rottenberg, ed. Peggy Kamuf and Elizabeth Rottenberg (Stanford: Stanford University Press, 2008), 27–62.

—, 'Implications: Interview with Henri Ronse', in *Positions*, trans. Alan Bass (Chicago: University of Chicago Press, 1981), 1–14; 'Implications: entretien avec Henri Ronse', in *Positions* (Paris: Minuit, 1972), 9–24.

—, 'Linguistics and Grammatology', *SubStance* 4.10 (1974): 127–81.

—, *Marges – de la philosophie* (Paris: Minuit, 1972).

—, 'Marx & Sons', in *Ghostly Demarcations: A Symposium on Jacques Derrida's Specters of Marx*, trans. G. M. Goshgarian, ed. Michael Sprinker (London: Routledge, 1999), 213–69.

—, *Memoirs of the Blind: The Self-Portrait and Other Ruins*, trans. Pascale-Anne Brault and Michael Naas (Chicago: University of Chicago Press, 1993).

—, 'Me – Psychoanalysis', in *Psyche: Inventions of the Other, Volume I*, trans. Richard Klein, ed. Peggy Kamuf and Elizabeth Rottenberg (Stanford: Stanford University Press, 2007), 129–42.

—, *Monolingualism of the Other; or, The Prosthesis of Origin,* trans. Patrick Mensah (Stanford: Stanford University Press, 1998).

—, 'My Chances/*Mes Chances*: A Rendezvous with Some Epicurean Stereophonies', in *Psyche: Inventions of the Other, Volume I*, trans. Irene Harvey and Avital Ronell, ed. Peggy Kamuf and Elizabeth Rottenberg (Stanford: Stanford University Press, 2007), 344–76; 'Mes chances. Au rendez-vous de quelques stéréophonies épicuriennes', in *Psyché: inventions de l'autre*, 2 vols (Paris: Galilée, 1998–2003) I: 353–84.

—, 'Nature, Culture, Ecriture: La violence de la lettre de Lévi-Strauss à Rousseau', *Cahiers pour l'Analyse* 4 (1966), 1–46.

—, 'A Number of Yes', in *Psyche: Inventions of the Other, Volume II*, trans. Brian Holmes, ed. Peggy Kamuf and Elizabeth Rottenberg (Stanford: Stanford University Press, 2007), 231–40.

—, *Of Grammatology*, trans. Gayatri Chakravorty Spivak (Baltimore: Johns Hopkins University Press, 1976); *Of Grammatology – Corrected Edition*, trans. Gayatri Chakravorty Spivak (Baltimore: Johns Hopkins University Press, 1997); *De la grammatologie* (Paris: Minuit, 1967). Other translations: *Della grammatologia*, trans. G. Dalmasso (Milan: Jaca, 1969); *Grammatologie*, trans. Hans J. Rheinberger and Hans Zischer (Frankfurt: Surkamp, 1974); *Kongen no Kanatani*, trans. Adachi Kazuhiro (Tokyo: Gendai Shichōsha, 1976).

—, *Of Hospitality, Anne Dufourmantelle Invites Jacques Derrida to Respond*, trans. Rachel Bowlby (Stanford: Stanford University Press, 2000).

—, *Of Spirit: Heidegger and the Question,* trans. Geoffrey Bennington and Rachel Bowlby (Chicago: University of Chicago Press, 1989).

—, 'On Cosmopolitanism', in *On Cosmopolitanism and Forgiveness*, trans. Mark Dooley (London: Routledge, 2001).

—, *On Touching – Jean-Luc Nancy*, trans. Christine Irizarry (Stanford: Stanford University Press, 2005).

—, '"Ousia" and "Grammé": A Note to a Footnote in *Being and Time*', in *Phenomenology in Perspective*, ed. F. Joseph Smith, trans. Edward Casey (The Hague: Nijhoff, 1970), 54–93.

—, 'Outwork, Prefacing', in *Dissemination*, trans. Barbara Johnson (Chicago: University of Chicago Press, 1981), 1–59; 'Hors livre: préfaces', in *La Dissémination* (Paris: Seuil, 1972), 7–68.

—, 'Parergon', in *The Truth in Painting*, trans. Geoff Bennington and Ian McLeod (Chicago: University of Chicago Press, 1987), 17–147.

—, '"Le Parjure," *Perhaps*: Storytelling and Lying', in *Without Alibi*, ed. and trans. Peggy Kamuf (Stanford: Stanford University Press, 2002), 161–201.

—, 'La parole soufflée', in *Writing and Difference*, trans. Alan Bass (Chicago: University of Chicago Press, 1981), 169–95; 'La parole soufflée', in *L'Écriture et la différence* (Paris: Seuil, 1967), 253–92.

—, *Positions*, trans. Alan Bass (Chicago: University of Chicago Press, 1981); *Positions* (Paris: Minuit, 1972).

—, *The Problem of Genesis in Husserl's Philosophy*, trans. Marian Hobson (Chicago: University of Chicago Press, 2003).

—, 'Psyche: Invention of the Other', in *Psyche: Inventions of the Other, Volume I*, trans. Catherine Porter, ed. Peggy Kamuf and Elizabeth Rottenberg (Stanford: Stanford University Press, 2007), 1–47.

—, 'Psychoanalysis Searches the States of Its Soul: The Impossible Beyond of a Sovereign Cruelty (Address to the States General of Psychoanalysis)', in *Without Alibi*, ed. and trans. Peggy Kamuf (Stanford: Stanford University Press, 2002), 38–80; *États d'âme de la psychanalyse: L'impossible au-delà d'une souveraine cruauté* (Paris: Galilée, 2000).

—, 'Punctuations: The Time of the Thesis', in *Eyes of the University: Right to Philosophy 2*, trans. Kathleen McLaughlin (Stanford: Stanford University Press, 2005), 113–28.

—, 'The Purveyor of Truth', *Yale French Studies: Graphies, Perspectives in Literature and Philosophy* 52 (1975): 31–113.

—, 'Qual Quelle: Valéry's Sources', in *Margins of Philosophy*, trans. Alan Bass (Chicago: Chicago University Press, 1982), 273–306.

—, 'Restitutions of the Truth in Pointing', in *The Truth in Painting*, trans. Geoff Bennington and Ian McLeod (Chicago: University of Chicago Press, 1989), 255–382.

—, *Right of Inspection*, trans. David Wills, photographs by Marie-Françoise Plissart (New York: Monacelli Press, 1998).

—, *Rogues: Two Essays on Reason*, trans. Rachel Bowlby (Stanford: Stanford University Press, 2005).

—, *Signéponge/Signsponge*, trans. Richard Rand (New York: Columbia University Press, 1984).

—, 'Some Statements and Truisms about Neologisms, Newisms, Postisms, Parasitisms, and Other Small Seismisms', in *The States of 'Theory': History, Art and Critical Discourse,* ed. and intro. David Carroll, trans. Anne Tomiche (New York: Columbia University Press, 1990), 63–94.

—, *Specters of Marx: The State of the Debt, the Work of Mourning, and the New International*, trans. Peggy Kamuf (London: Routledge, 1994).

—, *Speech and Phenomena: And Other Essays on Husserl's Theory of Signs*, pref. Newton Garver, intro. and trans. David B. Allison (Evanston: Northwestern University Press, 1973); *La Voix et le phénomène* (Paris: Presses universitaires de France, 1967).

—, *Spurs: Nietzsche's Styles/Éperons: Les Styles de Nietzsche*, trans. Barbara Harlow (Chicago: University of Chicago Press, 1979).

—, 'Structure, Sign and Play in the Discourse of the Human Sciences', in *The Languages of Criticism and the Sciences of Man: The Structuralist Controversy*, ed. Richard Macksey and Eugenio Donato, trans. Richard Macksey (Baltimore: Johns Hopkins Press, 1970), 247–64; also in *Writing and Difference*, trans. Alan Bass (Chicago: University of Chicago Press, 1978), 278–93.

—, 'Telepathy', in *Psyche: Inventions of the Other, Volume I*, trans. Nicholas Royle, ed. Peggy Kamuf and Elizabeth Rottenberg (Stanford: Stanford University Press, 2007), 226–61.

—, 'Le théâtre de la cruauté et la clôture de la représentation', *Critique* 230 (1966): 595–618.

—, '"There is No *One* Narcissism" (Autobiophotographies)', in *Points . . . Interviews, 1974–1994*, trans. Peggy Kamuf, ed. Elisabeth Weber (Stanford: Stanford University Press, 1995), 196–225.

—, '"This Strange Institution Called Literature": An Interview with Jacques Derrida', in *Acts of Literature*, ed. Derek Attridge, trans. Geoff Bennington and Rachel Bowlby (London: Routledge, 1992), 33–75.

—, '"To do justice to Freud": The History of Madness in the Age of Freud', in *The Work of Mourning*, trans. Pascale-Anne Brault and Michael Naas (Chicago: University of Chicago Press, 1998), 80–90.

—, 'To Speculate – on "Freud"', in *The Post Card: From Socrates to Freud and Beyond*, trans. Alan Bass (Chicago: University of Chicago Press, 1987), 257–409.

—, *The Truth in Painting*, trans. Geoff Bennington and Ian McLeod (Chicago: University of Chicago Press, 1987).

—, 'Typewriter Ribbon: Limited Ink (2)', in Jacques Derrida, *Without Alibi*, ed. and trans. Peggy Kamuf (Stanford: Stanford University Press, 2002), 71–160.

—, 'Ulysses Gramophone: Hear Say Yes in Joyce', in *Acts of Literature*, trans. Tina Kendall and Shari Benstock, ed. Derek Attridge (London: Routledge, 1992), 256–309.

—, 'Violence and Metaphysics: An Essay on the Thought of Emmanuel Levinas', in *Writing and Difference*, trans. Alan Bass (Chicago: University of Chicago Press, 1978), 79–153; 'Violence et métaphysique: essai sur la pensée d'Emmanuel Levinas', *Revue de métaphysique et de morale* 69.3–4 (1964): 322–45, 425–73.

—, 'What Remains by Force of Music', in *Psyche: Inventions of the Other: Volume 1*, ed. Peggy Kamuf and Elizabeth Rottenberg (Stanford: Stanford University Press, 2007), 81–89; 'Ce qui reste à force de musique', in *Psyché: Inventions de l'autre* (Paris: Galilée, 1987), 95–104.

—, 'White Mythology: Metaphor in the Text of Philosophy', *New Literary History* 6.1 (1974): 5–74; 'White Mythology: Metaphor in the Text of Philosophy', in *Margins of Philosophy*, trans. Alan Bass (Chicago: University of Chicago Press, 1990), 207–71.

Derrida, Jacques and Geoffrey Bennington, *Jacques Derrida* (Paris: Seuil, 1991).

Derrida, Jacques and Robert Bernasconi, 'Remarks on Robert Bernasconi's "Descartes in the History of Being: Another Bad Novel?"', *Research in Phenomenology* 17 (1987): 97–8.

Derrida, Jacques and Hélène Cixous, 'From the Word to Life: A Dialogue between Jacques Derrida and Hélène Cixous', trans. Ashley Thompson, *New Literary History* 37.1 (2006): 1–13.

Derrida, Jacques, Kirby Dick and Amy Ziering Kofman, *Derrida*, DVD, US edn (Jane Doe Films, 2002).

Derrida, Jacques, Maurizio Ferraris and Giorgio Vattimo, 'I Have a Taste for the Secret', in *A Taste for the Secret*, ed. Jacques Derrida and Maurizio Ferraris, trans. Giacomo Donis (Cambridge: Polity, 2001), 3–92.

Derrida, Jacques and Dominique Janicaud, 'Entretien', in *Heidegger en France,* 2 vols (Paris: Hachette, 2005), II: 89–126.

Derrida, Jacques and Richard Kearney, 'Deconstruction and the Other', in *Dialogues with Contemporary Continental Thinkers*, ed. Richard Kearney (Manchester: Manchester University Press, 1984), 105–26.

Derrida, Jacques and Catherine Malabou, *Counterpath: Travelling with Jacques Derrida*, trans. David Wills (Stanford: Stanford University Press, 2004).

Derrida, Jacques and F. Joseph Smith, 'Jacques Derrida's Husserl Interpretation: Text and Commentary', *Philosophy Today* 11.2–4 (1967): 106–23.

Descartes, René, 'Rules for the Direction of the Mind' (*Regulae ad directionem ingenii*), trans. Dugald Murdoch, in *The Philosophical Writings of Descartes*, Vol. I (Cambridge: Cambridge University Press, 1985), 9–78.

Donato, Eugenio, '"Here, Now"/"Always Already": Incidental Remarks on Some Recent Characterizations of the Text', *Diacritics* 6.3 (1976): 24–9.

—, 'Structuralism: The Aftermath', *SubStance* 3.7 (1973): 9–26.

Fink, Eugen, *Nietzsche's Philosophy*, trans. Goetz Richter (London: Continuum, [1960] 2003).

—, 'The Phenomenological Philosophy of Edmund Husserl and Contemporary Criticism', in *The Phenomenology of Husserl: Selected Critical Readings*, ed. and trans. R. O. Elveton (Chicago: Quadrangle, 1970), 73–147.

—, *Spiel als Weltsymbol* (Stuttgart: W. Kohlhammer, 1960); *Le jeu comme symbole du monde*, trans. Hans Hildenberg and Alex Lindenberg (Paris: Minuit, 1966).

Foucault, Michel, *The History of Madness in the Classical Age*, ed. Jean Khalfa, trans. Jonathan Murphy and Jean Khalfa (Abingdon: Routledge, 2006).

Freud, Sigmund, 'Delusions and Dreams in Jensen's *Gradiva*', in *The Standard Edition of the Complete Psychological Works of Sigmund Freud*, 24 vols, ed. and trans. James Strachey (London: Hogarth Press, 1953–74), 9: 1–96.

—, *The Future of an Illusion*, in *The Standard Edition of the Complete Psychological Works of Sigmund Freud*, 24 vols, ed. and trans. James Strachey (London: Hogarth Press, 1953–74), 21: 1–56.

—, 'The Uncanny', in *Pelican Freud Library*, trans. James Strachey (Harmondsworth: Penguin, 1985), 14: 339–76; 'Das Unheimliche', in *Gesammelte Werke* (London: Imago, 1947), 12: 229–68.

Gaston, Sean, 'An Inherited Dis-Inheritance', in *Derrida, Literature and War: Absence and the Chance of Meeting* (London: Continuum, 2009), 15–33.

—, *The Impossible Mourning of Jacques Derrida* (London: Continuum, 2006).

—, 'A Series of Intervals', in *Derrida, Literature and War: Absence and the Chance of Meeting* (London: Continuum, 2009), 1–11.

Geertz, Clifford, *The Interpretation of Cultures* (New York: Basic Books, 1973).

Gelley, Alexander, 'Form as Force: Jacques Derrida, *De la grammatologie*', *Diacritics* 2.1 (1972): 9–13.

Gourgouris, Stathis, *Dream Nation: Enlightenment, Colonization and the Institution of Modern Greece* (Stanford: Stanford University Press, 1996).

Granel, Gérard, 'Jacques Derrida et la rature de l'origine', *Critique* 246 (1967): 887–905.

Heath, Stephen, *The Nouveau Roman: A Study in the Practice of Writing* (London: Elek, 1972).

Heckman, John, 'From Telling Stories to Writing', *MLN* 86.6 (1971): 858–72.

Heidegger, Martin, *Being and Time*, trans. John Macquarrie and Edward Robinson (Oxford: Blackwell, 1990).

—, *Contributions to Philosophy (From Enowning)*, trans. Parvis Emad and Kenneth Maly (Bloomington: Indiana University Press, 1999); *Beiträge zur Philosophie (Vom Ereignis)* (Frankfurt am Main: Klostermann, 1989).

—, 'Letter on Humanism', in *Basic Writings*, trans. Frank A. Capuzzi and J. Glenn Gray, ed. David Farrell Krell, 2nd edn (New York: HarperCollins, 1993), 213–66.

—, *The Principle of Reason*, trans. Reginald Lilly (Bloomington: Indiana University Press, 1991); *Der Satz vom Grund* (Pfullingen: Neske, 1957).

—, *What is Called Thinking?*, trans. Fred D. Wieck and J. Glenn Gray (New York: Harper and Row, 1968); *Was Heisst Denken?* (Frankfurt am Main: Vittoria Klostermann, 2002).

Heraclitus, *Early Greek Philosophy*, ed. and trans. Jonathan Barnes (London: Penguin, 1987), 100–26.

Hochman, Jhan, *Green Cultural Studies: Nature in Film, Novel, and Theory* (Idaho: University of Idaho Press, 1998).

Holz, Richard C., 'Does Nature Have Historical Agency: World History, Environmental History, and How Historians Can Help Save the Planet', *The History Teacher* 37 (2003): 9–28.

Jacobs, Carol, 'Walter Benjamin: Image of Proust', *MLN* 86.6 (1971): 910–32.

Jameson, Fredric, *The Prison-House of Language: A Critical Account of Structuralism and Russian Formalism* (Princeton: Princeton University Press, 1972).

Janicaud, Dominique, *Heidegger en France*, 2 vols (Paris: Hachette, 2005).

Keats, John, *The Letters of John Keats*, ed. Robert Gittings (Oxford: Oxford University Press, 1970).

Klein, Richard, 'Prolegomenon to Derrida', *Diacritics* 2.4 (1972): 29–34.

Kofman, Sarah, *Lectures de Derrida* (Paris: Galilée, 1984).

Lacoue-Labarthe, Philippe, 'In the Name of . . .', in Philippe Lacoue-Labarthe and Jean-Luc Nancy, *Retreating the Political*, ed. Simon Sparks (London: Routledge, 1997), 55–78.

—, 'La scène de l'origine', in *Poétique de l'histoire* (Paris: Galilée, 2002), 13–66.

Laporte, Roger, *Fugue*, in *Une Vie* (Paris: P.O.L, 1986), 249–329.

Lavers, Annette, 'Man, Meaning and Subject: A Current Reappraisal', *JBSP* 1.3 (1970): 44–9.

Lawlor, Leonard, *Derrida and Husserl: The Basic Problem of Phenomenology* (Bloomington: Indiana University Press, 2002).

Leavey, Jr., John P., 'Destinerrance: The Apocalyptics of Translation', in *Deconstruction and Philosophy: The Texts of Jacques Derrida*, ed. John Sallis (Chicago: University of Chicago Press, 1987), 33–43.

Leibniz, G. W., *Monadology*, in *Philosophical Texts*, trans. Richard Francks and R. S. Woolhouse, intro. R. S. Woolhouse (Oxford: Oxford University Press, 1998), 267–84.

Leroi-Gourhan, André, *Gesture and Speech*, intro. Randall White, trans. Anna Bostock Berger (Cambridge: MIT Press, 1993).

Levinas, Emmanuel, 'The Trace of the Other', in *Deconstruction in Context: Literature and Philosophy*, ed. Mark C. Taylor, trans. A. Lingis (Chicago: University of Chicago Press, 1986), 345–59; 'La trace de l'autre', in *En découvrant l'existence avec Husserl et Heidegger*, 3rd edn (Paris: Vrin, 2001), 261–82.

Luther, Martin, *Luther's Works*, ed. Jaroslav Pelikan (St. Louis: Concordia, 1956).

McNeill, John R., *Something New under the Sun: An Environmental History of the Twentieth Century* (New York: Norton, 2000).

McQuillan, Martin, *Paul de Man* (London: Routledge, 2001).

Macann, Christopher, 'Jacques Derrida's Theory of Writing and the Concept of Trace', *JBSP* 3.2 (1972): 197–200.

Macksey, Richard, 'Anniversary Reflections', in *The Structuralist Controversy: The Languages of Criticism and the Sciences of Man – 40ᵗʰ Anniversary Edition* (Baltimore: Johns Hopkins Press, 2007), ix–xiv.

Macksey, Richard and Eugenio Donato, eds, *The Languages of Criticism and the Sciences of Man: The Structuralist Controversy* (Baltimore: Johns Hopkins Press, 1970).

Marks, Robert, *The Origins of the Modern World: A Global and Ecological History* (Lanham: Rowman and Littlefield, 2002).

Mehlman, Jeffrey, 'Introductory Note', *Yale French Studies* 48 (1972): 73–4.

Miller, J. Hillis, 'Beginning With a Text', *Diacritics* 6.3 (1976): 2–7.

—, *For Derrida* (New York: Fordham University Press, 2009).

—, 'Geneva or Paris? The Recent Work of Georges Poulet', *University of Toronto Quarterly* 29 (1970): 212–28; 'Geneva or Paris: Georges Poulet's "Criticism of Identification"', in *Theory Now and Then* (Hemel Hempstead: Harvester Wheatsheaf, 1991), 31–62.

—, 'The Geneva School: The Criticism of Marcel Raymond, Albert Béguin, Georges Poulet, Jean Rousset, Jean-Pierre Richard, and Jean Starobinski', in *Theory Now and Then* (Hemel Hempstead: Harvester Wheatsheaf, 1991), 13–29.

—, 'The Still Heart: Poetic Form in Wordsworth', *New Literary History* 2.2 (1971): 297–310.

Mookerjee, Nayanika, *The Spectral Wound: Sexual Violence, Public Memories and the Bangladesh War of 1971* (Durham: Duke University Press, forthcoming in 2011).

Nancy, Jean-Luc, *Le Partage des voix* (Paris: Galilée, 1982).

Nietzsche, Friedrich, *Ecce Homo*, in *Basic Writings of Nietzsche*, ed. and trans. Walter Kaufmann (New York: Modern Library, 1968), 655–791.

—, *The Pre-Platonic Philosophers*, ed. and trans. Greg Whitlock (Champaign: University of Illinois Press, 2000).

—, *Writings from the Late Notebooks*, ed. Rüdiger Bittner, trans. Kate Sturge (Cambridge: Cambridge University Press, 2003).

Paulhan, Jean, 'Alain, ou la preuve par l'étymologie', in *Œuvres complètes* (Paris: Le Cercle du livre précieux, 1966–70), III: 261–303.

Paulson, Ronald, 'English Literary History at The Johns Hopkins University', *New Literary History* 1.3 (1970): 559–64.

Poulet, Georges, *Studies in Human Time*, trans. Elliott Coleman (Baltimore: Johns Hopkins University Press, 1956).

Powell, Jason, *Jacques Derrida: A Biography* (London and New York: Continuum, 2006).

Quignard, Pascal, *La Leçon de musique* (Paris: Hachette, 1987).

Ricoeur, Paul, *Husserl: An Analysis of His Phenomenology*, trans. Edward G. Ballard and Lester E. Embree, intro. David Carr (Evanston: Northwestern University Press, 2007).

—, *Time and Narrative, Volume 3*, trans. Kathleen Blamey and David Pellauer (Chicago: University of Chicago Press, 1988).

Rousseau, Jean-Jacques, *Confessions*, ed. and intro. Patrick Coleman, trans. Angela Scholar (Oxford: Oxford University Press, 2000); *Les Confessions*, in Jean-Jacques Rousseau, *Œuvres complètes*, vol. I, ed. Bernard Gagnebin, Marcel Raymond and others (Paris: Gallimard, 1969), 1–656.

—, *Discourse on the Origin and Foundations of Inequality Among Men*, in *The Discourses and Other Early Political Writings*, ed. and trans. Victor Gourevitch (Cambridge: Cambridge University Press); *Discours sur l'origine et les fondements de l'inégalité parmi les hommes*, in *Œuvres complètes*, vol. III, ed. Bernard Gagnebin, Marcel Raymond and others (Paris: Gallimard, 1964), 109–237.

—, *Émile ou de l'éducation*, in *Œuvres complètes*, vol. IV, ed. Bernard Gagnebin, Marcel Raymond and others (Paris: Gallimard, 1969), 239–868.

—, 'Essay on the Origin of Languages', in *The Discourses and Other Early Political Writings*, ed. and trans. Victor Gourevitch (Cambridge: Cambridge University Press, 1997), 247–99; 'Essai sur l'origine des langues', in Jean-Jacques Rousseau, *Œuvres complètes*, vol. V, ed. Bernard Gagnebin, Marcel Raymond and others (Paris: Gallimard, 1995), 371–429.

—, *Lettre à d'Alembert*, in Jean-Jacques Rousseau, *Œuvres complètes*, vol. V, ed. Bernard Gagnebin, Marcel Raymond and others (Paris: Gallimard, 1995), 1–125.

—, *The Social Contract*, in *The Social Contract and Other Later Political Writings*, ed. and trans. Victor Gouvrevitch (Cambridge: Cambridge University Press, 1997), 39–152; *Du contrat social*, in Jean-Jacques Rousseau, *Œuvres complètes*, vol. III, ed. Bernard Gagnebin, Marcel Raymond and others (Paris: Gallimard, 1964), 347–470.

Rousset, Jean, *Forme et signification: essais sur les structures littéraires de Corneille à Claudel* (Paris: José Corti, 1962).

Said, Edward W., 'Abecedarium Culturae: Structuralism, Absence, Writing', *Triquarterly* 20 (1971): 33–72; 'Abecedarium Culturae: Absence, Writing, Statement, Discourse, Archaeology, Structuralism', in *Beginnings: Intention and Method* (New York: Basic Books, 1975), 279–343.

—, 'Notes on the Characterization of a Literary Text', *MLN* 85.6 (1970): 765–90.

—, 'The Problem of Textuality: The Two Exemplary Positions', *Critical Inquiry* 4.4 (1978): 673–714.

Said, Edward W. and Imre Salusinszky, 'Interview with Edward Said', in Imre Salusinszky, *Criticism in Society* (New York: Methuen, 1987), 122–48.

Saussure, Ferdinand de, *Course in General Linguistics*, trans. Wade Baskin (Glasgow: Fontana/Collins, 1974); *Course in General Linguistics*, trans. Roy Harris (Chicago and La Salle, Ill: Open Court, 1986); *Cours de linguistique générale* (Paris: Payot, 1987).

Schultz, William R. and Lewis L. B. Fried, *Jacques Derrida: An Annotated Primary and Secondary Bibliography* (New York and London: Garland, 1992).

Spivak, Gayatri Chakravorty, 'Can the Subaltern Speak?', in *A Critique of Postcolonial Reason: Toward the History of A Vanishing Present* (Cambridge, MA: Harvard University Press, 1999), 248–311.

—, 'Notes toward a Tribute to Jacques Derrida', in *Adieu Derrida*, ed. Costas Douzinas (London: Palgrave Macmillan, 2007), 47–60.

—, 'Responsibility – 1992: Testing Theory in the Plain', in *Other Asias* (Boston: Blackwell, 2008), 58–96.

—, 'Translator's Preface', in Jacques Derrida, *Of Grammatology* (Baltimore: Johns Hopkins University Press, 1976), vii–lxxxvii.

Starobinski, Jean, 'Note sur l'établissement du texte', in Jean-Jacques Rousseau, 'Essai sur l'origine des langues', *Œuvres complètes*, vol. V, ed. Bernard Gagnebin, Marcel Raymond and others (Paris: Gallimard, 1995), cxcvii–cciv.

—, *Jean-Jacques Rousseau: Transparency and Obstruction*, trans. Arthur Goldhammer, intro. Robert J. Morrissey (Chicago: University of Chicago Press, 1988); *Jean-Jacques Rousseau: la transparence et l'obstacle* (Paris: Plon, 1958).

Syrotinski, Michael, *Deconstruction and the Postcolonial* (Liverpool: Liverpool University Press, 2007).

Vannier, Bernard, 'Et Pictural', *MLN* 84.4 (1969): 627–45.

Wortham, Simon Morgan, *Counter-Institutions: Jacques Derrida and the Question of the University* (New York: Fordham University Press, 2006).

Young, Robert C., 'Deconstruction and the Postcolonial', in *Deconstructions: A User's Guide*, ed. Nicholas Royle (Basingstoke: Palgrave, 2000), 187–210.

—, *White Mythologies: Writing History and the West* (London: Routledge, 1990).

INDEX

Abraham, Nicholas and Maria
  Torok 45
  The Wolf Man's Magic Word 45
absence 46, 138, 180
accent 145–7, 149–50
actuality 130, 131, 135, 136
ahistoricism xx, 10, 11
Alain 26
Algeria 8, 9
Allison, David xix
almost, nearly (*presque*) 160–1
anasemic 45–6
animal xxxv, 47, 143, 163, 164, 167,
  168, 171
anthropocentric 36, 164, 165, 167
anthropologism xxxviii
arbitrary 26, 44, 58–68
L'Arc 75
Aristotle xvi, 40, 130–1, 135
  De Anima xvi
Aron, Raymond xvi–xvii
Artaud, Antonin xv, 180
articulation 15, 41, 42, 43, 44, 49,
  74, 75, 84, 91, 92, 102–3, 122,
  143, 146, 149, 50, 151, 154
Attridge, Derek 58–68, 136, 184
  Acts of Literature 136
Aufhebung xviii, xxi, 10, 187
Augustine 192
auto-affection 125, 127, 135,
  154, 159
auto-eroticism xxxix, 125

Badiou, Alain 19, 25–6
  Français 25–6
Barthes, Roland xvii, xxiii, 184
Baskin, Wade 60
Bass, Alan xxii, xxv, 33, 35
Bataille, Georges xv, 72, 124, 180
Bennington, Geoffrey xi, 77, 137–45,
  184–5, 196n. 3, 197n. 11
  'Derridabase' 74
  Interrupting Derrida 77
Bergson, Henri xviii
Bernasconi, Robert 186
biology 13, 14, 164
bizarre xxvi, 51–7, 143
Blanchot, Maurice xvii, 27, 73, 75,
  174, 192
  The Book to Come 174
  Death Sentence 192
  The Instant of My Death 75
  'Rousseau' 174
  The Space of Literature 174
  The Step Not Beyond 73
  The Writing of the Disaster 27
Bloom, Harold 193
book xvii–xix, xxvi–xxvii, 31–6
  closure/end of the book 34, 35
  idea of the book 32–6
Braudel, Fernand xvii
Brault, Pascale-Anne 72
breach/broach/open up/initiate
  (*entamer*) 102–3, 104–5, 106–7,
  108–9, 119–23

breath (*pneuma*, spirit,
    souffle) 28–31, 121, 191
Bugead, General Thomas-Robert 8
Burt, Ellen 193
Butades 151–3

Cahiers pour l'Analyse xvi
calculation 11, 83, 86, 179, 180
Calvin, Jean 182
catastrophe 161–2, 163, 165, 166
chance xxx, 164
Char, René xvii
Christianity xxxv
cinders 6
Cixous, Hélène 31, 170, 171
    'From the Word to Life' 31
    Insister 170
    Portrait of Jacques Derrida 170
Clark, Timothy 161–8, 185
Clarke, James 190
climate/environment 161–8
'Collection' Critique xv, xvii
colonialism 8
Condillac, Etienne Bonnot,
    abbé de 124
Connors, Clare 131–3, 149–50,
    160–1, 185–6
Critical Inquiry xxi
Critique xv, xvi–xvii, xix, xxvi, xxxiv,
    23, 33, 34, 78, 96, 189, 191
Crosby, Alfred W. 164
    Ecological Imperialism 164
Crusoe, Robinson 47, 51
Culler, Jonathan xi, 184, 198n. 27
culture/nature 122–3, 161–2, 164
Cupidi, Richard 194
cybernetics 12–13, 91–3

D'Alembert, Jean le Rond 182
Davies, Paul 81–91, 204–5
death xiii, xx, 30, 49–50, 51, 70,
    76, 77, 78, 94, 114, 121, 122,
    136, 140, 149, 150, 178, 180,
    181, 182

decolonization 3–5, 8, 9
deconstruction xiii, xxx, xxxii,
    xxxiv, 6, 7, 8, 9, 19, 23, 36–7,
    39, 42, 66, 81, 115, 119, 137,
    154, 168
Deconstructions: A User's Guide 7
Defoe, Daniel 47, 49
Deguy, Michel xvii
Deleuze, Gilles xxxi, 40, 191
    A Thousand Plateaus 40
Dening, Greg 186
de Man, Paul xxiii–xxiv, xxv, xxix,
    xxxi–xxxii, xxxvii, 7, 9, 60, 163,
    190, 193
    Allegories of Reading 163
    'The Rhetoric of Blindness' xxiv,
    xxxvii, 7
Derrida, Jacques xiii, 171, 201n. 2
    'Abraham, the Other' 57
    'Afterword: Toward an Ethic of
    Discussion' 198n. 28
    *The Animal That Therefore
    I Am* xxxviii
    Archive Fever 8
    *The Beast and the Sovereign,
    Volume 1* 167–8, 197n. 8
    La bête et le souverain II 47
    'Cogito and the History of
    Madness' xxi
    'Circumfession' 8, 96
    'Deconstruction and the
    Other' 57
    'De la grammatologie I' xv, xvi,
    xxvi, 23, 34
    'De la grammatologie II' xv, xvi,
    xxvi, 23, 77, 95
    Demeure 75
    'Des Tours de Babel' 201n. 52
    'Differance' xviii, xx, xxxvii, 56, 76
    Dissemination xxii, 74, 189
    'Dissemination' xvii
    'The Double Session' 57
    Du droit à la philosophie (*Right to
    Philosophy* 1 and 2) xx

The Ear of the Other 70, 174
'Edmond Jabès and the Question of the Book' xv, 169
Edmund Husserl's Origin of Geometry 33, 198n. 23
'Ellipsis' 35, 36
'The Ends of Man' xix, xx, xxxiv
'Entretien' (with Dominique Janicaud) 198n. 24
'Envois' 97, 137, 198n. 23
'Et Cetera' 57, 58
'Le facteur de la vérité' xix
'Faith and Knowledge' 122
'Force and Signification' xv, xxiii, 54, 56
'Form and Meaning' xx
'For the Love of Lacan' 53
'Freud and the Scene of Writing' xix, xxiv, xxxiv, xxxviii, 115
'From Restricted to General Economy' 72
'From the Word to Life' 97, 169
Geschlecht I' xxxiv
The Gift of Death 51
Glas 7, 57, 59, 71, 116, 180
'Heidegger's Ear' xxxiv
'Heidegger's Hand (*Geschlecht* II)' xxxiv
'I Have a Taste for the Secret' 57
'Implications' xvii, 32, 33, 77
Limited Inc 72
'A "Madness" Must Watch Over Thinking' 96
Margins of Philosophy xvii
'Marx and Sons' xxxvii
Memoirs of the Blind 152
'Me – Psychoanalysis' 57
Monolingualism of the Other 6, 8, 57, 59
'My Chances/*Mes chances*' xxx, xxxiii, xxxvi, xxxxviii
'Number of Yes' 57
Of Hospitality 8

Of Spirit xxxiv, xxxv, 70
On Cosmopolitanism and Forgiveness 8
On Touching – Jean–Luc Nancy 92, 197n. 7
The Origin of Geometry: An Introduction xv, xvii
The Other Heading 72
'*Ousia* and *Grammē*' xix, 186
'Outwork' 74
'Parergon' 15, 198n. 23
'"Le Parjure", *Perhaps*' xxxvii
'La parole soufflée' 28
Positions xxiv
The Post Card 137, 189
The Problem of Genesis in Husserl's Philosophy 198n. 23
'Psyche: Invention of the Other' 57, 58
'Psychoanalysis Searches the States of Its Soul' 196–7n. 6
'Punctuations: The Time of the Thesis' 196n. 3
'Qual Quelle: Valéry's Sources' 53
La Question de l'histoire xx
Right of Inspection 57, 58
Rogues 116
Signéponge/Signsponge 65
'Some Statements and Truisms' 200n. 46
Specters of Marx 8, 57, 167, 198n. 23
Speech and Phenomena xiv, xv, xvii, xix, xx, 23, 33, 77, 121, 125, 143, 158, 186, 191
Spurs: Nietzsche's Styles xxxix, 74
'Structure, Sign and Play' xix, xxiii, 4, 69, 77
'The Supplement of Copula' xix
'Telepathy' 57
'There is No *One* Narcissism' 57, 72

Derrida, Jacques (*Cont'd*)
'The Theatre of the Cruelty and
the Closure of
Representation' xv
'This book is therefore devoted to
the bizarre' xxvi–xxvii, 52
'This Strange Institution Called
Literature' 136, 169
'To do Justice to Freud' xxxii
'To Speculate – on "Freud" ' 57
'Typewriter Ribbon' xxxvii,
55, 60
'Ulysses Gramophone' 57
'Violence and Metaphysics' 186,
198n. 23
'What Remains by Force of
Music' 74, 76, 147
'White Mythology' xix
Writing and Difference xiv, xv,
xvii, xviii, 32, 33, 35, 43, 97,
125, 158, 189
Derrida, Marguerite 158, 159
Descartes, René xxxv, 25, 26, 68,
84, 88, 117, 118, 124, 139, 175
*Regulae ad Directionem
Ingenii* 117–18, 175
desire 22, 129, 131, 132, 163,
180, 188
destinerrance xxxi, 41
Derathé, Robert 135
Dhaka xxxi
Diacritics xxiv
Dick, Kirby 23, 95, 158
Derrida 23, 95, 158
différance xiii, xviii, xix, xxi, xxvii,
xxxiii, xxxiv, 6, 35, 38, 40, 41,
42, 43, 49, 61, 67, 68, 76, 77,
78, 91, 94, 95–6, 108–9, 115,
116, 119, 120–1, 122, 135, 145,
155, 204n. 2
dissemination 6, 25, 122
DNA 13, 91, 162
Donato, Eugenio xxiii, xxiv, 189,
200n. 50

Dostoyevsky, Fyodor xxv
doubling 15, 16, 17, 54
drawing 151–4
Duclos, Charles Pinot 124
Durkheim, Emile 135

economic xxii
economy 43, 133, 178
Ehrmann, Jacques 192–3
Ellmann, Maud 184
L'Encyclopédie 124, 183
energeia 135
Entfernung 143
environment, *see* climate
environmental history 164–5
Epicurus xxx
epoch/age xxxiii, 3–5, 11, 17, 21,
30, 69, 81, 83, 84, 85, 87, 99,
104–5, 106–7, 119, 120, 126,
139, 161, 170, 205n. 4
ethics xxxiii, xxxiv, 6, 7, 116,
117, 168
ethico-political 6, 7, 8
ethnocentrism 3–4, 5–6, 8, 80, 82,
84, 91
être juste avec xxxiii, xxxvii
etymology 26–7, 33, 147
event xxxiv, xxxv, 5, 45, 60, 96, 157,
205n. 4
evolution 91–3
Exergue 3, 10, 68
experience 70–2, 114
eye 118, 152, 154–7, 158, 171,
176–7, 182

face xxxiii, 91–2, 114, 152
Felman, Shoshana 193
feminism 6
festival 138, 139, 180
Février, James 124
finitude/finite/infinite xvi, 15, 17,
20, 76–8, 166
Fink, Eugen 45, 69–70
Nietzsche's Philosophy 69–70

'Phenomenological
  Philosophy' 70
Spiel als Weltsymbol 45
force 131–3, 149, 156
Foucault, Michel xv, xvii, xxi, xxxi,
  36, 74, 98–9
Frege, Gottlob 87
Freud, Sigmund xv, xxx, xxxvi,
  xxxviii, 7, 38, 64
  *Beyond the Pleasure
  Principle* 76
  Delusion and Dream 115
  The Future of an Illusion 115
  *The Interpretation of
  Dreams* 64, 192
  'The Uncanny' 38
Fried, Lewis L. B. 198n. 29

gap xi, xv, xix, 102–3, 153, 155,
  157, 180, 196n. 3
Gaston, Sean xiii–xxviii, 10–11,
  68–70, 129–31, 173–5, 179–81,
  186–7, 196n. 2–3
Geertz, Clifford 186
  *The Interpretation of
  Cultures* 186
Gelley, Alexander xxiv
gesture 91–2, 151–4, 179
Geneva School xxiii
geography 137, 140, 144
gesture 91–2, 151–3
globalization *see also*
  mondialisation 8
God 30, 39, 50, 78, 87–90
Godel, Robert 66
Gourevitch, Victor 152
grammarians 45, 55
grammatology xxxiv, xxxvi, 7, 23,
  28, 30, 31, 53, 62, 79–81, 90,
  91, 92, 94–5, 98–9, 104–5,
  108–9
Granel, Gérard xvii
Greco-Christian 30
Guattari, Félix 40

habitation des femmes 126–8,
  182–3
habitation in general 93–5, 126–8,
  154, 181–3
hand 91–2
Harris, Roy 60
Hartman, Geoffrey 193
hauntology 6
hearing 10, 69, 152, 178
Heath, Stephen 199n. 36
Heckman, John xxii
Hegel, G. W. F. xiv, xvi, xvii–xviii,
  xxxv, 6, 7, 10, 11, 21, 28, 62,
  83, 180, 190
  absolute knowledge xviii, xxxv
Heidegger, Martin xiii, xiv, xvi,
  xviii, xx, xxv, xxxiii, xxxiv,
  xxxv, xxxvi, 7, 10, 22, 23, 24,
  25, 26–7, 39, 40, 49, 50, 51,
  68, 69, 70, 81–3, 85–6, 88,
  98–9, 100–1, 104–5, 106–7,
  143, 180, 186
  Being and Time xxxv, 23
  Contributions to Philosophy 98–9
  'Letter on Humanism' xxxv
  The Principle of Reason 85
  What is Called Thinking? xxxiv
Heraclitus 69
hinge (*brisure*) 33, 35, 38, 41–3, 44,
  48, 51, 73–6, 113
historical closure/closure of an
  epoch xxxiv, xxxvi, 3
historical context 3, 16
Historicism/ahistoricism xv, xx, 10,
  11, 27
history xvii, xix, xxii, xxvii, 6, 10,
  11, 21, 23, 25, 27, 80, 81, 82,
  83, 84, 85, 119, 126, 131, 132,
  144, 164, 165, 169, 172
Hjelmslev, Louis 44–5, 71
Hochman, Jhan 161–3, 165, 166
  Green Cultural Studies 161
Holtz, Richard C. 165
Homer 124

human 79–81, 91, 92, 94–5, 130, 161, 164, 167–8
human sciences 4
Husserl, Edmund xv, xvi, xx, xxiii, 7, 10, 24, 39, 70, 77, 82, 93, 181
Hyppolite, Jean xxiii

I 117–18, 123–4, 124–5, 158, 159, 175–6
imagination 129–31, 124, 136, 154, 156
incest 159–60
inhabiting 36–7, 128, 154, 183
in-habitation 134, 154
inscription xvi, 16, 22, 25, 29, 31, 34, 35, 37, 61, 77, 94, 95, 156, 181, 182
intervals xi, xv, xix, 42
iterability xxx, xxxiii, 15, 22, 78, 203–4n. 2, 205n. 1

Jabès, Edmond 97, 169
Jacob, François and Jacques Monod 13
Jacobs, Carol xxii
Jameson, Fredric xxv
   The Prison-House of Language xxv
Janicaud, Dominique 198n. 24
Jaspers, Karl 68
Johns Hopkins Conference 1966 xiii, xxii–xxiii, xxiv, xxix, 43, 189
   The Languages of Criticism and the Sciences of Man: The Structuralist Controversy xxiv
Johns Hopkins University xxiii
Johns Hopkins University Press xxii, xxx
Johnson, Barbara xxv, 193
Johnson, Christopher 3–5, 11–14, 79–81, 91–3, 187–8

Journal for the British Society for Phenomenology 199n. 36
Julia set 137

Kafka, Franz 68, 124, 173–4
Kaluza, Theodor 144
Kamuf, Peggy 36–7, 93–5, 126–8, 133–4, 154–7, 176–7, 181–3, 188
Kant, Immanuel xxxiv, xxxv, xxxvii, 93, 145, 181
   Critique of Pure Reason xxxiv
Keats, John 136
khora 21
Klein, Melanie 96, 124, 159, 171, 172
Klein, Richard xxiv
Kofman, Sarah 15

Lacan, Jacques xix, xxiii
Lacoue-Labarthe, Philippe xxv, 75, 191, 179
   'Entretiens sur Roger Laporte' 75
   'La scène de l'origine' 179
language xv, xvi, xx, xxi, xxvi, xxxv, xxxxviii, 7, 10, 12, 14, 16, 20, 26, 28, 30, 39, 42, 44, 49, 60, 61, 62, 63, 64, 68, 69, 70, 74, 86, 88, 114–15, 140–2, 146, 149, 151, 152, 159, 168, 169, 173
Lanson, Gustave 124
Laporte, Roger 41, 42, 74, 75, 124, 147, 189
   'Bief' 75
   Fugue 75, 147
   Supplément 147
   La Veille 74
Latin 25–6, 42
Lavers, Annette 199n. 36
Leibniz, G. W. 10–11, 81–91, 124, 179
   characteristica universalis 10–11, 83, 84, 86–90, 179

Letter to the Princess
Elizabeth 81, 89–91
Monadology 81, 86, 87, 88,
89, 90
Leroi-Gourhan, André 80, 91–3,
124, 188
Gesture and Speech 91–2
Levinas, Emmanuel xv, xx, 49, 187
'The Trace of the Other' 49, 187
Lévi-Strauss, Claude xiv, xvi, xxxvi,
xxxvii, xxxviii, 3, 9, 67, 68, 79,
80, 113, 117, 124, 164, 167,
187, 191, 194
life 13, 28, 29, 30, 50, 51, 70, 91,
94, 109, 113, 114, 115, 121,
122, 124, 125, 136, 164, 169,
179, 181
linguistics xiii, xxiii, xv, xvi, 12,
21, 22, 38, 44, 45, 58–68,
71, 114
literary modernity 173–4
literary theory xxi
literature xv, xxii, xxiv, 57, 75, 84,
136, 173–4, 193
Littré 113, 127, 176
logos xvi, xxxiv, 4, 6, 10, 11, 16,
23–5, 27, 28, 29, 30, 43, 69, 77,
86, 95, 98 9, 102–3, 104–5,
115, 185, 205n. 3
logocentrism xiii, xvi, xxxiv, xxxvi,
3, 5, 6, 7, 10, 11, 17, 19, 21, 22,
23, 24, 28, 30, 39, 40, 42, 49,
79, 81, 82, 90, 93, 98, 99, 102,
103, 114, 120, 161, 162
love 97, 129, 132, 137, 149, 152,
153, 178
lure/delusion/illusion
(*leurre*) 113–17, 122
Luther, Martin 30

Macann, Christopher 199n. 36
machine xxxviii, 11, 13–14, 50, 55,
75, 91, 92, 165, 179

Maclachlan, Ian 32–6, 70–2, 74–6,
76–8, 109, 188–9
McNeill, John 164, 166
Something New Under the Sun 164
Mallarmé, Stéphane xxxv
Mandelbrot set 138
mark/re-mark xiii, xxxiii, xxxviii, 3,
15, 17, 18, 19, 21, 31, 35, 47,
48, 50, 53, 73, 83, 85, 87, 96,
117, 125, 131, 133, 134, 135,
137, 149, 150, 163, 171, 182,
185, 203n. 2, 205n. 1
Marks, Robert 164
*The Origins of the Modern
World* 164
Marxism 6, 36
Masson, Oliver 124
meaning 24, 25, 27, 26, 28, 42, 44,
46, 47, 48, 50, 51, 59, 61, 83,
101, 105, 109, 113–14, 119,
120, 134, 138, 151, 156, 168,
173, 203n. 2
Mehlman, Jeffrey xxiv
metaphor 35, 155, 156, 157, 173–4,
175, 177
metaphysics xxiv, 3, 4, 5, 6, 10, 11,
13, 14, 18, 19, 22, 23, 25, 27,
30, 39, 46, 49, 50, 66, 68, 70,
71, 77, 80, 81, 83, 85, 90, 95,
114, 120, 131, 134, 135, 177,
180, 181
Michelman, Steve 190
Miller, J. Hillis xi, xxiii, xxiv,
xxv, xxx, 38–51, 189–9, 193,
199n. 34, 200n. 50
For Derrida 38
'Geneva or Paris? The Recent
Work of Georges Poulet' xxiv
MLN xxii
Moby Dick xxxiii
Mookerjee, Nayanika xxxi
The Spectral Wound xxxi
mondialisation 145

monstrous future 3, 5, 56, 68, 97
Morlock, Forbes 22–3, 95–6,
    117–18, 123–4, 124–6, 147–9,
    158–60, 190

Naas, Michael 28–31, 72, 113–17,
    151–4, 190–1
naïveté 176–7
name xxxiii, 53, 58–60, 64, 67, 73,
    83, 94, 95, 96, 105
Nancy, Jean-Luc xi, 75, 98–108,
    147, 191–2
    'Entretiens sur Roger
    Laporte' 75
    Le Partage des voix 147
natural 29, 59, 61, 62, 63, 64, 65,
    113, 129, 130, 158, 177
nature 34, 62, 65, 122, 123, 124,
    129, 132, 133, 134, 135, 146,
    155, 161–8, 176, 179
need/passion 141–3, 149, 150,
    155, 158
New Literary History xxiii
Newmark, Kevin 193
New Testament 29
Nietzsche, Friedrich xxxv, 7,
    69–70
    Ecce Homo 69
    Late Notebooks 69
    The Pre-Platonic Philosophers 69
North and South 140–4, 149, 180
nothing xx, xxi, xxii, xxxiii–xxxvii,
    46, 52, 75–6, 105–9, 137, 147,
    153, 177–8, 179
    almost nothing 153, 160–1
    space where nothing shows 179
    textual blank xxxiii, xxxv, 106–7,
    108–9

O'Brien, Flann 144–5
opening xxxiii, xxxv, 5, 6, 35,
    100–9, 119, 157, 192
orientation 140

origin xxvii, 5, 20, 24, 47, 49, 50,
    52, 69, 73, 92, 116, 121, 122,
    140–3, 146, 156
Otto, Peter 187
Oxford Literary Review 184, 192

painting 136, 146
Parmenides xxxiv
partage 35
passion 141–3, 146, 149, 150, 155,
    156, 158, 159, 175
Patel, Shailja xxxv
Paulhan, Jean 26–7
    'Alain, ou la prevue par
    l'étymologie' 26–7
Paulson, Ronald xxiii
Peirce, Charles Sanders 46,
    62, 124
Penelope xxxv
periodicity 179–81
pity 129–31, 134
play (*jeu*) xx, 15, 16, 38, 40, 41,
    43–7, 49, 51, 53, 69, 70,
    118, 122, 138, 163, 166, 176,
    178, 188
    games 44–5, 138, 166
    play/game of the world 44, 69, 166
pneumatology 28–31
phantasm/illusion 29, 113–17,
    121, 154
pharmakon xxxvi, 6
phenomenology xiv, xv, xxiii, xxvii,
    23, 24, 25, 39, 156
    Geneva School xxiii
philosopheme 100–1
philosophy 4, 11, 21, 23, 25–6, 79,
    84, 99, 100–1, 103, 106–7,
    108–9, 119
phonetic/phonocentrism 3, 4, 5, 11,
    19, 28, 39, 58, 59, 62, 63, 67,
    68, 83, 93, 114
    non-phonetic 4, 10–11, 28, 83,
    84, 86, 87, 179

Piel, Jean xv
Plato 10, 40, 44, 63, 66, 83, 98–9
  Sophist 119
Pliny the Elder 152
  Natural History 152
Poe, Edgar Allan xix
political xxii, 6
  politics of the institution xx
Ponge, Francis 7, 65, 75
  La Fabrique du pré 75
positive science xxx, xxxvi–xxxvii,
  14, 79–81
postcolonialism 6, 8, 9
potentiality 130–1, 135
Poulet, Georges xxiii, 189, 190
  Etudes sur le temps
    humain xxiv
power (*dynamis*) 129–31, 134–6
Preface (*Of Grammatology*) xxvi,
  xxxi, 6, 7
preference 131–3
presence xxxvi, 21, 28, 49, 50, 71,
  72, 83, 84, 85, 93, 108–9, 114,
  117, 120, 121, 130, 139, 166,
  168, 170, 177, 180–1
  non-presence 49, 94, 130
Pre-Socratics 10, 83
print/stamp/engraving
  (*estampe*) 136
program 12, 91, 94
proper/figurative 156–7, 159, 163,
  173, 178
proper name xxx, xxxviii, 95
psychoanalysis xxiv, xxx, xxxvi,
  31, 115
punctuations xi, xiv–xv

Quignard, Pascal 145
  La Leçon de musique 145

racism 8
Rameau, Jean-Philippe 67
Rand, Nicholas 45–6

reading xi, xiv, xv, xxiii, xxxi, xxxii,
  xxxiii, xxxvii, 10, 14, 18, 20, 31,
  32, 44, 54, 55, 82, 123–6, 132,
  133, 138–9, 143, 145, 149–50,
  155, 158, 159, 171, 175–6, 185,
  186, 193
reason xvi, 11, 24, 25, 43, 81, 82,
  85, 87–8, 90, 99, 127
reception of *Of Grammatology* xiv–xv,
  xix–xxi, 6
  as essay xvii–xix
  back cover xxii, xxvi–xxvii
  criticism of xxv
  il n'y a pas de hors-texte xx–xxii
  in America xxi, xxii–xxv
  in Britain 199n. 36
  in France xvii, xxv
    French context xvi–xvii
  more and less than a
    book xvii–xix, xxvi–xxvii
  political/apolitical debate xx–xxi
  translation xix, xxv–xxvi, xxx–xxxi,
    3–4, 6, 43, 53, 64, 70, 113
referral (*renvoi*) 43, 46, 56–7,
  64, 168
Regnault, Jean-Baptiste 152
  Butades Tracing the Portrait of
    Her Shepherd or the Origin of
    Painting 152
Reimann, Bernhard 144
representation xxii, xvi, xxvi–xxvii,
  19, 52, 53, 62, 66, 104–5, 130,
  132, 138, 152, 176–8, 180, 190,
  203n. 2
reserve 130
responsibility xxxii, xxxiii, xxxiv
  Revue de métaphysique et de
    morale xv
rhizomes 40
Ricoeur, Paul 187
  Time and Narrative 186
Ronse, Henri xviii
Rousset, Jean xxiii

Rousseau, Jean–Jacques xvi, xviii,
    xxiii–xxiv, xxvi, xxxi–xxxii,
    xxxvi, xxxvii, 6, 7, 10, 26, 28,
    29, 30, 34, 52, 53, 54, 55,
    56, 57, 67, 68, 83, 84, 93, 95,
    113, 116, 117, 119, 120, 121,
    123–4, 125, 126–8, 129–36,
    138–57, 159–73, 173–83,
    190, 192, 194
  Confessions 123, 125, 127, 139,
    160, 169
  Émile 29, 34, 127, 134, 160, 166
  'Essay on the Origin of
    Languages' xiv, 7, 129, 131,
    139, 140, 147, 148, 151, 152,
    155, 156, 157, 159, 160, 168,
    169, 172, 173, 175
  Letter to d'Alembert 139, 176,
    178, 182–3
  Reveries of a Solitary Walker 128
  Second Discourse (*Discourse on
    Inequality*) 129, 131, 132
  The Social Contract 176
Royle, Nicholas xi, 51–8, 192, 204

Said, Edward xxi, xxii, xxv
  'Abecedarium Culturae' xxv
Salusinszky, Imre 198n. 25
same 42, 43
Sartre, Jean–Paul 8
Saturnalia 180
Saussure, Ferdinand de xiv, xvi, 28,
    42, 44, 51, 52, 54, 55, 56, 57,
    58–68, 71, 124, 194
  Anagrams 67
  Cours de linguistique générale 39,
    58, 59, 60
scattering xix, 25, 196n. 3
Schultz, William R. 198n. 29
science (*epistēmē*) 4–5, 6, 11, 14,
    24, 30, 38, 79, 93, 94, 98–9,
    106–7, 120
  human sciences/sciences of
    man 79–81, 91–3, 94

seasons 180
sense 102–3, 106–7
series xvii
sexual difference xxxix
shibboleth 6
sign xvi, xxvii, xxxiii, 10, 14–22, 24,
    28, 31, 35, 41, 43, 46, 47, 49,
    58–68, 104–5, 136, 151, 153,
    154, 157, 176
  arbitrary 11, 26, 58–68, 137, 144
  immediate sign 151–4
  signified and signifier 24, 28, 31,
    35, 41, 43, 46, 58–68, 97, 113,
    114, 138, 168, 175
  signifier of the signifier 14–22
signature 6
Smith, Robert 185
Smock, Ann 72–4, 136–7, 145–7,
    177–9, 192–3
soul xvi, 13
sound 28, 31, 52, 55, 59, 61, 137,
    150–2, 158, 171
South and North 140–4, 149
sovereignty 116, 180
space xviii, xxiv, 39, 42, 43, 50, 54,
    93–4, 119, 120, 176, 181, 182,
    204n. 2
  spacing (*espacement*) 15, 29, 38,
    42, 50, 95, 115, 116
spectral logic 57
speech xvi, xxvi, 10, 11, 28–31, 52,
    56, 62, 63, 65, 91–2, 114, 115,
    116, 117, 121, 146, 151, 155,
    156, 157, 177, 178, 181
  speech and writing xxxviii,
    xxvi–xxvii, 3, 7, 29, 39, 56, 58,
    63, 64
speech act theory 55
Spinoza, Baruch 81–2, 85
Spivak, Gayatri Chakravorty xi, xiv,
    xix, xx, xxv–xxvi, xxix–xxxix, 6,
    7, 10,16, 43, 53, 55, 64, 67, 70,
    123, 184, 190, 193, 201–3
  'Can the Subaltern Speak?' xxxi

Starobinski, Jean xxiii, 123, 129, 178, 199n. 39
  Jean-Jacques Rousseau: la transparence et l'obstacle xxiii, 124, 178
  'Note sur l'établissement du texte' 129
Stevens, Wallace 39
structuralism xv, xvi, xxi, xxiii, xxiv, xxvi, 3, 12, 79, 187
  structural anthropology 4, 80
subject 26, 38, 118, 124, 180
subjectile 6
SubStance xx
supplement xxvi, 6, 12, 17, 19, 24, 25, 57, 62, 63, 66, 113, 121, 122, 126–7, 129, 130, 131, 132, 134, 138, 139, 141, 143, 145, 146, 147, 148, 149, 155, 163, 166, 178
Suvée, Joseph–Benoît 152
  Butades or the Origin of Drawing 152
Syrotinski, Michael 5–10, 23–8, 193
  Deconstruction and the Postcolonial 7

tactile 42
Taylor, Mark C. 187
  Deconstruction in Context 187
technology 92–3, 94, 167
tekhnē 11, 92
Tel Quel xv, 184, 188
text xx, xxi, xxii, xxxiii, xxxv, 56, 78, 106, 107, 126, 139, 147, 148
textual blank xxxiii, xxxv, 106–7, 108–9
theatre 138, 177–9, 179–81
  theatre without theatre 177–9
theology 30, 50
theoretical matrix 20–1, 22
thing xxxiii, 106–7

thinking/thought xxxiii–xxxiv, xxxv, xxxvi, xxxvii, 13, 83, 93, 98–9, 100–1, 104–5, 176–7, 188
thought weighing, saying nothing xxxiii–xxxiv, xxxv, xxxvi, xxxvii, 100–1, 104–5, 106–7
time xviii, xxiv, 17, 20, 39, 42, 43, 47, 69, 86, 94, 96, 105, 119, 120, 154, 160, 170, 180–1, 203–4n. 2
  to 98–9, 106–7
  to come xxxv, 21, 98–9
  today 17, 21, 31, 104–5
trace xxxiii, xxxiv, xxxvi, xxxvii, xxxviii, 6, 13, 38, 39, 40, 42, 47–51, 61, 64, 65, 67, 72–4, 91, 94, 95, 96, 104–5, 119, 120–1, 137, 156, 162–3, 181
  arche–trace 72–4
transgression 98–9, 100–1, 104–5, 106–7
translation xix–xx, xxv–xxvi, xxxv, 24–6, 74
truth xxii, xxxvi, 10, 24, 26, 27, 83, 97, 114, 175, 179

Ulysses xxxv
uncanny xxvi, 38, 41
undecidability 15, 18
under erasure (*sous rature*) 8, 40, 42, 50, 71
universal xxxiv

Vannier, Bernard 199n. 30
Vernant, Jean-Pierre xxiii
violence 8, 9, 32, 61, 81, 114, 123, 148
virtuality 129–31, 135
visible/visibility 10, 42, 49, 121, 154, 155, 156, 177–8, 179, 180
voice 7, 10, 11, 17, 28–31, 58, 113–14, 117, 121, 124, 137, 145, 146, 147, 155, 169, 177, 178, 191
Vocabulaire européen des philosophies 25

Wagner, Richard 44
Warburton, William 24
Warminski, Andrzej 193
water-hole (*point d'eau*) 168–72
Watson, James and Francis
Crick 13
we 158, 175
Weber, Samuel 72
Wiener, Norbert 13, 14
Cybernetics 14
The Human Use of Human Beings 14
Wimsatt, W. K. 31
Wittgenstein, Ludwig 44
Whal, Jean xvii
wholly other 6, 19, 4
Wolfreys, Julian 14–22, 193–4, 203–4
Wood, Sarah 31–2, 96–7, 168–72, 194
Wordsworth, Ann 185
Wordsworth, Jonathan 185
world 43, 46, 68–70, 106–7, 166
Wortham, Simon Morgan 198n. 22
writing xiii, xxvi–xxvii, xxxiii, xxxv, xxxvii, xxxviii, 3, 6, 9, 10–11, 12, 15, 16, 17, 19, 23, 28, 29, 30, 31, 32–3, 34, 35, 38, 48, 54, 55, 56, 60–2, 64, 63, 65, 68–70, 71, 74, 83, 91–3, 95, 96–7, 102–3, 106–7, 114, 115, 116, 120, 124, 132, 143, 146, 147, 148, 149, 150, 155, 156, 158, 162, 171, 172, 173
arche-writing xxxviii, 6, 38, 49, 71, 106–7
Chinese writing 11, 83–4
good writing 31–2, 34, 96–7, 172
natural writing 26, 29
non-phonetic 10–11, 28, 83, 86, 87, 179
phonetic writing 4, 5, 39, 58, 63, 93
speech and writing xxxviii, 3, 7, 29, 39, 56, 58, 63, 64
violence 9
writing in general xiii, xxxiii, xxxviii
writing science 25

Yale French Studies xxiv
yes 57
Young, Robert 7, 8, 184
'Deconstruction and the Postcolonial' 8
White Mythologies 7–8